BATTLE OF STALINGRAD

BATTLE OF STALINGRAD

THE BEGINNING OF THE END
FOR HITLER IN THE EAST

DMITRY DEGTEV

FRONTLINE
BOOKS

First published in Great Britain in 2024 by Frontline Books
An imprint of Pen & Sword Books Ltd Yorkshire – Philadelphia

Copyright © Dmitry Degtev, 2024
ISBN 978 1 39905 235 1

Typeset by Lapiz Digital Printed and bound in the UK by
CPI Group (UK) Ltd, Croydon, CR0 4YY.

Printed on paper from a sustainable source by
CPI Group (UK) Ltd, Croydon, CR0 4YY

Pen & Sword Books Limited incorporates the imprints of Archaeology,
Atlas, Aviation, Battleground, Digital, Discovery, Family History,
Fiction, History, Local, Local History, Maritime, Military, Military Classics,
Politics, Select, Transport, True Crime, Air World, Claymore Press, Frontline
Publishing, Leo Cooper, Remember When, Seaforth Publishing,
The Praetorian Press, Wharncliffe Books, Wharncliffe Local History,
Wharncliffe Transport, Wharncliffe True Crime and White Owl.

For a complete list of Pen & Sword titles please contact

PEN & SWORD BOOKS LTD
47 Church Street, Barnsley, South Yorkshire, S70 2AS, England
E-mail: enquiries@pen-and-sword.co.uk
Website: www.pen-and-sword.co.uk

Or

PEN & SWORD BOOKS
1950 Lawrence Rd, Havertown, PA 19083, USA
E-mail: uspen-and-sword@casematepublishers.com

CONTENTS

LIST OF PLATES

INTRODUCTION

Hitler and his generals were naively sure that after the capture of Stalingrad, victory in the war would certainly come. And Stalin and his generals thought that since the Wehrmacht stubbornly climbed into these ruins, regardless of time and losses, it meant that the Germans knew more about this city than they did. In fact, the strategic importance of Stalingrad was greatly exaggerated. And the campaign to the Volga turned into a complete disaster for the Hitlerite armies. After the Soviets struck back, Hitler declared the city a 'fortress' and ordered it to be supplied by air. But for the 6th Army, this 'fortress' gradually turned into an 'afterlife'. That's what Friedrich Paulus called it shortly before the surrender . . .

The battle for Stalingrad has attracted military historians, history buffs, journalists and ordinary citizens for many years. It impresses everyone with its geographical scale and scope. First there was an impressive breakthrough by the Wehrmacht deep into the Soviet Union – to the very border of Asia. Then there was an unprecedented and bloody battle for a huge city. And it all ended with the biggest military disaster in the history of Germany and a turning point during the Second World War.

The author of this book visited Volgograd (formerly Stalingrad) for the first time at the age of 10. I was amazed by the outstanding beauty of this southern city and its expanses. At the same time, I was shocked by the preserved ruins of one of the buildings, and a line of turrets of T-34 tanks mounted on granite pedestals in different parts of the city. These turrets mark the symbolic front line in Stalingrad as of 19 November 1942. It was these terrible ruins and harsh tank turrets on the streets that aroused my interest in the Second World War and especially the battle for Stalingrad. When, years later, the question arose where to go on a honeymoon with my wife, the answer was obvious – by tourist vessel on the Volga – to Stalingrad!

The author has been working on this topic for many years, studying hundreds of Soviet and German documents and eyewitness accounts.

As a result, I became convinced that almost all books about Stalingrad are a mixture of real facts with numerous legends. Take at least the popular stories about sniper duels in the city, about which they even made feature films. In fact, the author could not find a single mention of snipers in any Soviet or German document! Apparently, no one paid attention to these lone shooters, and their individual murders had absolutely no effect on the course of the battle. That's why you won't find a single line about snipers in this book. Also in all the books, the success of Operation Uranus, as a result of which the 6th Army was surrounded, is explained by good planning, good training of the Red Army and the use of a large amount of artillery. In fact, it turned out that there was no artillery, and the Russian offensive did not differ in any way from similar highly incompetent attacks undertaken by the Russians in other sectors of the front.

There are no memoirs of Soviet generals and soldiers in this book, because they were all written in the Soviet era, when strict censorship was in effect in the USSR. There are no memoirs of German soldiers and generals in the book, because they also greatly distorted reality. As a result, you will see a completely different, unusual battle for Stalingrad, a battle without myths and legends.

This book is the most detailed chronicle of the battle, shown from both sides. At the same time, it reflects in detail the efforts of all branches of the armed forces: tanks, artillery, infantry, aviation and the Russian river flotilla for the first time.

- The events are depicted day by day, reflecting not only the storming of the city, but also what was happening on the flanks, as well as actions on the huge communication routes leading to Stalingrad.
- For the first time, the efforts of the Luftwaffe to destroy Russian logistics routes, the Russian oil industry and to prevent Russian shipping on the Volga are described.
- The study is compiled from a huge number of archival sources, many of which have never been published
- The book describes for the first time the true state of the German infantry and panzer divisions advancing on Stalingrad and depicts their tactics.
- For the first time, the exact ratio of the losses of the Red Army and the Wehrmacht in Stalingrad has been calculated (these figures will shock everyone).
- The author will answer the question for the first time, did Hitler try to rescue Paulus from Stalingrad?

Chapter 1

JUNE AGAIN, 'SURPRISE' AND BLITZKRIEG . . .

'We will do everything to meet this 4th Panzer Army properly'
By the beginning of the main summer offensive of 1942, the German land forces were much worse prepared than for Operation Barbarossa. Despite the fact that by May a total of 1,100,000 men had arrived on the Eastern Front, the German divisions were still short of 625,000 soldiers. And although most of the replacements were sent to Army Group South, even there the number of units reached 50 per cent of the level of 1941. During the campaign, this indicator was increased to 70 per cent, while in Army Groups North and Centre, on the contrary, it was reduced to 35 per cent. Army Group South also received most of the tanks and self-propelled artillery (assault guns) sent to the Eastern Front, including the new models of the Panzer III and Panzer IV.

In total, by the time Operation Blau began, it consisted of 46 infantry divisions, nine panzer divisions, four jäger divisions, five motorised infantry divisions, two mountain divisions and two SS divisions. Also, Army Group South was assigned 25 divisions from the allies of the Third Reich, but most of them were to arrive in their designated areas only in the autumn. But the Luftwaffe, on the contrary, significantly increased in comparison with the beginning of the Eastern Campaign. As of 20 June 1942, there were 2,644 aircraft on the Eastern Front, that is, almost 1,000 more than at the beginning of Operation Barbarossa! At the same time, 60 per cent of aviation was concentrated in Luftflotte 4.

According to the original plan, Operation Blau was divided into three phases. In the first stage (Blau I), it was supposed to deliver a powerful blow to the troops of the Soviet South-western Front from the Kursk and Belgorod region and capture Voronezh, an important railway junction and industrial centre. After that, Army Group South was to be divided into two new groups: Army Group A under the command of Field Marshal Wilhelm List and Army Group B under the command of Field Marshal Fedor von Bock. Then, during the second stage (Blau II), the German troops would turn to the south-east and, advancing along the Don, cut off the Soviet troops defending along the Seversky Donez River. During the third stage (Blau III), the tank wedges of Army Groups A and B would surround all Soviet troops in the big bend of the Don. After that, the offensive was to begin directly to the Caucasus, and in parallel along the Volga River – to Astrakhan. Interestingly, Stalingrad was not listed as a priority target in the plan.

On the morning of 24 June, Generaloberst Wolfram von Richthofen arrived at Luftflotte 4 headquarters in Kursk. He had only four days to explore the new combat area and hold appropriate meetings and conferences. And it was traditional to fly his small Fi 156 'Storch' aircraft along the front line. Richthofen's career was on the rise during this period, as Hitler regarded him as 'his specialist' and helped him in every way. Thanks to recent victories, the commander of Fliegerkorps VIII became the most famous Luftwaffe commander, whose fame eclipsed all others, including Reichsmarschall Göring himself. Richthofen had the 'winter crisis' behind him, during which, despite the terrible frosts and snowstorms, the Luftwaffe was able to provide the necessary support to their divisions and help them hold their extended defensive positions. Then there was the 'spring renaissance', when German aviation quickly regained strength and conducted two major operations – the defeat of Soviet troops on the Kerch bridgehead and the assault on Sevastopol, simultaneously inflicting heavy losses on the Soviet Black Sea Fleet.

Over the Crimea, the Luftwaffe again completely dominated the sky, repelling all attempts by Soviet aviation to interfere with their actions. And in all this there was considerable merit of Richthofen, a brilliant tactician and professional organiser of massive support of ground forces from the air, and along the way a bloodthirsty sadist who did not hide his pleasure at the sight of fields strewn with thousands of corpses and cities turned into a pile of incinerated ruins. Already during the operation to capture Sevastopol – the Führer decided that it was Richthofen who would 'lead the armies of Mordor into battle', that is, lead the reinforced Luftflotte 4 during the new summer offensive.

Richthofen himself was incredibly excited; at last again there was not a short tactical operation or an assault, but a full-scale offensive in the spirit of the blitzkrieg strategy. And he lead an entire air fleet into battle, at that time the most powerful in the Luftwaffe. The hot summer weather, the huge number of planes at airfields, the roar of hundreds of tanks moving to their starting positions, all this recalled the events of a year ago, when German troops began their campaign against the Soviet Union. Although the Red Empire could not be crushed during one military campaign and then the 'winter crisis' arose, the German army withstood the blow. And the recent successful operations in the Crimea and on the Don inspired almost all Germans with excessive optimism.

One of the flights along the front line almost ended the career of Hitler's favourite 'specialist'. When Richthofen's Fi 156 flew at low altitude over the positions of the 387th Infantry Division, its soldiers mistakenly started shooting at it. As a result, the fuel tank was punctured, and the wings of the aircraft received many holes. After an emergency landing, Richthofen sent the division commander a 'thank you', in which he wrote that he was pleased to see how the morale of the German ground forces was being restored. 'I ask these troops to direct their morale against the Red Air Force,' he wrote. 'Visibility was excellent, and the aircraft had clear markings, perhaps the shelling was intended to provide a welcome. In this case, the commander of Fliegerkorps VIII expresses his gratitude for this and at the same time wishes that the logical congratulations in the future will be carried out with blank cartridges.' In his diary, Richthofen was less tactful: 'Damn dogs! They are not shooting at the Russians, but at my "Storch"!'

The preparations of the Germans were not a secret for the Soviet command. On 19 June, an incident similar to what happened to Richthofen occurred with the officer of the operational department of the 23rd Panzer Division, Major Reichel. He flew in a Fi 156 to the location of one of the units, got a little lost and eventually came under fire from the ground. The 'Storch' made an emergency landing in the neutral zone and was completely wrecked. A German patrol sent to the crash site found that the Russians had got to the plane first. In Reichel's briefcase was a detailed plan for the first phase of the upcoming offensive (Blau I), including 'demonstrations' (in which area the false attack will be launched), the routes of the offensive of panzer divisions, the names of all units that would take part in the operation, and the first goal – Voronezh.

However, Stalin considered this 'gift of fate' to be disinformation, and the Bryansk Front headquarters and army headquarters only took note of the document. Some Russian officers were sure that they would be able to repel a blow if anything happened. 'I will do everything to meet this 4th Panzer Army properly,' the Chief of Staff of the 40th Army, Major General Zinovy Rogozny, confidently declared in discussions with the higher command. But in any case, the preparation of the Germans for a major offensive to the east of Kursk was as obvious as the year before on the border. This was indicated by the increased radio exchanges, the intensification of the actions of German reconnaissance groups, the hum of vehicle engines that did not stop at night, the frequent flights of German aircraft over the front line areas and the rear, and many other signs. Soviet reconnaissance planes recorded a sharp increase in the number of German aircraft at the nearest airfields, including in Bryansk and Kursk, as well as busy round-the-clock traffic on the roads.

On 25 June, Soviet pilots saw a large movement of transport from Kursk in the direction of the city of Shchigry, and infantry scouts saw camouflaged wooden descents to the water made on the west bank of the Tim River. The next day, reports were received of the appearance of numerous camouflaged positions of German long-range artillery in the same sector. At dawn on 27 June, a Russian reconnaissance aircraft recorded a 40km-long transport column on the Kursk–Shchigry Road. In the afternoon, a report was received from the foreign intelligence service that several aviation groups of German fighters and bombers were based at airfields in Bryansk and Kursk. At the same time, information was received that German aircraft were flying en masse from the rear to advanced airfields located near the front line. All this indicated that a thunderstorm was about to break out...

On the decisive day of 28 June, Richthofen got out of bed at 01.45, an hour and a half before the start of Operation Blau. And at 03.00 his small plane was already cutting through the morning sky. Soon the summer silence was broken by the sirens of diving Ju 87 Stuka bombers and the roar of artillery. At the same time, the first targets of the bombers were the headquarters of the Russian 40th Army and a communications hub near the village of Efrosimovka. During the targeted airstrikes, all radio stations and walkie-talkies were destroyed, and the staff suffered heavy losses. The radio operators simply scattered. The commander of the army, General Parseghov, only survived by a miracle. There was also an air strike on the command post of the Bryansk Front in Yelets, on which 140 high-explosive bombs were dropped. The quarter of the city in which this objective was located was completely destroyed, several fires broke out and dozens of people were killed. As a result, the management of the Soviet troops was completely disrupted for a whole day.

As at the beginning of Operation Barbarossa, German planes attacked airfields, artillery positions, warehouses and oil storage facilities, causing fires and destruction everywhere. Then, raising large clouds of dust, tanks and armoured personnel carriers of the 48th Panzer Corps of General Werner Kempf rushed deep into Soviet territory. Having broken through the defences at the junction of the 13th and 40th Armies in the first half of the day, the advanced units of the Germans seized the bridge over the Tim River intact and moved to the opposite bank at noon. Richthofen, who saw all this from the air, felt optimistic: 'I have a feeling that everything will go smoothly.'

While Bf 109 fighters patrolled the entire airspace above the offensive front, twin-engine bombers attacked railways, supply bases and reserve concentrations on the right bank of the Don. The navigator of an He 111 bomber, Hans Reif from 3./KG27, wrote:

Now our summer offensive extends to the entire Southern Front from Kursk to the Azov Sea, which we must support as flying artillery. On Sunday, June 28, we were woken up at 1.00 . . . At 3.25 we took to the air for the first time and finished at 20.12, returning after the fifth departure. The front was located only 20-30 km from our airfield, at the beginning of this offensive, and then began to shift rapidly to the east. During these missions, we witnessed the rapid advance of our troops.

The war diary of the Bryansk Front reported:

The enemy air force, numbering up to 300 aircraft, in the area of the 121st and 160th Rifle Divisions of the 40th Army, it continuously attacked the combat formations of units and command posts. Up to 200 aircraft operated at the same time . . . Some of the weapons did not have time to fire a single shot, as they were destroyed or disabled by enemy aircraft. The enemy determined the location of artillery batteries by the flashes of the guns and suppressed them. Enemy aircraft shackled the actions of the artillery of the 40th Army on the first day of the battle.

But the busiest day was had by the German Bf 110 'Zerstörers', which were used as ground-attack aircraft, firing at roads, ferry crossings, artillery positions and clusters of Soviet troops from low altitude. Konstantin Pavlenkov, at that time commissar, instructor of the political department of the 91st Tank Brigade, told the author of this book:

One platoon of soldiers lay on the ground, it was impossible to get them moving. Another platoon escaped. I took everyone I could gather into the forest. The mood is panicked, everyone is shouting – we must run . . . It got to the point that a wandering herd of horses or cows was mistaken for Germans. And then these 'Messerschmitt-110' appeared, which I remembered for the rest of my life. They approached in groups, and then singly searched for their targets, diving and firing at us from cannons and bullets.

It was a terrible thing, and purely psychologically, a twin-engine plane rushing at you at low altitude, roaring with its engines, caused panic and horror. When this thing turned in your direction and began to descend, even I, an adult, literally pooped in my pants, and the soldiers in general screamed like women!

In the Soviet Union, propaganda emphasized that political workers and commissars were personally responsible for the morale of soldiers and were the first to go into battle, setting an example to others. Western historians, on the contrary, portrayed the commissars as demonic villains who only sought out 'enemies of the people'. There is also an opinion that all Stalin's commissars were Jews, which is why the Germans shot them in the first place. In fact, commissars were recruited from people with a good education (even teacher training), with a lot of life and professional experience. Being older and more cultured people, they were called upon by their mere presence to give confidence to untrained recruits who perceived them as fathers.

Konstantin Pavlenkov was called up for political service in the Red Army having been a rural schoolteacher. Having gone to war at the age of 32, he became a real front-line father for young fighters. 'All the officers and soldiers literally huddled up to me. On the first day, I realized three things: I don't understand anything about the war, I am responsible for the frightened soldiers, 19-year-old soldiers are completely helpless and need constant "paternal" care. So, I had to become a "father" for an entire battalion', he recalled.

Meanwhile, on 30 June, the 6th Army of General Friedrich Paulus also went on the offensive. 'The enemy is almost exactly implementing its plan outlined in the directive captured on 19 June. The direction of the main strike is Voronezh, the strike in the direction of Livni, Yelets and Zadonsk is a cover for the strike of the main direction,' the headquarters of the Bryansk Front stated. However, the Soviets could not understand the further intentions of the German command, since a direct road to Tambov, Saratov, perhaps even Kuibyshev (now Samara) opened up to the Germans through Voronezh. And Stalin was afraid that this was a new offensive against Moscow!

When on the evening of 2 July, the operational group of the Bryansk Front headquarters, which had gone to Voronezh to lead the left flank stretching to the east, arrived in this city, the officers saw a frightening picture there, painfully reminiscent of the nightmare summer a year ago. There were traces of bombing everywhere, many buildings lay in ruins, huge columns of smoke from fires rose into the sky, which for some reason no one extinguished. There were corpses of horses and scraps of wire everywhere in the streets, and endless columns of refugees, mostly women, wrapped in bundles and with crying children, stretching along the highway leading to the east. After reading propaganda articles in newspapers about the brutal atrocities of the Nazis in the occupied territories, most Voronezh residents fled the city in panic.

Already in the evening of 3 July, having covered 130km from the starting positions in six days, the leading units of the 24th Panzer Division and the Großdeutschland Division reached the Don in the area of Semiluki and Gremyachye. By that time, the Soviet 40th Army had been completely defeated and divided into three isolated parts. Some units retreated to the south, several divisions were in the enemy's rear in the area of Kastorny, and only the 232nd Rifle Division managed to withdraw to the eastern bank of the Don. Therefore, on the morning of the next day, the Germans, without encountering resistance, forced the river, and by the evening the vanguard group penetrated into the Long Grove, located on the southern outskirts of Voronezh, from where they began to shell the streets of the city. They even managed to hit several high-ranking officers: for example, the head of the artillery department of the Bryansk Front, Major General Dmitriev, was wounded.

According to the original plan of Operation Blau, the German troops were not supposed to get involved in the battles for Voronezh, but to immediately turn south. However, the commander of the Army Group South, Field Marshal von Bock, could not resist the temptation to capture the city, which he had failed to take in November 1941. In addition, Voronezh was located on an elevation that dominated the entire surrounding area, and was convenient in terms of creating a new defensive line. Relying on the optimistic reports of the military, Hitler eventually made a compromise decision: all panzer divisions should move south – along the Don – and the infantry should continue the offensive on Voronezh.

On 5 July, the Luftwaffe carried out massive air attacks against the city and its surroundings, which lasted from morning until late at night. In addition, German planes bombed the railways on the Voronezh–Gryazi, Voronezh–Liski and Otrozhka–Michurinsk lines, among others. Dive-bombers and Zerstörers bombed and shelled trains with evacuated property, wounded and refugees, completely paralyzing traffic in places. From 4 July to 6 July, the Grafskaya railway station was repeatedly subjected to air strikes, while from 05.30 to 20.00 on 6 July alone, 19 attacks by groups of 6 to 30 aircraft were recorded. As a result, all station tracks and buildings, a water tower, a depot and a power plant and a telephone exchange were destroyed, 71 cars and one locomotive were destroyed, and all communication wires were cut. Movement was paralyzed for three days. As a result of an air attack on the Usman railway station on 5 July, an ammunition train exploded on the rails, all tracks and buildings were destroyed by the shockwave and fires, and 1,500 unexploded mines and shells were scattered throughout the area. There, traffic was paralyzed for 22 hours. On the same day, the Gryazi-Stalingradskiye station was also subjected to massive bombing. As a result, over 800m of tracks, a railway depot, a blacksmith's shop and a locksmith's shop of a car repair plant were destroyed, and 26 cars and nine locomotives were damaged (one was thrown off the track). Most of the stations had no air defences, so the Luftwaffe acted with virtual impunity.

After the capture of most of Voronezh on 9 July, the High Command of the Wehrmacht (OKW) disbanded Army Group South, replacing it with two separate Army Groups, A and B. The second, contrary to the original plans, was headed by Field Marshal von Weichs. Von Bock suddenly received a telegram from the Führer with the words: 'Congratulations on your retirement.' This rather ridiculous and unmotivated action was the first in a series of strange personnel changes that accompanied the entire summer campaign of the Wehrmacht in 1942. A whole epoch had ended with von Bock. He was the last of the major German military leaders involved in the brilliant fast-moving offensive operations of 1940–1 still 'in business'. And it is no coincidence that the departure of von Bock, who conducted the first phase of Operation Blau brilliantly, coincided with the fact that the strategy of the German command (both in terms of the use of ground forces and aviation) finally lost any grounding in reality.

On 9 July, the second stage of the offensive began. The Soviet troops continued to withdraw, and the Wehrmacht command, despite the small number of prisoners, was optimistic. 'We are ready to inflict a crushing defeat on the enemy here, in the big bend of the Don. A great success is clearly visible,' wrote the commander of the 9th Anti-aircraft Division, General Wolfgang Pickert, in a note.

A strange offensive

On 11 July, the Germans captured Kantemirovka and Starobilsk and their leading units were 320km from the Volga. But it was not possible to fully implement the plan of the second phase of the operation – the encirclement of Soviet troops in the Seversky Donets area. The first reason was the rapid flight of the Russians, the second was the previously-mentioned delay of part of the German units near Voronezh. Nevertheless, the situation looked favourable for the Germans. There were no more large formations of Soviet troops or defensive lines ahead.

On 12 July, by order of Stalin, a new Stalingrad Front was formed under the command of Marshal Semyon Timoshenko. It included the 21st, 62nd, 63rd and 64th Armies. However, at that moment it was more of an improvised barrier than a full-fledged Front. The 21st Army had been pretty battered in the battle that had just ended and had retreated to the north bank of the Don. The 63rd Army, which was still in the formation stage, also hastily manned defences along the bank of the Don from Babki to Serafimovichi. These armies covered the direction to Kamyshin and Saratov rather than the path to Stalingrad. And only one army, the 62nd (the former 7th Reserve Army), was located from north to south along the Kletskaya–Kalmykovsky-Surovikino line. At that time, it had only six rifle divisions, numbering 74,600 men, 1,340 mortars and 504 artillery guns. The south-western approaches to Stalingrad were not covered at all, and the units of the 64th Army were still on the way, and in trains moving in different directions. There were almost no anti-aircraft guns in this area, there was nothing to fight off the German planes with . . . According to the list of combat and numerical strength, as of 15 July, the entire Stalingrad Front had only 65 anti-aircraft guns, of which 48 were in the 21st Army, that is, on the northern bank of the Don.

Meanwhile, the Wehrmacht continued to advance like a steamroller. Whole armies that got in its way were rolled out like asphalt. For example, the Soviet 28th Army, which received the main blow of Paulus's 6th Army in early July, suffered huge losses. In complete chaos, being subjected to constant air attacks, by mid-July it withdrew to the Cantemirovka area. And there it came under attack by the rapidly advancing units of the 4th Panzer Army. As a result, the 28th Army was practically destroyed and scattered over a wide area. On 13 July, units of the German 40th Panzer Corps moving from the north-west and units of the 3rd Panzer Corps moving from the west met in the Millerovo area. The resulting pocket included parts of the Russian 9th and 38th Armies, as well as the remnants of the 28th Army. And although a significant part of these troops, who abandoned their artillery and other heavy equipment, managed to escape from the encirclement, five rifle divisions were completely defeated and 73,500 men were captured. As trophies, the Germans got 422 artillery guns and 109 tanks.

The fate of the Russian 38th Rifle Division, which was formed in the spring of 1942 in Alma-Ata (Kazakhstan), was typical. Such units, without delving into the diversity of nationalities living in the Soviet Union, were usually called 'Mongolian' by the Germans. In May, as part of the 28th Army, the division participated in an unsuccessful offensive on Kharkov, where it suffered heavy losses. At the beginning of July, the remnants of the unit managed, experiencing numerous hardships, to walk to the vicinity of Millerovo, where they still found themselves surrounded. 'On July 13, the division was finally surrounded by the enemy and dispersed. It was not possible to establish communication, the division did not have ammunition, food and fuel. The men scattered and in small groups began to exit the encirclement. In this environment, the division lost up to 90 per cent of personnel and materiel,' says the miraculously preserved (but not complete) division's war diary. As a result, on 16 July, only about 60 people reached the positions of the 62nd Army (later several smaller groups came out). After that, the remnants of the 38th Division were sent to rest – on the bank of the Volga River near the village of Rynok in Stalingrad, where replacements arrived.

Meanwhile, the German 48th Panzer Corps, which included the 24th Panzer Division and the 29th Motorised Infantry Division, continued its rapid offensive. But not to the east – to Stalingrad – but to the south-east! Already on 15 July, having travelled 125km across the open steppe in three days, German tanks broke into the village of Morozovskaya, which was half-destroyed by air attacks, located exactly in the middle between Rostov-on-Don and Stalingrad. And after that, the tank corps, which had every chance to reach the Volga in 10–12 days, turned south – to Tsimlyanskaya.

The fact is that after the capture of Voronezh and the breakthrough to the Don, Hitler decided that the Soviet defence had collapsed, like last summer. Therefore, there was no need to 'waste time' consistently achieving your goals. Having removed von Bock from command, who personally participated in the development of the operation and insisted on the original version, he ordered the 4th Panzer Army to turn south immediately, without waiting for a breakthrough to the Volga, and then quickly advance on Baku.

The Soviet command also did not assess the situation correctly and made serious miscalculations. Fearing that the Germans would cross the Don and move north to Tambov and Saratov, it sent the lion's share of available reserves to this sprawling area, despite the fact that the Germans first defended the bank of the Don with only weak barriers, and then gradually transferred it to second-rate allied troops. The fact that by mid-July the leading units of the Germans had not yet reached the Kletskaya–Surovikino line, although by all rough calculations their tanks should have already been rolling over the hastily assembled divisions of the Stalingrad Front, both pleased and alarmed the Soviet generals at the same time. Where have they gone, these devils? Are they really planning some new and insidious roundabout manoeuvre?!

The 629th Fighter Aviation Regiment (629th IAP), based at Surovikino airfield, was assigned to conduct reconnaissance and determine the location of the Germans. Already on the morning of 12 July, a pair of I-16 fighters, having flown over a fairly large area, discovered the advance units of the Germans. They were located in the village of Bokovskaya, 75–80km from the area where the 62nd Army was digging in. Over the next two days, Russian planes regularly overflew the area. At the same time, there were no German planes in the air, and no movement of Germans to the east from Bokovskaya was visible. What a strange offensive!

In fact, the pilots observed only small advance detachments of the 100th Jäger Division and the 113th Infantry Division in the Bokovskaya area, which had stopped due to a lack of gasoline for their vehicles and while waiting for the rest of the units of the 6th Army, which were still at Starobilsk. Therefore, a kind of neutral strip 70km wide was formed between the Wehrmacht and the Red Army! But the German 24th Panzer Division, advancing south after the advanced units of the 48th Panzer Corps, was detained in Morozovskaya and later transferred to the 6th Army. It became the first unit that the troops of the 62nd Army later met with.

On 18 July, the headquarters of the Stalingrad Front, which had not yet had time to prepare for defence, received an unexpected order to go on the offensive along the railway to Morozovskaya and Tatsinskaya, in order to hit the flank of the German troops advancing to the south! The next day, the advance detachments of the 62nd Army, which had not yet had contact with the enemy, began advancing to the Osinovka-Oblivskaya–Tormosin line. On 20 July, continuing this strange offensive, the Russian detachments reached the Chir River, and almost reached Morozovskaya to the south (6km remained to the city), and without contact with the enemy. Inspired by this unexpected success, Tymoshenko ordered the 64th Army, which had not yet finished concentrating, to seize Tsimlyanskaya by a surprise attack and establish contact with the troops of the North Caucasus Front. These days, a 'strange war' was going on in the steppes to the west of Stalingrad. The Germans were moving in one direction, not meeting

Russians on their way. And the Russians were moving in another direction, without meeting the Germans!

The oddities continued until 22 July. On this day, the advanced detachments of the Russian 62nd Army met with the same advanced detachments of the German 6th Army, after which fierce battles ensued between them. On that day, German intelligence for the first time established that the troops of the Stalingrad Front, including the 62nd and 63rd Armies, were defending themselves in the bend of the Don. At the same time, the Germans gave very precise characteristics to some of the opposing Soviet units:

> The 181st Rifle Division (186th and 195th Rifle Regiments), formed in May in Stalingrad from low-quality personnel (penal guards and inexperienced troops), for the first time at the front. 192nd Rifle Division (676th Rifle Regiment). It was formed in May under Rostov on the basis of the 102nd Rifle Brigade. In the companies of the 676th Regiment – 130 men each, 6 light machine guns, several 5-centimeter mortars.

On 24 July, the Luftwaffe launched the first powerful air strike on the positions of the 62nd Army, mainly on the right flank adjacent to the Don. In addition, the bridge of the Don in Kalach was heavily bombed, on which several raids were carried out and about 300 high-explosive and fragmentation bombs were dropped. The next day, the Stukas repeatedly attacked the same target again. As a result, the bridge was damaged by near-misses but remained open. A mill, a district hospital and several residential buildings were destroyed in the city. By 25 July, the German 14th Panzer Corps and the 8th Army Corps broke into the Verkhnebuzinovka area, surrounding the right wing of the 62nd Army, and the 3rd Motorised Infantry Division reached the approaches to Kalach-on-Don.

The Battle for Verkhnebuzinovka

The two-week delay in the German offensive allowed the Soviets to come to their senses, transfer new troops to the steppes and move to active operations themselves. The Russians hastily formed the 1st and 4th Tank Armies from the remnants of the previously defeated 28th and 38th Armies and four newly-raised tank corps. On 25 July, Soviet tankers launched a counter-attack on the tip of the German wedge, cutting the supply routes of the German 14th Panzer Corps of General Gustav von Wietersheim. Other German units that broke through to Verkhnebuzinovka suddenly found themselves in a difficult situation. The headquarters of the 6th Army had to request urgent air support: 'An attack by all aviation forces on the enemy north of Kalach and north of Ryzhov (Rychkovsky). The position of the 3rd and 60th Motorised Divisions is critical! The main efforts of the Fliegerkorps VIII will be directed to support the 3rd Motorised Division.'

Meanwhile, Paulus personally went to the headquarters of the 24th Panzer Corps, located in the Lipovsky farm. From Verkhnyaya Makeyevka, he flew to one of the advanced bases of tactical reconnaissance aircraft, from where, accompanied by several light tanks, he drove by car. Paulus was surprised by the sight of the area south of the Don, resembling an African desert. He was also surprised that there was not a single German soldier in the vast spaces! At Wietersheim's headquarters, a decision was made: to recognise the current situation as critical and to abandon the planned rapid bridging of the Don in the Kalach area by tank divisions, followed by a rush to Stalingrad. Paulus decided to first bring up the infantry divisions that had fallen behind, clear the western bank of the Don from the Russians, and only then systematically move towards the goal.

'At night and early in the morning, the enemy, with the support of numerous tanks, made several attacks, some of which were successful,' the 14th Panzer Corps reported on the morning of 26 July. But by lunchtime, a turning point had come in the battle around Verkhnebuzinovka. From morning to evening, the German ground-attack planes struck Soviet tanks, which were visible in the steppe, as in the palm of their hand. And Ju 52 transport aircraft, accompanied by fighters, dropped containers with ammunition and fuel to the positions of the tankers. The 9th Anti-aircraft Division of the Luftwaffe also actively participated in the battles. During the day, the 3rd Battery of the 8th Anti-aircraft Regiment alone destroyed and 'immobilised' four tanks and one 'rocket launcher', while losing one person killed, three wounded and a Kfz.81 car.

As a result, some of the Russian units were cut off and ended up in a pocket. These events, which took place in the steppe, resembled Erwin Rommel's battles in Africa. On the wide plain, tanks moved quickly and easily entered the enemy's rear. But then the enemy made a similar manoeuvre. In these conditions, the main importance was the well-established system of unit management. And by this indicator, the Germans were much superior to the Russians. Interaction with aviation, and the ability of pilots to quickly recognise the situation and identify the necessary targets, also played an important role.

The Russians scolded their aviation, blaming it for the failure of the operation. 'The actions of the 1st Tank Army were severely hampered by the actions of enemy aviation. The reason for the poor results of the actions for July 26 should be considered poor interaction, mainly with aviation. Khryukin (the commander of the 8th Air Army) needs to be explained firmly regarding interaction, he does not understand it, since modern combat requires it,' the war diary of the Stalingrad Front reported. The commander of the 62nd Army, Major General Vladimir Kolpakchi, was also blamed for the lack of success, and was replaced by Lieutenant General Anton Lopatin. A few days earlier, Marshal Tymoshenko had also been removed from the post of commander of the Stalingrad Front without explanation and replaced by the former commander of the 21st Army, Lieutenant General Vasily Gordov.

Stalin constantly demanded that the generals not only stubbornly defend themselves, but also constantly launch counter-attacks and 'restore the situation'. The Soviet leader naively believed that a numerical advantage in tanks and the 'determination' of the commanders were all that was needed to 'crush' the enemy. 'The Front has a three-fold advantage in tanks, an absolute predominance in aviation. If desired and able, it was possible to smash the enemy to pieces . . . If the Military Council of the Stalingrad Front is not capable of this matter, let it declare it directly and honestly,' said Stalin's telephone message received at 01.45 on 26 July. In response to which Gordov and Commissar Nikita Khrushchev, a member of the Military Council, both promised to fix everything.

On 28 July, the Russian 1st Tank Army managed to break through to Verkhnebuzinovka and partially unblocked the 184th and 192nd Rifle Divisions and the 40th Tank Brigade. The next day, the vanguard units of the Germans again found themselves in a crisis situation. A group of 30–40 Soviet tanks managed to crush a Croatian battalion and units of the 16th Panzer Division, reaching the command post of the 14th Panzer Corps. The vanguard was still being supplied only by air, since all land routes were cut. On top of everything else, as a result of the heat and constant fires, the steppe in the Verkhnebuzinovka area broke out in flames, and German soldiers had to escape not only from enemy tanks, but also from the advancing wall of fire everywhere.

The Luftwaffe supported the units in a difficult situation with all the forces available in this sector of the front. Stukas and ground-attack Bf 109Es and Hs 123s attacked the positions of Soviet troops and tanks on the west bank of the Don. In addition, the Stukas continued to fiercely bomb the Kalach pontoon bridge, inflicting heavy losses on the columns of Soviet troops crossing the river.

The culmination of the first battle on the outskirts of Stalingrad came on 30–31 July. The units of the Russian 13th Tank Corps and several rifle divisions, which managed to break out of the pocket, being subjected to constant air attacks retreated in disorder to the north-east to the Golubaya village. 'The units are morally exhausted, the commanders are panicked. Colonel Zhuravlev, who was entrusted with this group, lost heart and did nothing,' the war diary of the Stalingrad Front reported.

Despite the setback, Gordov and Khrushchev managed to inflict serious losses on the German vanguard, who had significantly detached themselves from their rear, and hold them up. For example, the 14th Panzer Corps lost 67 tanks and self-propelled artillery pieces from 23 July to 2 August, including three Panzer IIs, 52 Panzer IIIs and three Panzer IVs. General Paulus' plan for the rapid capture of Stalingrad by the forces of the tank and motorised divisions thrown forward failed. Already at the end of July, the headquarters of the 6th Army, having analysed the condition of the units of the 14th Panzer Corps, recognised all four divisions included in it (the 16th Panzer, 3rd and 60th Motorised, 113th Infantry) as only being 'suitable for limited offensive tasks'. In Wietersheim's corps, after a heavy battle, there were 205 tanks (26 Panzer IIs, 149 Panzer IIIs, 30 Panzer IVs) and 17 self-propelled artillery pieces.

The condition of the 51st Army Corps operating to the south was somewhat better: infantry battalions had from 40 to 60 per cent of their combat strength (according to the German scale), and the 24th Panzer Division retained 85 per cent of its combat strength. The corps had 138 tanks (27 Panzer IIs, 84 Panzer IIIs, 27 Panzer IVs) and 17 self-propelled artillery pieces and was considered suitable for any offensive tasks.

The Luftwaffe anti-aircraft artillery had also been heavily engaged. From 26 July to 3 August, the 9th Anti-Aircraft Division reported 26 downed aircraft, the destruction of 35 tanks, three multiple rocket launchers, 13 guns and 91 machine-gun nests. 'In two cases, after a defensive battle with the advancing enemy infantry, 500 dead were counted on the battlefield in front of heavy batteries,' the report said. The German anti-aircraft gunners' own losses amounted to 6 guns (five 88mm anti-aircraft guns and six 20mm calibre), 13 vehicles, and 28 killed and 114 wounded.

The battle of Verkhnebuzinovka allowed the Germans to evaluate the quality of new Russian tanks delivered from the Urals and the nearby Stalingrad Tractor Plant. They were of frankly low quality and were assembled in a hurry in conditions of shortage of raw materials. 'Recently, T-34 tanks have been destroyed mainly from 3.7 and 4.7 cm anti-tank guns,' the 6th Army's combat operations magazine said.

The fact is that the Soviet industry produced a very limited amount of nickel, ferrosilicon and ferromanganese, which were necessary for the smelting of grade 8-C steel from which the armour of the necessary strength was made. In the summer of 1942, due to the increase in the production of tanks, the shortage of raw materials began to be felt especially acutely. As a result, the Red Army Armour and Tank Directorate decided to search for a cheaper substitute for Grade 8-C steel. The nickel content in armoured steel was reduced from 2.5–3 per cent to 0.8–1 per cent. The new steel grade was assigned the «ФК» (FC) index. However, the quality of the armour was steadily declining. During the field tests, the Soviet armour-piercing 45mm projectile easily penetrated the frontal and side armour plates of the T-34 tank.

However, the quality of German tanks coming from the factories of the Third Reich had also noticeably deteriorated! The surprised Paulus learned about this from the tankers' stories about the recent battle. Meanwhile, south-east of Oblivskaya, the southern wing of the 6th Army went on the offensive. The Germans immediately managed to break through the front, after which their tanks rushed to Nizhnechirskaya. At the same time, the pontoon bridges over the Chir and Don were attacked several times by dive-bombers during 26 July, as a result of which the departing Russian units suffered heavy losses. The deputy commander of the 64th Army, Major General Broud and the head of the operational department of the Army staff, Lieutenant Colonel Sidorin, were killed. Subunits of the 71st Infantry Division reached the Don and captured a bridgehead on the eastern shore in the area of Logovsky.

However, Paulus could not immediately continue the offensive on Stalingrad. 'After the fighting on the West Bank, the army's forces will be too weak to carry out further tasks, namely the capture of Stalingrad,' stated the headquarters of the 6th Army on 30 July. Paulus informed the command that a further offensive was possible only with the participation of the 4th Panzer Army, after replenishing divisions and restoring normal supplies. All these days, gasoline and ammunition for tanks that went to the Don were delivered only by transport planes carrying about 200 tons of fuel per day. Landing and unloading were carried out at several sites in the steppe to the south-east of Verkhnebuzinovka and in the Nizhnechirskaya area. Since it took at least five days to deliver the 1,000 tons of cargo requested by Paulus, he asked the command for a six-day pause before launching a new offensive.

It is characteristic that during the fighting to the west of the Don, the Soviets did not complain about the total dominance of German aviation, as it had a month before near Voronezh. Bombers and ground-attack planes appeared over the battlefield only sporadically. The Russians carried out transportation in the near rear without hindrance, moved supplies without interruption, and in the sky, one could often see the flights of Russian ground-attack planes and fighters inspiring the troops.

The fact is that in late July and early August Stalingrad was not a priority target for the Luftwaffe. On 20 July, Richthofen arrived at the new headquarters in Mariupol, located on the coast of the Sea of Azov. The next day, he finally officially took command of Luftflotte 4. The appointment was directly signed by the Führer himself and was to come into force on 3 July, but for some reason it was held up by Reichsmarschall Göring. Fliegerkorps VIII was headed by Richthofen's protégé General Martin Fiebig.

Richthofen took over Luftflotte 4 at the moment when the Operation Blau plan was 'thrown into the trash'. Instead of consistently achieving its goals, the Wehrmacht launched an offensive in rapidly diverging directions. Starting on 8 July, Rostov and the Don River bridges became the main targets of the bombers and ground-attack planes. Raids on these targets were carried out almost continuously for two weeks, and the power of air attacks was increasing every day. So, on 15 July, according to Soviet data, 400 high-explosive and fragmentation bombs were dropped on Rostov, the Bataysk railway junction (located south of Rostov) and bridges. The next day, Ju 88s, He 111s and Ju 87s dropped 500 bombs of all sizes on the same targets, and on 17 July, 600. On 18 July, the Luftwaffe dropped about 1,000 high-explosive, fragmentation and incendiary bombs on railway facilities and bridges, including high-powered weapons like the SD1700 and SC1800. As a result, the railway bridge across the Don was severely damaged and two floating bridges were destroyed.

On 21 July, 1,500 bombs of all calibres were dropped on Rostov, Bataysk and the crossing Soviet troops. The bombing campaign culminated on 22–23 July, during which the Russian air surveillance posts (VNOS) recorded 1,200 flights of German aircraft in the Rostov region. Three thousand bombs were dropped on Soviet troops, railway junctions and lines! At the same time, the 2nd Battalion of the 'Brandenburg' Special Purpose Regiment captured the crossings in the Don Delta, opening the way for tanks to the south.

Hitler was elated. Rostov fell so quickly, and his troops had captured so much territory, that the resistance of the Red Army seemed finally broken. On 23 July, the Führer announced that the 'Soviets had been defeated' and signed the famous Directive No. 45. According to the new Edelweiss plan, German troops were to encircle and destroy Soviet units that had fled across the Don. This was to be followed by the capture of the entire coastline of the Black Sea, including naval bases. Then the final phase followed. Panzer formations would advance south-east to Grozny and further, along the coast of the Caspian Sea, to Baku.

Chapter 2

CUT STALINGRAD OFF FROM THE WORLD

The Shadow of the Luftwaffe over the Volga

In 1942, Caucasian oil was supplied to the central regions of the USSR only through two transport arteries: on oil tankers on the Volga and tank wagons on the Astrakhan–Urbach single-track railway. This line ran east of Stalingrad, along the border of Kazakhstan. The smooth functioning of these logistics routes was of great strategic importance for the Soviets. In addition to tankers and oil barges, passenger steamers, military transports and other vessels regularly sailed along the Volga. On average, about 20 ships passed through Stalingrad's river port every day in the summer of 1942. The transportation of petroleum products was carried out by the Volgotanker ship company, which had approximately 170 self-propelled and non-self-propelled barges.

On 10 July, He 111 bombers from KG55 relocated to the Kramatorsk air base in Donbass. On the same evening, the commander of this Kampfgeschwader, Oberstleutnant Benno Kosh, received an order 'to disrupt the day and night movement of ships along the Volga from Astrakhan to Saratov'. However, it was impossible to fulfil it immediately, as first it was necessary to bring a sufficient supply of aerial mines (Luftminen) to the airfield. It took ten days. As a result, the headquarters of Fliegerkorps IV decided to start laying mines on the night of 23 July, simultaneously carrying out an air raid on Stalingrad.

Around midnight, an air alert was announced in the city. Following this, at 00.15, the first planes appeared, playing the role of pathfinders. They dropped incendiary bombs on the northern industrial zone of Stalingrad. After that, twenty Ju 88A dive-bombers from KG51

19

'Edelweiss' attacked the Stalingrad Tractor Plant, dropping 40 high-explosive SC500 bombs on it. As a result, several workshops were partially destroyed, 21 people were killed and 85 injured.

At about the same time, a soldier of the air surveillance post (VNOS) Ivan Sitnikov, while on duty near the village of Stupinsky Yar, heard the hum of planes flying over the Volga. It lasted for several minutes, after which it gradually subsided. Having made entries in the observation log and indicated the time, Sitnikov stared intently at the sky. Suddenly he noticed against the background of the stars several parachutes descending directly on the Volga. At first Sitnikov thought that German troops were descending on parachutes, then he saw that cylindrical objects were attached to them. Soon, quiet splashes of water were heard and the ominous 'gifts' quickly sank into the water. 'Mines!', it dawned on the foreman, and he immediately ran to the nearest phone to report what he had seen.

Indeed, simultaneously with the raid on Stalingrad, several groups of He 111s dropped mines in the area of Gorny Balykley and in the Solodniki–Cherny Yar area. The deadly metal cylinders smoothly sank to the bottom and lay in wait for their victims. The Germans laid LMA, LMB and BM1000 mines. They were equipped with various types of fuses, including acoustic ones. Explosive charges weighing from 300kg to 680kg were guaranteed to destroy any type of river ship.

The next night, German planes dropped mines in the areas of Antipovka (30km south of Kamyshin), Dubovka and Solodnikov. According to Soviet information, the bombers operated in groups of 2–3 aircraft. The mining was carried out between 21.20 and 23.50. The first victim was the steamer *Smolensk*, which was going upstream with the oil barge *Kondoma* in tow. On the evening of 25 July, she was blown up by a mine in the area of Gornaya Proleika. The entire ship's crew and passengers, including the children of the crew members, were killed.

On the night of 26 July, the mission continued. The first planes were spotted over the Volga at 20.53, and mines were laid in the Kamyshin–Dubovka section, in the area of Krasnoarmeysk and at Tsagan-Aman. Ninety bombs were dropped on steamers and barges on the river. The barges *Talovka* and *Vesta*, carrying automobile oil, were sunk, and in the area of the Bykovo farm (40km south of Kamyshin), bombers dropped incendiary bombs on the passenger steamer *Alexander Nevsky*, on board which there were 300 passengers. The captain of the vessel, Nikolay Kharlamovich, immediately turned the ship towards the high shore, and soon he buried the bows in the sand. People rushed to the shore in panic, and only 15 people died in the fire. On the same night, three tugs, four dry-cargo barges and two oil barges were sunk. In the area of Kamenny Yar, the tugboat *Adjaristan* was sunk, on which 20 people were killed.

On the night of 27/28 July, the Luftwaffe was particularly active. Planes appeared over the Volga for five hours from 21.00 to 02.20, and the dropping of mines and the bombing of ships were noted on the stretch of 400km from Kamyshin almost to Astrakhan. Experienced crews of torpedo bombers from II./KG26 and bombers from I./KG100 and III./LG1 participated in the missions. Departing from the Crimea, He 111s dropped 31 mines into the Volga. According to German information, two barges sailing upstream were damaged. In fact, the oil barges *Buryat* and *Ob* (with a cargo of 10,000 tons of kerosene each) were blown up in the Stalingrad area (at the same latitude as the Yerzovka). A huge column of smoke rose over the steppes, burning fuel flowed down the Volga, and the movement of ships along the river was greatly hampered. A convoy of three barges with military cargo was sunk in the area of Solenoye Zaimishe.

The Soviets on the Volga had a military flotilla under the command of Rear Admiral Dmitry Dergachev. It was formed back in 1941, when the Russians were first afraid of a German breakthrough to the Volga. By the end of July, the flotilla had 18 powerful tugs armed with anti-aircraft guns, as well as seven gunboats, 14 armoured boats, 33 minesweepers, two floating anti-aircraft batteries and two marine battalions. On 26 July, Dergachev received an order to escort river vessels moving along the river and provide anti-aircraft defence.

Frightened by reports of the mass loss of ships, the Volgotanker shipping company suspended the departure of oil barges from the port of Astrakhan. But dozens of ships were already on their way. On 26 July, People's Commissar (Minister) of the USSR River Fleet Zosima Shashkov made a report at a meeting of the State Defence Committee. He asked for urgent measures to strengthen ships and strengthen air defence. But all this took a lot of time. The situation was catastrophic for the Soviets. At night, more and more 'infernal machines'[1] descended into the waterways, and bombers attacked ships and docks. In total, from 25 to 31 July, Russian air surveillance posts recorded the fall of 231 mines into the river.

But, despite the danger, heavy oil barges slowly crept upstream. On 29 July, 220,000 tons of oil products were in transit on the Astrakhan–Kamyshin section. At night, German planes appeared over the river again and mined the Bokovo–Astrakhan section, simultaneously dropping bombs on ships, wharves and coastal villages. For example,

---

1 This is the term the Russians used for mines.

the passenger steamer *Turgenev* left Astrakhan, heading to Stalingrad for the wounded. The passage to Enotaevka was uneventful, but at night the sailors saw an approaching plane astern (on the bright side of the horizon). It was flying low over the river from the south-east. The watchmen for a while asked, whose is it, Russian or German? All doubts were dispelled by the bomb, which separated from the belly of the plane. A huge column of water rose on the port side, showering the deck with many fragments.

The sailors of the *Turgenev* did not have time to come to their senses, as the plane returned, and, making a second approach, fired at the ship with machine guns. Tracer bullets penetrated the upper deck and caused a fire in the 2nd class cabin. The sailor Alexander Rakov clearly saw the faces of the German pilots, and crosses and swastikas on the fuselage. Two minutes later, the He 111 came on a third approach and dropped another bomb, which exploded astern of the ship. As a result, the deck superstructure was severely damaged. After the bomber disappeared over the horizon, the captain of the *Turgenev* decided to return to Astrakhan for repairs.

At the end of July, Luftflotte 4 intensified attacks against Russian ships on the Volga. KG27 'Boelcke' joined the operation. One of the pilots of the 2nd Staffel wrote:

> One bright moonlit night, when we could clearly distinguish both the river and the cities, and the ships on the river, I was flying at an altitude of about 200m above the Volga. I managed to 'put' two 250kg bombs near one vessel, but without any visible result. The shell explosions of the Russian light and medium anti-aircraft artillery were far behind me, without hits. On the next approach, I ordered my navigator to fire a side machine gun at the target ahead of the course, while I was trying to drop the other two bombs. It was a fatal mistake, because I represented a very good target for the Russians. That's what happened: we got a direct hit. The radio operator shouted: 'The flight control surfaces were blown away! No, they seem to be here again!' Despite the very dangerous situation, we burst out laughing. A lucky accident left our plane manageable. We managed to get out of it, and I climbed to a height of 4,000m.

After six hours of flight, the bomber landed safely in Kursk.

The first serious losses of the Luftwaffe were noted on the night of 30/31 July, when four bombers did not return from dangerous missions over the Volga. Among them was the He 111H-6 W. Nr. 7382 'G1+AP' (crew commander Feldwebel Martin Wallrabenstein) from the 6th Staffel KG55. He took off from the Kramatorsk airfield, but did not return to his base. The entire crew of the bomber has since been considered missing. In fact, the He 111 made an emergency belly landing in Russian territory. Subsequently, the remains of the bomber were taken to Stalingrad and put on public display on the Central Square. There this plane lay for the whole battle, becoming the subject of numerous photographs, legends and then films!

In early August, the steamer *Turgenev* again went on a voyage to Stalingrad. This time, all the sailors were on their guard, cautiously looking at the sunny August sky. The river presented a depressing sight. Oil slicks floated everywhere on the surface, interspersed with clusters of dead fish. From time to time fragments of ships, lifebuoys and mutilated corpses of people floated past the sides. In some places, the skeletons of sunken ships could be seen sticking out of the water. The voyage to Kamenny Yar passed without incident, and about 120km remained to the destination. But on the morning of 6 August, the anchored steamer *Viktor Kholzunov* appeared ahead. He left Astrakhan three days earlier. Her captain Yevgeny Kistovich reported that the Volga was mined, and it was too dangerous to continue the journey.

Turgenev stopped next to *Viktor Kholzunov*. An anchor splashed into the river. Anchored in the middle of the river, the vessels were an easy target for bombers. But everything was quiet, and the peaceful steppe landscape did not portend any adventures. Soon a boat was lowered, and the captain went on it to his colleague. Together, they radioed the Stalingrad port, and they were ordered from there that the *Viktor Kholzunov* urgently go on, regardless of the danger. This was the end of the short rendezvous between the two ships. *Victor Kholzunov* went around the stern of the *Turgenev* and headed along the waterway. Thick black smoke poured out of the funnel, and the ship began to move away to the north-west. But then the unexpected happened. After the *Viktor Kholzunov* overtook another ship, it sailed on for 200m and then a mine exploded under her, a huge column of water rising up and the echo of the powerful explosion rolling across the steppe.

The sailors on the *Turgenev* were horrified to see how the *Viktor Kholzunov* began to quickly go down by the bows, the surviving crew members jumping overboard. A few more seconds passed, and the hull of the sinking vessel broke with a crash, the aft part stood on an even keel for a short time, and then began to inexorably sink into the abyss. Soon, only clouds of smoke and steam remained above the water, as well as desperately floundering sailors. The captain of the *Turgenev* immediately ordered all boats to be lowered and the survivors to be rescued. Half an hour later, everything was quiet on the river and nothing reminded of the disaster, except for the huge spot of fuel oil that spread.

In addition to the *Victor Kholzunov*, that day, the steam cargo longboat *Kulturik* was lost, which was sunk by aircraft at Sadkovsky Yar. On 7 August, the cargo and passenger ship *Academic Timiryazev* blew up and sank near Yashin Island. The next day, the cargo and passenger steamer Kommunistka, with 400 passengers on board, was blown up by a mine. The ship went down so quickly that most people did not even have time to leave their cabins. As a result, only one in five managed to escape and reach the shore. In addition, the cargo steam launch *Energichniy* and the passenger boat *Gvardeyets* were sunk by aircraft in the Sarepta harbour.

In total, from 25 July to 10 August, 302 vessels passed through the mined section of the Volga, of which 79 were blown up by mines or were sunk by bombs. Thus, every fourth ship was sunk. At the same time, hundreds of people were killed, a significant amount of cargo lost and 115,000 tons of petroleum products spilled down the river! This was the obvious success of Richthofen's Luftflotte 4, which put Russian logistics routes at risk.

The Volga military flotilla was not ready to deal with the mine danger on the river. The conversion of vessels into minesweepers took place hastily, the installed trawls quickly demonstrated their unsuitability, and the crews lacked any experience in dealing with mines.

Final Destinations on Fire

When Hitler decided to launch offensives on the Caucasus and the Volga at the same time, and it became clear that the battle for the 'city of Stalin' could not be avoided, the Luftwaffe applied a strategy already tested in the Crimea. First, isolate the objective from the outside world, destroying all communications leading to it, then concentrate all the power of aviation on the 'stronghold' itself. Simultaneously with the mining of the Volga and air attacks against ships, German planes struck at the Soviets' land logistics routes.

The main goal of the Luftwaffe was the 500km railway line running north of the Don River through the stations of Borisoglebsk and Povorino to Stalingrad. At that time, this huge railway, laid in a sparsely populated area, had become the main transport corridor connecting Moscow and the central regions of Russia with the south. It was only through it that troops and equipment could get directly to the overstretched front along the Don.

The first air attacks were carried out on 12 July, and then repeated many times a day. The Luftwaffe bombed the large railway stations at Ilovla, Log, Archeda and Frolovo as a priority. Air attacks were carried out at the same intervals every 36 to 48 hours. The restoration of the damage took at least 10–12 hours. As a result, by the beginning of August, Russian railway communications began to collapse. Huge congestion and 'traffic jams' appeared on the railway tracks in the Stalingrad area. Railways tracks, stations and sidings were clogged with empty cars that had nowhere to go. Russian railwaymen were forced to simply push many cars off the rails or dump them into ditches. The speed of cargo delivery decreased every day, and some trains moved at a speed of no more than 10–15km per day.

The Russians had to send trains to detour along the 270km Balashov–Kamyshin railway line. But it was single-track and in a neglected state. Old rails on dilapidated rotten sleepers allowed trains to move only at a speed of 15–20km/h. Accidents were constantly occurring, steam locomotives and wagons being derailed. In addition, the area along the railway was sparsely populated, and there were no sidings and loading platforms at the few stations. That's why the cars that came off the tracks and the steam locomotives that failed had to be simply pushed into the ditches.

As the German armies approached Stalingrad, the air attacks against this railway line intensified. For example, on the morning of 13 August, Ju 88 bombers attacked Rakovka station twice. At 12.15, a raid was made on the Kotluban station, on which 30 high-explosive bombs were dropped. Twenty wagons with military cargo and 11 wagons with grain were burned there. The Upper Lipki, Log and Ilovlya stations were also attacked. On the morning of 16 August, He 111 bombers attacked Rakovka station twice, and in the evening air attacks were carried out against Ilovlya and Archeda stations. On 17 August, the Germans bombed the stations at Rakovka, Log, Archeda, Lipki, Kachalino and Panshino. Especially terrible consequences were caused by the explosion of 48 railway carriages loaded with rockets, which completely destroyed an entire section of the track 1.5km long.

During these missions, the Ju 88s and He 111s operated at an altitude of 1,000m and without fighter escort. But Russian fighters could not oppose them. When attacked, the bombers gathered in a tight formation and consistently conducted barrage and aimed fire from their numerous machine guns. The main responsibility for scaring off enemy fighters lay with the planes on the extreme left and extreme right, which in the jargon of German pilots were called 'chain dogs'. Attacking the He 111 formations at close range was suicidal, so the Soviet pilots preferred to shoot at them from afar and launch rockets at them. Such tactics were ineffective.

The efforts of the Luftwaffe brought serious effects. Railway transportation worked with great interruptions; trains arrived with a significant delay from the schedule. The Russians had to unload troops and cargo 100–130km from the battlefields.

For example, in mid-August, the Russian command decided to transfer five regiments of Guards BM-13 rocket launchers ('Stalin organs') to Stalingrad at once. Loading was carried out in Moscow on four trains during 16–18 August. According to the plan, the rocket launchers should have arrived at the Samodurovka and Polyana stations (in the Povorino area) on 19–21 August, and from there they had to go on their own to the Ilovlya sector – to the outer defensive perimeter of Stalingrad. However, in fact, the trains reached their destination only at the beginning of September, and the 'Stalin organs' did not reach the front until 15 September.

However, the Soviets have always been prone to improvisation. In the middle of summer, the Russians began to build a new railway line along the western bank of the Volga. It passed through Ulyanovsk–Saratov–Kamyshin to the northern outskirts of Stalingrad. In addition to railway troops and construction battalions, the entire local population, even 12-year-old schoolchildren, participated in the large-scale construction. The track was built in two months and was in operation by the beginning of September. Among the Russians, it was called the 'Volga Rockade'.

Chapter 3

THE LONG ROAD
IN THE SANDS

'Our progress continues unstoppably'
Shortly after German troops crossed the Manych Canal in the last days
of July 1942, which at that time was considered the border between
Europe and Asia, various representatives of the command fell into
euphoria and made the optimistic conclusion that the battle for oil had
already been won. On 29 July, Luftflotte 4 headquarters reported to the
Wehrmacht High Command: 'The Russian Air Force is demonstrating
its weakness in front of the right flank of the army Group South. Stuka
dive bombers carry out their attacks without fighter escort, and are
not attacked by Russian fighters.' According to OKW's assessment
of 4 August, 'the Soviet command is obviously creating defences
south of the Kuban River to protect the Maykop district and the naval
bases of the Black Sea Fleet. Nevertheless, the forces of the enemy are
scattered . . . Panzer units are moving forward on Baku everywhere.'
On 4 August, the medical officer of III./KG27, Dr Keller, wrote to
his wife: 'Encouraging prospects in the Caucasus. This is again a big
pocket, from which the Russians have only one way left through the
Black Sea to Batum. The big oil deposits of Maykop will also be in our
hands in the coming days!' This doctor was by no means on the front
line, but in the quiet rear, and he received information from the various
gossip of pilots sharing impressions and news. Therefore, Keller's
opinion reflected the mood prevailing in the Third Reich at that time.

Ten days later he wrote to his wife again: 'Now I definitely believe
that this year we will defeat the Russians, so they can no longer be
dangerous for us. After all, they have 10 million fewer soldiers, they
have lost the most important agricultural areas, the largest industrial

and oil centres are in our hands, and despite Stalin's firm orders not to retreat another step, our progress continues unstoppably.'

After the rapid capture of Krasnodar and Maykop, Hitler and his entourage decided that the Soviet troops in the Caucasus had been defeated. The Wehrmacht command, under the influence of the Führer, believed that the capture of Stalingrad was of great strategic importance. '. . . When the city falls, Stalin will have to seek peace,' Franz Halder wrote in his diary. The chief of the OKW operations section, General Alfred Jodl, also announced that 'the fate of the Caucasus will be decided at Stalingrad'. Richthofen also believed this. Soon he issued an order, more like a proclamation: 'The struggle for Stalingrad, the red stronghold, is heating up. The Luftwaffe must use destructive strikes to bring this battle to a solution. I expect from the commanders of Luftflotte 4 units and formations in the air and on the ground, at the front and in the rear areas, ultimate dedication and a firm will to win.'

The Soviet command also believed that it was in the area of Stalingrad (and not Rzhev, Leningrad, Voronezh or Novorossiysk) that the fate of the world would be 'decided'. On 7 August, the commander of the newly formed South-eastern Front, Colonel-General Eremenko, wrote a proclamation:

> Comrades! We have the honour to defend the city of Stalin. The hated and brutal hordes of fascism poured blood over the occupied regions. Rivers of blood and tears have been shed: so much innocent blood and tears have been shed that all Hitler's bloodthirsty bandits can be drowned in them. Hitler's bandits disgraced and dishonoured our girls and wives . . . In the battle of Stalingrad, we will mark the beginning of the end of the extermination of Hitlerism.

On the evening of 9 August, Stalin signed a directive stating: 'The defence of Stalingrad and the defeat of the enemy coming from the west and from the south to Stalingrad is crucial for our entire Soviet Front. Spare no effort and stop at no sacrifice in order to defend Stalingrad and defeat the enemy.' On the same day, Eremenko received extraordinary powers, commanding two Fronts at once – the Stalingrad and the South-Eastern.

Stalingrad (formerly Tsaritsyn) was founded in the sixteenth century as an intermediate point on the Volga trade route. The city was initially built near the mouth of the Tsaritsa River flowing into the Volga. The terrain here was quite specific and determined the features of the development of the city for centuries. The high Volga bank was cut by numerous deep ravines running perpendicular to the Volga and dividing the area into several separate plateaus. On the shore, at some distance from the river, several huge gentle hills rose up, towering tens of metres above the surrounding fields. In the following centuries, the city experienced many important historical events, including the peasant uprisings of Stepan Razin and Emelyan Pugachev.

The city gradually expanded along the bank of the Volga. During the First World War, as part of a programme to dramatically increase armaments production, the British company Vickers built a large artillery factory on the northern outskirts of Tsaritsyn. This was the beginning of the northern industrial zone, which later played an important historical role. During the Russian Civil War, major battles between the White Army and the Red Army took place in the Tsaritsyn area. One of the leaders of the defence at that time was Stalin, after whom the city later received the honorary name Stalingrad. During the years of Stalin's 'industrialisation', two more large enterprises were erected on the steep Volga bank: the Stalingrad Tractor Plant (STZ) and the 'Red October' metallurgical plant. Soon the factories were surrounded by typical workers' settlements, consisting of private one-story houses, multi-apartment brick buildings, 'zasypushki',[1] 'shields' and barracks. In the southern suburbs, the large StalGRES power station was built in Beketovka in 1930.

By 1940 Stalingrad consisted of four separate parts, which was due to its historical development and peculiar landscape. From the Tsaritsa River to the Mamayev Kurgan hill stretched the central part of the city, built of tall brick houses, including high-rise buildings, visible for tens of kilometres. Further to the north, along the entire high bank of the Volga, there was an industrial zone, where large workshops were interspersed with loading docks, oil storage facilities and warehouses. Monotonous blocks of housing stretched away from them in a westerly direction. To the south of the centre, behind the Tsaritsa, there was the ancient historical part of Stalingrad, consisting of houses built in the seventeenth to nineteenth centuries. The tallest building here was an grain elevator, towering over the one- or two-storey houses like a colossus. This had been erected right before the war according to a standard design. Further to the south, settlements that were part of the Kirovsky district of the city were scattered on several hills: Beketovka, Sarepta, Krasnoarmeysk. They were crowned by the buildings of the StalGRES power station, which were visible for tens of kilometres.

---

1 A 'zasypushka' is a house made of planks, in which ordinary earth was used as insulation.

By the beginning of the war, almost 450,000 people lived in Stalingrad, and 126 industrial enterprises were operating. The city had 124 schools, four universities, four theatres, a circus and many cinemas. The centre of trade in the city was the central department store. The industrial zone was connected to the central quarters by several tram routes and railways.

By the summer of 1942, Stalingrad was one of the most important industrial centres of the Soviet Union. The Tractor Plant produced half of all T-34 tanks, and the 'Red October' Metallurgical Plant was the main producer of high-quality steel for the tank, aviation and bearing industries. Factory No. 221 'Barricades' at that time was the main manufacturer of divisional artillery, producing 76mm USV-BR guns. In mid-July, when it became clear that Stalingrad was the main target of the German offensive, defensive lines and structures begun in the autumn of 1941 were hastily restored or completed. At the end of July, over 57,000 people worked on the construction of the city's defensive lines. Everything necessary for them was mined on site.

But at the beginning of August Stalingrad was still living a relatively peaceful life, the approaching danger only indicated by the glare of artillery cannonades visible at night in the west, the fumes from fires coming from the Don steppes, the shiny strip of spilled oil constantly stretching along the Volga and the frequent flights of German reconnaissance planes over the city. Not until 5 August, for the first time since the beginning of the war, a daytime air attack was made against Stalingrad. At 08.09, a single aircraft dropped six high-explosive bombs on the site of the 'Barricades' plant. Two residential buildings were destroyed, seven civilians were killed and 35 wounded.

It is interesting that the Germans studied the situation in the city, including articles in the Soviet press! 'An enemy newspaper with details of the situation in Stalingrad has been captured,' the 6th Army's 1 August summary says.

In the first week of August, there was a relative lull on the Stalingrad front. The Germans were pulling straggling infantry divisions and reinforcements into the big bend of the Don-river, and the Soviet troops maintained constant counter-attacks against the wedge directed towards Kalach-on-Don. However, due to the heavy losses suffered, these attacks were carried out by weak forces and mostly led only to further losses. And then the Russians were again under the threat of encirclement.

On 6 August, the commander of the 62nd Army, Major General Lopatin, directly stated to the Front headquarters that 'if we continue to be here, we will remain fools, as it was before'. He was referring to a large bridgehead on the western bank of the Don west of Kalach, which was held by Soviet troops, despite the obvious threat of being outflanked. However, in response, Lopatin received an order: 'not a step back'! Meanwhile, a day earlier, the Führer, who had previously been interested only in the rapid advance of Army Group A into the Caucasus, suddenly became concerned about the slowness of the 6th Army and expressed fears that the Soviet troops would have time to evacuate their bridgehead. Despite Paulus' objections, the next day he ordered an operation to encircle the 62nd Army on the morning of 7 August.

Since the summer nights at this time were very short, the Germans began the offensive at 03.00 Berlin time. This time, the 6th Army met with complete success, and the prediction of Major General Lopatin turned out to be prophetic. Fliegerkorps VIII supported the attack of tanks with all its might, striking artillery positions, columns of tanks and infantry. Stukas and Hs 123s bombed bridges and floating pontoon bridges across the Don at Kalach, as well as reinforcements coming from the east.

As early as 15.30, the 16th Panzer Division, advancing from the north, reached the hills located 5km west of Kalach, and, raising clouds of dust, the first Panzer II light tanks burst in there. At 18.00, the 24th Panzer Division, advancing towards them from the south, also reached the hills south-west of the Kalach bridge. On this day, the weather was clear and hot, the sun warming the air to +35°. Therefore, in the clouds of dust and smoke rising high into the sky, German soldiers could not see their comrades for a long time. And it was only by midnight that it was possible to establish contact between the leading units and completely 'cover' the resulting pocket. As a result, the entire Russian 1st Tank Army and most of the 62nd Army (five rifle divisions, several tank brigades, five artillery regiments and other units) were completely surrounded.

The delighted Paulus, who decided that a turning point had finally come in the protracted battle, immediately presented a plan for a further offensive to OKH (in fact to the Führer). He suggested, without waiting for the pocket to be cleared, first strike in a north-eastly direction – towards Kachalinskaya – in order to finally throw the Russians behind the Don, and at the same time seize bridgeheads on the eastern shore. In the second stage, the 14th and 24th Panzer Corps were to rapidly advance on Stalingrad in order to encircle the remaining Soviet troops in the Karpovka area, connect with the forward units of the 4th Panzer Army at Voroponovo and reach the Volga north and south of the city. The left flank was to be covered by the 8th Army Corps, which was ordered to advance north-east to the Berdiya River. Paulus intended to start the first stage on 11 August and the second on the 14th in order to complete the operation to capture Stalingrad by the middle of the month.

The destruction of the pocket took several days. The fiercest fighting took place in the area of Surovikino. The 51st Army Corps had to attack this village for three days, suffering serious losses at the same time. The capturing of numerous ravines in which the Russians were sheltering from air attacks and artillery shelling, and at the same time the unbearable heat (fixed to +45°!), took a lot of time and effort for the Germans, delaying the concentration for Paulus's further offensive. 'The Russians continue to resist stubbornly but hopelessly in ravines and heavily fortified positions. Strong attempts to break through to the south-east, east and north-east were repulsed with bloody losses for the enemy,' as the 6th Army headquarters assessed the situation in the pocket on 10 August. By this time, the remnants of the 62nd Army held only a small area north of Surovikino. Like black crows, German Fw 189 reconnaissance planes, which the Russians nicknamed 'Rama' ('Frame'), circled above them in a casual manner. Taking advantage of impunity and the lack of air defences, these planes periodically dropped bombs on suitable targets.

Soviet aviation made no attempt to supply the encircled troops. The Russians limited themselves to visual observation of what was happening and the delivery of officers with radios to the pocket (twelve were dropped on the night of 11 August). However, none of them got in touch. On 12 August, Russian pilots reported that fighting was going on on the west bank of the Don, but no detailed information was received. On 13 August, several groups of Red Army soldiers managed to cross to the eastern shore. But they could not really describe what was happening. In fact, most of the 62nd Army and 1st Tank Army surrendered on 11 August. According to German information, 57,000 prisoners were captured during this battle, and 1,100 tanks and 750 guns were shot down and captured. The last group of Russians, mainly senior officers and commissars, tried to break through to the east on 14 August in the area east of Rychkovskaya, but 70 men were killed 'in a fierce battle', and 40 were captured, including the chief of staff of the 229th Rifle Division. But General Anton Lopatin was not among the prisoners and fallen. It was customary for the Russians to save the generals first of all, abandoning the soldiers to their fate. Lopatin was evacuated from the pocket by plane.

This defeat was the first result of the application of Stalin's well-known order 'Not a step back', issued on 27 July. Another consequence of this 'inspiring' document was a sharp increase in the number of defectors. Having got into a difficult situation and not being able to fulfil obviously unrealistic orders, many soldiers preferred to lie down in no man's land, and then go over to the Germans in the dark. The alternative for them was to be shot with machine guns or be court-martialled. It seemed to the German command that numerous defectors were a sure sign of an imminent victory. 'I inform you that soon we will be fulfilling the new tasks set by the Führer. I am sure that the troops subordinate to me will fulfil them. Long live the Führer!': so ended the pathetic order of General Paulus to the army following the end of the battle.

Through the desert

While the battle in the big bend of the Don reached its climax, the threat to Stalingrad suddenly loomed from the south. The fact is that at the end of July the 4th Panzer Army of Generaloberst Hermann Hoth had already managed to cross the Sal River and rushed to the Caucasus. But then it was suddenly stopped. On Hitler's orders, the 48th Panzer Corps and the 4th Army Corps were turned to the east and ordered to move to the Volga. Their route ran along the railway line Salsk–Kotelnikovo–Stalingrad. At first, this operation, which took place in a deserted steppe, developed fantastically rapidly. The vanguard of the 14th Panzer Division set an absolute Blitzkrieg record, covering a distance of 150km in 15 hours! On 3 August, tanks and armoured vehicles reached the Yesaulovsky Aksai River, from which only 90km remained to Stalingrad. Previously, such movements were possible only in North Africa! At that moment it seemed that Hoth could outrun Paulus in this 'race to the Volga'.

When the headquarters of Yeremenko and Khrushchev learned that the enemy was approaching from the south-west, they were shocked. At first, they had nothing to oppose the Germans, except for the scattered air attacks of the 8th Air Army. On 4 August, Il-2 ground-attack planes and single-engined Su-2 bombers struck the first blows at Hoth's vanguard. Although the German units did not suffer any serious losses as a result of these air attacks (not a single bomb hit on armoured vehicles was recorded), these bombardments and shelling still had a strong psychological impact on the soldiers. In the middle of a huge desert, tanks and armoured personnel carriers were clearly visible, Soviet pilots easily found them and attacked them from different directions, making several approaches. After some time, new groups of ground-attack planes appeared from the north, and everything started over again.

Despite the air attacks, the advance of Hoth's army did not slow down. On 6 August, the 14th Panzer Division reached the outer defensive perimeter of Stalingrad without encountering any troops there. Then the tanks reached the '74 Kilometre' railway junction and the vicinity of the Tinguta railway station. With binoculars, the German tankers could already see the shiny ribbon of the Volga, visible beyond the plain located ahead to the right. At that moment, this adventurous raid into the Russian rear resembled an adventure. One of the tankers wrote in his diary: 'Through the heat of 58 degrees and columns of dust, we continue to move along the Kalmyk steppe to the north-east. During the day we did not meet a single settlement. Our skin is black from dust and sunburn. There are no roads. We drive through the mounds by compass. The Kalmyk steppe absorbed us into itself.' The supply of Hoth's vanguard, located in the middle of a huge desert, was carried out by air. Ju 52 transport planes regularly dropped containers with fuel and provisions. Often even water had to be delivered in this way!

However, soon the safe adventure for the Germans ended. On 6 August, Yeremenko and Khrushchev learned from aerial reconnaissance that German tanks were only 40km from Stalingrad. The emergence of a new threat forced the Soviets to take urgent measures. On the same day, the Stalingrad Front was divided into two parts: the defence of the southern sector was assigned to the South-eastern Front as part of the 64th, 57th and 51st Armies. Four tank brigades (150 tanks) and three rifle divisions were sent to the area of the Tinguta station, additionally reinforced by the personnel of three military schools. In addition, Eremenko sent two armoured trains to meet the Germans. The operation was prepared very carefully, the transfer of troops took place only at night, and the tanks delivered to the front were effectively camouflaged.

Luftwaffe reconnaissance did not notice these movements, as a result of which Hoth's vanguard, which was in the middle of an empty desert, got into a very dangerous position. In the lead were only the 14th Panzer Division with 50 tanks and half of the 29th Motorised Infantry Division. All the other units of the 4th Panzer Army (two infantry divisions and Romanian troops), for various reasons, were stretched far in the rear to the north-east and south-east of Kotelnikovo. Until 7 August, the Germans did not meet serious resistance in the Kalmyk steppes, but already on that day the 'peaceful expedition' of the 48th Panzer Corps of General Werner Kempf across the vast wasteland ended. The vanguard groups were suddenly attacked by numerous Soviet tanks, which seemed to have risen up from under the sand and dust. The Germans immediately took up a circular defence and began to shoot back. The attacks, repeated the next day, were repelled.

At dawn on 9 August, an Fw 189 reconnaissance aircraft flew around the area of the Tinguta railway station. Down below, the navigator of the plane saw a frightening sight. Columns of vehicles were moving towards the front from Stalingrad, and there was lively activity around the clearly-visible positions of the 14th Panzer Division. Dozens of T-34, KV-1 and T-60 tanks were in readiness for attack. The message was transmitted to the ground troops, and already at 04.50 columns of tanks were moving from the steppe from almost all sides to the German positions. Behind which, with wild shouts of 'hurrah', the chains of soldiers were running. A fierce battle unfolded, taking place over a fairly large area.

At 08.30, the headquarters of the 48th Tank Corps had already received a message about the withdrawal from the front positions and a desperate request for air support. At first these reports were considered exaggerated, but at 10.40 the headquarters of the 4th Panzer Army passed a message to the headquarters of Fliegerkorps VIII: 'We ask you to support ground-attack planes and "Stukas" leading a heavy defensive battle to the 48th Panzer Corps.' By lunchtime, ten German tanks had been lost in the fighting. Soon, Ju 87s appeared, which struck at the Soviet troops at the '74 Kilometre' railway junction and an armoured train, but the air attack only slowed down the onslaught of the Russians. By 15.30, the position of the 14th Panzer Division had already become critical. Ten more tanks were lost in three hours, and the number of combat-ready tanks in the outflanked flanked and retreating unit was reduced to 23. At the same time, the long-barrelled 50mm guns of the Panzer III tanks could not penetrate the armour of heavy Soviet KV-1 tanks, and the armour-piercing projectiles simply stuck into it like nails! 'There are numerous enemy tanks operating. Please send aviation!', the commander of the 14th Panzer Division, General Heim, shouted in panic over the radio.

At this time, Richthofen's 'Storch' landed near the command post of the 48th Panzer Corps. After studying the situation, he began to call his subordinates and get into the air all the planes that were not engaged in combat. After 17.00, Stukas finally appeared overhead, and then ground-attack Bf 109Es and Hs 129s, which struck Soviet tanks for three hours. The Hs 129s formed a big circle, and then alternately descended and fired their guns, aiming at the engine compartments of KV-1 and T-34 tanks. One by one, the hulking armoured monsters froze, enveloped in smoke.

As a result, the situation was stabilised by nightfall, and the 14th Panzer Division was able to systematically withdraw south to Plodovitoye, evacuating most of its artillery and equipment. The previously-mentioned Soviet 38th Rifle Division also took part in this battle. The fighters who came out of the encirclement in the Millerovo area had only five days to rest, after which the hastily replenished unit was sent south in a forced march through Stalingrad–Beketovka–Nariman–Zety–Tinguta. Moreover, the replenishment continued along the way, the division picking up scattered groups and even single soldiers who they came across on the way. In the attack on 9 August, the 38th Division under the command of Colonel Safiulin supported the 13th and 133rd Tank Brigades, while losing eight guns and 40 men.

On 10 August, the situation in the area of the Tinguta railway station stabilised. The commander of the 48th Panzer Corps, General Kempf, coincidentally was awarded the Knight's Cross with Oak Leaves (for his previous numerous services). The Germans breathed a sigh of relief, although there was nothing to rejoice about. Despite the fact that the Soviet tankers failed to completely defeat the 14th Panzer Division, and the Russian tank brigades themselves suffered heavy losses in this battle (80 per cent of tanks were lost), at Abganerov and Tinguta, Yermenko achieved the same as Gordov earlier at Verkhnebuzinovka. Instead of a quick raid to Stalingrad by the tank vanguards thrown out in advance, the Germans were forced to change their plans again at the final stage of the offensive, regroup and gradually break through enemy defences, wasting precious time.

'Beautiful bloodshed!'

Yeremenko and Khrushchev had very little time to grieve about their recent defeats and guess where the enemy would strike next. Already at dawn on 15 August, 'Stukas' appeared in the sky again, which, with sirens howling, attacked the positions of the Russian 4th Tank Army in the sector between Kletskaya and Peskovatka. At 05.30 the Germans went on the offensive and quickly broke through the front. The Russian command lost contact with subordinate units. 'The reasons for the loss of communication are that when moving command posts, no one was in charge of the units. Everyone moved where they wanted and how they wanted, while not reporting to anyone,' says the war diary of the Stalingrad Front.

The next day, contrary to Eremenko's order to hold the bridgehead on the west bank of the Don at all costs and counter-attack the enemy who broke through, the 'movement' turned into a stampede. Of the nine rifle divisions that were part of the Russian 4th Tank Army, three were completely destroyed, one was surrounded, and the rest fled in disorder, being subjected to constant air attacks. For example, soldiers of the 39th Guards Division and the 18th Rifle Division tried to dig in on the hills on the west bank of the Don. However, at 13.00, fifty German tanks appeared, then the terrifying howl of Ju 87 sirens was heard from out of the sun. Soon the soldiers, forgetting Stalin's order 'Not a step back', abandoned all heavy weapons and equipment, then ran to the river in complete disorder.

The result of this offensive for the Germans was the capture of almost the entire small bend of the Don south of Ilovlya. As trophies, they got 12,835 prisoners, 47 tanks and 252 guns. 'Mostly young and fanatical communists,' was how the intelligence department of the 6th German Army described one of the captured groups. The 6th Army itself suffered minimal losses this time. For example, the 16th Panzer Division lost 21 men killed and 79 wounded on 15 August, and the 3rd Motorised Infantry Division lost two men killed. The total losses of the army amounted to 239 killed and missing, over 1,100 wounded and only six tanks.

Satisfied, Paulus issued an army order on 16 August to attack Stalingrad. In general, it corresponded to his previous plans only with modified deadlines. Five days were allotted for preparation. In those days, when the heat was unbearable in the Don steppes, the soldiers, as if in a desert, suffered from thirst and clouds of dust that resembled sandstorms. It seemed to them that nothing was impossible for the Wehrmacht. And there, in a city only 50km away, they would soon be celebrating the long-awaited victory over the Soviets. No one could have imagined that there would come a time for the 6th Army when water would be in excess, but everything else would be scarce!

The Soviets were frantically trying to strengthen their defences on the eastern bank of the Don. But this was prevented by the continuous air attacks of the Luftwaffe. In groups of 20–30 aircraft, accompanied by Bf 109 fighters, the Germans bombed field defence positions, railway stations, Volga ferry crossings, artillery battery positions and airfields. For example, on 20 August, the Luftwaffe bombed the villages of Solodcha, Trudolyubie, Sovetsky, Dmitrievka, Zety, Novy Rogachik, Serebryakovo and Krasnoarmeysk, and the Sarepta railway station. 'Enemy aircraft bombed the battle formations of the army during the day, making up to 500–600 sorties . . . the 138th Rifle Division fought fierce battles with enemy infantry and tanks during the day on August 20, being subjected to continuous attacks from the air,' the 64th Army war diary says.

The next day, massive air attacks continued. For example, at 08.45 seven Hs 123 biplanes bombed the area of Sovkarevka, at 09.34 12 He 111s raided Yerzovka (a grain warehouse, a hospital and 15 residential buildings were destroyed), at 12.19 nine He-111s bombed Beketovka, and at 15.00 nine Ju 88A dive-bombers attacked the same target. Most of the German planes bombed the positions and the immediate rear of the Soviet troops. Hauptman Herbert Pabst, commander of the combat training air group Erg.Gr./StG77, recalled: 'Since early morning we have been constantly over the advancing tanks, helping them with our bombs and machine guns. We landed, refuelled, received bombs and ammunition and immediately took off again.' The 64th Army war diary reports: 'Enemy aircraft continuously bombed and shelled the battle formations of divisions. Bombarded Krasnoarmeysk, a dairy farm, Big Chapurniki.' In the afternoon, Richthofen flew his 'Storch' over the steppe to the west of Stalingrad. He witnessed his bombers dropping fragmentation bombs on Soviet troops. This sight caused the bloodthirsty Richthofen great delight. 'Beautiful bloodshed!' he wrote in his diary that evening.

A similar picture developed the next day. This unbroken domination of German aviation, as before in Sevastopol, near Kharkov and in the Voronezh region, had a powerful demoralising effect on Soviet soldiers. Ground-attack planes, fighters and bombers circled over the steppe for days, freely attacking any targets, chasing even individual solders and cars. One of the Red Army soldiers, frightened by the continuous air attacks, wrote to his family in despair:

> Today, the whole day, the German aviation did not give any rest, even if you dig into the ground for 100–1,000 metres, it will still get you. Our planes have not been seen all day, and this is not only today, but it was yesterday and will be tomorrow. There is no resistance, what they want, they do with ground troops ... German planes are shelling our troops and civilians in the rear

It happened that German pilots, flying at low level, opened their cockpits and fired at the infantry with pistols!

Chapter 4

'UNDIVIDED DOMINATION'

'By evening, the Volga was already in sight'

While the Soviet commanders were discussing how and with what forces to fulfil Stalin's next categorical order – to 'restore the situation' – at 03.00 on 21 August, units of the German 51st Army Corps began crossing the Don in the area of Peskovatka and Vertyachy. Basically, the Germans met weak resistance, and only the 76th Infantry Division suffered serious losses during the crossing (several assault boats were sunk by fire from the eastern shore). At 11.35 Paulus arrived at the forward command post of 51st Corps on the bank of the Don. The west bank at this point is much higher than the east, and he clearly saw numerous explosions, fires and signal-rocket launches on the bridgehead, as well as work on building a bridge across the river. In the distance, a chain of small hills could be seen receding over the horizon – to the Volga. Later, Paulus went to the command post of the commander of the 14th Panzer Corps, General von Wietersheim. There they decided to start a dash to the Volga on the morning of 23 August.

By evening, with the massive support of the Luftwaffe, the Germans had expanded the bridgehead to 6–8km in depth, surrounding two battalions of the 98th Rifle Division in the area of Vertyachy. At 16.00, the first pontoon bridge across the river was completed. The commander of the Russian 62nd Army, General Anton Lopatin, saw all this through binoculars. Then he honestly reported to Eremenko that the army, actually formed anew after the defeat on the west bank of the Don, would not be able to repel further attacks. Lopatin again acted as a prophet, warning that the next morning German tanks could reach Kotluban or Karpovka.

At night, the Russians threw in all available bombers to attack the bridges across the Don at Peskovatka and Vertyachy. At the same time, artillery opened fire on them. This slowed down the crossing of the German troops a little, but did not stop it. By dawn, the 16th Panzer Division and the 3rd Motorised Infantry Division had already taken up their starting positions west and north of Vertyachy. At 04.00 the Luftwaffe carried out a massive raid on the positions of the 62nd Army. The 87th and 98th Rifle Divisions and the 28th Tank Corps suffered the most from it. The artillery of the 62nd Army alone lost 79 men, 12 guns and 14 tractors due to air attacks.

When the smoke and dust cleared, at 04.45 German tanks rushed to the offensive. Having quickly crushed the demoralised Soviet units, at 06.00 they broke out into the open steppe. Already at 08.00, a huge column, raising a whole veil of dust, followed north of Bolshaya Rossoshka. At 11.15, the vanguard of the 16th Panzer Division reached the Povorino-Stalingrad railway between the Konny station and the '564th Kilometre' siding (the junction of the railway from Povorino with the Stalingrad Ring Railway). 'Under the attack of tanks, weak Soviet forces are retreating to the south and north, but strong pockets of resistance remain in the valleys of Rossoshka (87th Rifle Division) and Kotluban (35th Guards Rifle Division and 28th Tank Corps),' the headquarters of the 14th Panzer Corps reported.

Having had lunch and rested a little under the cover of fighters constantly patrolling in a clear sky, the Germans drove on. At 15.30, having covered another 15km, Wietersheim's tanks crossed the Stalingrad–Saratov highway, along which traffic was still driving. Half an hour later, the vanguard reached the hills to the north of the suburban village of Rynok, and at 17.00 (19.00 Moscow time), the tanks left for a large plateau south of the village of Vinnovka. Although the headquarters of the 6th Army reported (and this information was transmitted to the Führer and to the summary of the Wehrmacht High Command) that the Volga had been reached, in fact the bank was still far away. The war diary of the 16th Panzer Division reports: 'By evening, the Volga was already in sight, a few kilometres west of the Volga, just north of Stalingrad, the division took up a circular defence in a rather narrow area centred about 2km east of point 722.'

Interestingly, the first combat vehicles to reach Stalingrad were the Panzer IIs from the 16th Panzer Engineer Battalion! It was these light tanks weighing 9.5 tons, armed with a 20mm cannon, that again found themselves on the edge of the blitzkrieg! Vividly refuting the well-known myths about the advantages of sloped armour and wide tracks . . .

The German breakthrough to the Volga bank was accompanied by large-scale air battles. Fliegerkorps VIII carried out 1,600 sorties during the day, dropping 1,000 tons of bombs on Soviet positions around Stalingrad. German pilots reported 73 aerial victories, 17 of which were claimed by I./ JG53. In fact, the Red Army Air Force lost 42 aircraft, including 25 fighters.

Russian aviation responded to the Germans with 607 sorties. 'Stalin's Falcons' reported 57 aerial victories. Another 27 downed 'vultures' were claimed by anti-aircraft artillery. The Soviets, as usual, lied about their successes, repeatedly overestimating them. In fact, the Luftwaffe lost only nine aircraft (six Bf 109s, one He 111, one Ju 87 and one Bf 110) of which three were shot down in air battles and four were shot down by ground fire, the rest crashing for technical reasons. It was another success of the Luftwaffe, which confirmed their complete superiority over the Russians. An important point, contrary to popular stories, no massive bombing attacks against Stalingrad were recorded on this day!

Meanwhile, the German command had every reason to be optimistic. In the evening, Paulus again visited the command post of the 51st Army Corps. There, in his presence, the chief of artillery of the 98th Rifle Division was interrogated, who had surrendered that morning. With a sullen face, this young Russian officer said that the situation of the Red Army was hopeless, and there was 'a big mess' in Stalingrad itself. At 21.30, the delighted Paulus received a directive from the headquarters of Army Group B. Field Marshal von Weichs ordered the 6th Army and the 4th Panzer Army to continue the offensive, unite on the hills located west of Stalingrad, and then seize the city with a joint strike. Weichs also asked Richthofen to bomb Stalingrad day and night 'in order to neutralise the governing bodies located there and complicate the organisation of the defence and counteroffensive troops located there'. Thus, it was Weichs (not Hitler, nor Richthofen) who authorised the subsequent massive air raids on the city.

At dawn on 24 August, the 16th Panzer Engineer Battalion conducted reconnaissance around the occupied bridgehead, and then the Germans began to clear the area. First of all, they captured a battery of 85mm anti-aircraft guns in a sudden attack. At 06.40, the assault groups began moving towards the Volga. The 1st Company moved along the ravine adjacent to the village of Latoshinka, past dense orchards, vineyards and country houses. Soon the sappers reached a 200m-wide steep descent covered with thickets of trees and shrubs, which led directly to the river. On the bank, the Germans saw a four-track railway, two piers and a railway ferry pier. Moreover, there was a lot of work going on there, and the Russian workers were extremely surprised when they saw soldiers running along the bank. With a quick attack, the sapper platoon captured the ferry pier and stopped the train that had already left for the city. In the wagons, the Germans found howitzers and ammunition for them. At the same time, German tanks broke into the village of Latoshinka, capturing another anti-aircraft battery still firing there. Following this, the village of Vinnovka was occupied, and armoured personnel carriers combed the orchards and vineyards.

At 11.00, the clearing of the bridgehead was completed. 'All the soldiers of the panzer engineer battalion were full of joy for an outstanding achievement: to be the first German soldiers to occupy the Volga bank,' the chronicle of the 16th Panzer Division stated. The weather was clear and hot, and from the high shore the Germans could clearly see the panorama of the eastern shore. They saw how in the distance several anti-aircraft batteries were firing at German planes, trains were moving, and Russian fighters were landing and taking off at the airfield located 6km away (Srednaya Akhtuba).

However, the tankers did not have time to enjoy the views of Asia[1] for long. After lunch, the dacha village of Latoshinka was subjected to the first air attack by Soviet ground-attack planes, and then a vessel appeared on the river from the south, described as a 'monitor' in the German report (in fact, it was an NKL-27 Poluglisser speedboat) with a landing party. But as it approached the bank, it was struck by fire from a Panzer III, and the soldiers who jumped onto the sandbank were cut down by 20mm anti-aircraft guns.

Meanwhile, the 51st Army Corps advanced to the hills near Bolshaya Rossoshka, and the 3rd and 60th Motorised Infantry Divisions took up positions along the narrow corridor leading to the Volga. But German commanders, even tankers, also had their own panic. Thus, the commander of the 14th Panzer Corps, General von Wietersheim, having learned that the offensive was not developing according to plan and his units were threatened with encirclement, already on the afternoon of 24 August proposed to retreat from the Volga the next night. They had admired the Asian expanses, shot at the ships, and that's enough! 'Otherwise, it may be too late.' But in response, Wietersheim received strict orders to hold the occupied area and act there independently. The next day, the general even requested 'night fighter cover' to protect against constant night raids by Russian bombers and ground-attack aircraft. To which he was told that there were no night fighters in Fliegerkorps VIII![2]

---

1 According to the geography of that time, the Volga was considered the border between Europe and Asia.
2 That wasn't entirely true. In fact, back in July, a night fighter unit of Luftflotte 4 (Nachtjagdschwarm der Luftflotte 4) was created on the basis of 9./KG27. Based at the Kursk

Since it had not yet been possible to create a solid front along the entire 30km long and about 8km wide corridor between Bolshaya Rossoshka and Latoshinka, the supply routes of the 16th Panzer Division on the Volga were cut that night. Because of this, Fliegerkorps VIII received an order to organise supplies by air. At 05.15, the drop point for containers was determined – 3km north of the village of Orlovka, on a small plateau. In the evening, several groups of Ju 52s under the cover of fighters reached a given area and dropped ammunition for tank guns. On 26 August, Wietersheim again raised a panic, demanding permission to withdraw from the Volga, citing the concentration of Soviet tanks to the north and an acute shortage of ammunition. 'Don't back down! I categorically order it!', Paulus replied again, surprised by his pessimistic assessment of the situation.

Due to the lack of cargo containers at Oblivskaya airfield, transport planes first flew to the Stalino airbase, took on board empty containers and flew with them to Oblivskaya, where they were loaded with tank shells. Then, with an escort of Bf 109s, the transport planes flew to the Volga bridgehead and dropped cargo at the positions of the 14th Panzer Corps. During the day, 39 containers were delivered there, 12 with 50mm shells and 27 with 75mm shells. The day itself passed relatively calmly on the riverbank, but when it got dark, the Germans suddenly saw three ships in the dark with their navigation lights turned off sailing upstream from Stalingrad. When they drew level with Latoshinka, fire was opened from 20mm anti-aircraft guns and anti-tank guns. The first two vessels, despite shells exploding close to them, managed to get through, but the third broke down and stopped. It was a full moon, and from the high shore it was clearly visible how people were jumping over the side and swimming to the shore. Then the huge burning skeleton was carried downstream. According to the intercepted calls for help, the Germans learned the name of the ship – *Joseph Stalin*.

It was the finale of a rather dramatic story. By 26 August, six passenger steam vessels were anchored off the eastern shore of the Volga opposite Stalingrad: *Paris Commune, Mikhail Kalinin, Joseph Stalin, Chicherin, Klim Voroshilov* and *Tajikiya*. On that day, a meeting was held with the participation of the People's Commissar (Minister) of the USSR River Fleet Zosima Shashkov, representatives of the Lower Volga Shipping Company and the command of the South-eastern Front. Some offered to send ships to Astrakhan, but Commissar Nikita

---

airfield, it was engaged in hunting Soviet bombers in the Voronezh region. At the same time, the crew of an He 111 (Oberfeldwebel Engelbert Heiner) was able to shoot down 11 aircraft in a short time.

Khrushchev and Shashkov insisted that it was necessary to break through to the north – towards Saratov. The main calculation was that the guns positioned by the Germans on a high plateau would not be able to shoot down at them. Therefore, if the steam vessels went near the west bank occupied by the Germans, they would only be threatened by small-arms fire.

As soon as it got dark, the steamer *Tajikiya* set off for a trial breakthrough. Having accelerated to maximum speed in the strait between the islands of Sporny and Denezny, the steamer suddenly dashed out from behind the coastal thickets and raced along the enemy bank. After a while, *Tajikiya* radioed: 'Shelled, there is damage, but got through.' After that, the *Paris Commune*, *Mikhail Kalinin* and *Joseph Stalin* began to prepare for a breakthrough. *Joseph Stalin* first approached the pier of the 'Red October' plant, where she took on board 1,000 passengers, mostly old men, women and children. When it was completely dark, around midnight the steamer weighed anchor and slowly moved to the starting position between Sporny island and the eastern shore.

Meanwhile, the *Paris Commune* and *Mikhail Kalinin*, following each other, passed by the 6km section occupied by the Germans in the same way as the *Tajikiya*. When the ships appeared, the Germans first fired a flare, then opened heavy fire. The steamers took a lot of hits and caught fire, but still managed to get away. After that, it was the turn of *Joseph Stalin*. It was no longer necessary to count on surprise, so Captain Ivan Rachkov decided to go right in the middle of the river. The Russians believed that the enemy would still not be able to fire guns directly, and machine-gun fire from a distance of 1km would be ineffective. However, they were wrong. On the edge of the plateau, the Germans had 20mm Flak-38 anti-aircraft guns, which could depress to -12°.

At 01.00, going at maximum speed, *Joseph Stalin* appeared from behind the Sporny Island. Here is how these events are described in the combat report of the 16th Panzer Engineer Battalion:

23.00. South of the Volga, three transport steam vessels were seen. When passing the first two, they found themselves in the zone of effective action of our weapons, however, despite numerous near-misses, they were able to escape to the north without much damage. The third steamer (with a displacement of about 500 tons) was going right in the middle of the current and after hundreds of shots from 20mm anti-aircraft guns caught fire. Approximately 500 people jumped into the water. Some of them swam to the sandbank.

Second Mate Konstantin Samoilov recalled:

> The flames from the fire engulfed the steamer more and more. Navigator Stroganov and I dumped into the water everything that came under our hands: lifebuoys, tables, benches. The fire was getting closer and closer, and we jumped overboard. The steamer was all in flames. We sailed along the side towards the bow, our heads were hot from the fire raging nearby. And then over the Volga there was a prolonged, as if a farewell whistle of a dying ship. Most likely, the base of the wheelhouse burned through, and it collapsed down, pulling the cable of the steam whistle . . . And we swam to the shoal, into which the steamer crashed with its nose. People jumped ashore, and they were shot from the shore with machine-gun fire.

In total, about 200 people managed to escape from the *Joseph Stalin*, but many of them suffered severe burns. The corpses of the passengers were then found in different places for a long time, and the body of Captain Rachkov was removed from the river only the following year, after the battle.

Stalin's unfulfilled 'advice'

Meanwhile, at dawn on 27 August, the Russians launched a counter-offensive. The 700th Marine Battalion, together with soldiers from other units and with the support of the gunboats *Usypkin*, *Chapaev* and armoured boats, launched an offensive from the village of Rynok to Latoshinka. The BT-7 tanks attached to the group were able to break through the defences of the 16th Panzer Engineer Battalion, crushing several guns and machine guns, and reach the gardens near the outskirts of Latoshinka, offloading a landing party of sailors there. The Germans only managed to hold their defences with great difficulty. And at 15.20, after a powerful Ju 87 raid on Rynok and Spartanovka villages, the newly-arrived 16th Motorcycle Battalion, with the support of sappers, launched an attack on these villages and was able to capture them by nightfall. The Russian Marines lost 70 per cent of their personnel in these battles and retreated. So, the bridgehead on the bank of the Volga was expanded, and in front – behind a large ravine – were the buildings of the Tractor Plant.

After that, the Germans mined the slope and blew up two railway bridges across the river flowing below. However, Spartanovka and Rynok turned out to be extremely inconvenient for defence, they were exposed to fire from the northern outskirts of Stalingrad and from the Volga, so on 29 August, having suffered serious losses, the Germans had to retreat to Latoshinka, take up defence there and shoot back in anticipation of further events.

All these days, Wietersheim's corps was still supplied mainly by air, as well as by convoys of trucks, which, accompanied by tanks, broke through the Soviet lines in the area of the Konny railway junction. On 27 August, transport planes dropped 28 containers of shells. In the morning of the next day, 52 more containers were dropped on the site 5km west of Vinnovka. On 29 August, Ju 52s taking off from Millerovo delivered 40 containers to the 14th Panzer Corps. This time they contained not only ammunition for artillery and tank guns, but also cartridges for rifles and machine guns, as well as cigarettes, the shortage of which the soldiers strenuously complained about.

As soon as Stalin learned about the German breakthrough to the Volga, he was literally enraged and immediately ordered them to be destroyed and to 'throw the enemy behind the outer rim'. 'I advise you! First, it is imperative that our troops firmly close the hole through which the enemy broke through to Stalingrad, surround the enemy who broke through and exterminate him. You have the strength to do this, you can and must do it,' said the 'advice' received at the headquarters of Yeremenko and Khrushchev at 04.55 on 24 August. At the same time, Stalin categorically 'advised' not to withdraw troops from other sectors of the front and to hold positions everywhere.

There was no time to prepare, so individual units that happened to be nearby were simply thrown into battle. In addition, it was impossible to concentrate troops in the open steppe and prepare for an attack in conditions of complete air supremacy of the German air force. 'Enemy aircraft, having undivided air supremacy, bombed and stormed our troops from any heights,' the war diary of the Stalingrad Front reported.

On the morning of 25 August, the Russian 4th Tank Army attempted to cut the enemy corridor to Stalingrad with a blow from the north. However, after the first shots, the sirens of Stukas were heard again in the sky, which did not bode well. From 08.00 to 14.00, the battle formations of the advancing regiments were subjected to continuous bombing. Moreover, there were 40–50 planes over the battlefield at the same time, which went in a circle and fired at the infantrymen from low level in turn, periodically dropping bombs. As a result, the Russians suffered heavy losses and could not advance far. Nevertheless, north of Bolshaya Rossoshka, they managed to cut the supply routes of the 14th Panzer Corps in a second place, increasing the gap to 6km, partially fulfilling the order of the leader.

The attacks launched the next day ended even more disastrously. Some of the Russian units did not take part in the battle at all, since the telephone connections, destroyed on 23 August, still did not work, and the messengers that were sent could not find the units. The Russian 4th Tank Corps mistakenly drove into its own minefield and suffered heavy losses. Those who did rise to attack were forced to lie down again. 'Enemy aircraft continuously bombed our units in groups of up to 50 aircraft,' complained the headquarters of the 4th Tank Army. The commanders did not have detailed maps of the area, which consisted of monotonous ravines and heights, and as a result, two local peasants had to be involved as guides.

'A strong offensive of 100 heavy and super-heavy enemy tanks from the Yerzovka-Grachi line in the south direction. Fliegerkorps VIII supported the defence of the army with strong blows and significantly reduced the tension of enemy attacks. The fighters maintained air superiority,' the combat operations magazine of the 6th German Army reported. Paulus's headquarters was literally inundated with panicked reports from the 14th Panzer Corps. At dawn, the head of the operations section of the army, Oberst Elhlepp, had to personally fly there to clarify the situation. General Wietersheim was in a panic again and said that if the Russians once again launched a large-scale offensive, it would not be possible to hold their positions.

The Soviets did indeed launch an offensive, but the same thing happened as the day before. German gunners and tankers knocked out 88 tanks, and three more were on the account of T-34 crews who defected to the Germans. Stukas struck attacking Soviet troops throughout the day. As a result, the 4th Tank Corps lost 140 tanks out of 160 available in three days! Eighty-four tanks were destroyed in the neighbouring 16th Tank Corps. After that, three tank brigades had to be merged into one 'demi-brigade'. In justification of his failure and heavy losses, the headquarters of the 4th Tank Army stated:

It should be noted the exceptional role of enemy aviation in restraining the offensive, which, having undivided dominance, bombs and storms our troops in groups and alone. Dozens of planes are continuously hanging over the battlefield, methodically bombing and shelling our troops, preventing them from getting off the ground. In addition, enemy aircraft bomb all roads leading to the front to a depth of 100 km. Daytime traffic is almost out of the question. Tanks also suffer heavy losses from aviation. Our aviation was completely absent from the front for two days. The rear also suffered heavy losses from enemy aircraft, especially of horses.

'The combat capabilities of the enemy as a whole are deteriorating. There are many defectors, including tankers. After two days of the offensive, the number and strength of the enemy as a result of heavy losses (230 tanks were hit) significantly decreased,' the headquarters of 6th Army reported to the Main Command of the Ground Forces. The Germans fairly accurately estimated the losses of the Soviet 4th Tank Army. At the same time, as part of the cut-off group of the German 14th Panzer Corps at that time there were only 106 tanks (including 77 Panzer IIIs, 21 Panzer IVs and 8 Panzer IIs) and 36 anti-tank guns.

While Soviet fighters were practically thrown out of the battle, Russian bomber aircraft in some cases acted quite effectively. On the afternoon of 24 August, Paulus and Richthofen, who were at the forward command post of the 76th Infantry Division, witnessed how four Il-2s attacked a road very close by. Through binoculars, they clearly saw the angry faces of the ground-attack planes' pilots, looking around and signalling each other with their hands (there were no radios in the cabins). Paulus was surprised by the courage of the pilots, who carried out attacking manoeuvres, almost touching the surrounding hills with their wings and firing at their targets. And on the ground, burning vehicles and drivers and soldiers running away were seen.

The communications of the 6th Army suffered the most from constant raids. On the night of 25/26 August, Soviet bombers managed to destroy one of the two bridges across the Don in the Akimovsky area. The following night, the pontoon bridge at the Trekhostrovskaya was damaged by direct hits. On the night of 28 August, bombers again damaged the newly-restored Akimovsky Bridge. Since the pontoon crossings were attacked at the same time, the Germans had to completely stop night traffic on them in the period from 23.00 to 01.00. The bridgehead on the Volga was also subjected to constant bombing and ground-attack planes. On the evening of 27 August, the Russian pilots managed to achieve direct hits into the control room (office) of the rear of the 14th Panzer Corps. Twenty-nine people were killed, including the quartermaster of the corps, Major von Wedel, the corps doctor and other officers. In the deep rear of the 6th Army, on the same evening Soviet bombers destroyed the Ostrogozhsk railway station, where an ammunition train exploded, blocking traffic for two days.

'The city is destroyed and stands without any further targets for bombing'

While fierce battles were going on around Stalingrad in various places simultaneously, the city itself was subjected to the first massive raid on 24 August. The main targets of the Luftwaffe were military facilities: a tractor factory, the 'Barricades' and 'Red October' factories, food industry enterprises, the grain elevator, the railway station, offices of the NKVD and the Bolshevik Party (in the city centre), positions of anti-aircraft batteries and piers. The air raid was supposed to paralyze the production of military equipment, the work of state bodies, hinder rail transportation inside the city and in its vicinity and sow panic among the remaining population.

The first He 111 bombers appeared over the city at about 07.00. People on the street saw a signal rocket fly out of the first plane, which was a signal to all other crews. After that, silvery objects fell out of the bomb hatches and scattered in fans. Soon they turned into huge 'umbrellas', so that the whole sky became milky white. These were special incendiary bombs, which the Russian Rescue Service (MPVO) called 'incendiary leaflets'. Tens of thousands of strips of foil coated with phosphorus, flaring up in contact with the air, slowly descended on the city centre and adjacent neighbourhoods. The fiery 'leaf fall' was approaching the roofs of houses. When in contact with the surface, the 'leaves' began to glow with a fierce blue-white flame of enormous temperature. And in a matter of minutes, dozens of fires had sprung up all over the city.

After a while, new groups of He 111s and Ju 88s appeared, and the sirens of Stukas were also heard. The war diary of 5./KG27 reports:

> The first attack as part of a compound with several links on the city of Stalingrad. Together with us attacked Stukas, ground-attack planes and fighters. The grandiose anti-aircraft defence of the Russians. We are flying at an altitude of 7,500m. The bombs were dropped at the drop point over the outskirts of the city, as otherwise they could hit their own planes flying below us.

The worst thing was when the oil storage tanks located on the Volga River near the Tractor Plant exploded. A huge column of flame shot up into the sky for hundreds of metres. Then, from the fire, the surviving oil tanks began to explode loudly, throwing up new columns of fire and smoke. After some time, burning petroleum flowed down the slopes to the water in a fiery stream. Massive fires began, the flames rapidly burned out everything in their path. Flaming oil flowed into the Volga, setting fire to steamships, barges and piers. Anti-aircraft gunner Anna Matveeva from the 748th Anti-aircraft Artillery Regiment recalled:

> On the Volga, it is still peeking through the veil of explosions, covering half the sky, a giant fountain of fire rises, the flame rushes up, there it

swirls in clouds, releases black smoke. The flames fly apart. The flame falls into the river. The flame licks the water, eats it, and a wide ribbon of fire flows along the Volga. I was stunned – the Volga is burning! Everything is burning – earth, sky, water. In this conflagration, nurse girls scurried, they carried the wounded from the battle on stretchers to the ferry and themselves fell under fire. The screams were no longer heard from the volleys of guns. The wounded jumped from the fifth floors, because the houses crumbled from the explosions . . . In order not to suffocate from the smoke, the anti-aircraft gunners took cotton wool from the sanitary instructors, soaked it in ammonia and brought it to their nose.

In the city centre, built up with new multi-storey buildings, the fires took on gigantic proportions. Due to the strong wind and hot weather, the fire burning over one building was connected to a neighbouring fire, fire tornadoes formed and as a result entire streets burned. The flames leapt from tree to tree, burst into apartments, onto stairwells, instantly burning everything in their path, jumping from roof to roof. Even the asphalt was burning! In the city centre, trying to escape from the flames, people jumped from the upper floors, climbed onto balconies and cornices, hung on drainpipes, but death overtook them there too. Fire trucks initially still tried to fight the fire, but due to lack of water and numerous blockages on the streets, their actions were completely ineffective. When it got dark, the fiery glow was visible 150km from Stalingrad: it was observed by the residents of Elton, Gornaya Proleika and Kamenny Yar. The Germans were also impressed. 'At dusk I advanced 14 kilometres, then spent the night in an open place against the background of incredible smoke and flames that illuminated Stalingrad. A fantastic landscape in the moonlight,' wrote the commander of the 9th Anti-aircraft Division of the Luftwaffe, Major General Pickert.

The representatives of the Soviet command, Georgy Malenkov and General Alexander Vasilevsky, who were on Stalin's instructions at the time in Stalingrad, were also very impressed. In their cipher message to the leader, they reported:

Today Stalingrad has suffered greatly from the bombing and the fires that have arisen from it. The city centre has completely burned down, the buildings of the regional office of the Bolshevik Party, the telegraph office, the House of Soviets, the prosecutor's office, the printing house of the regional newspaper, the House of Defence and many residential quarters have burned down, fires continue. Factories suffered from the bombing: at the 'Barricades' plant – six workshops, at the Stalingrad

Tractor Plant – three workshops and oil storage facilities were set on fire, at the 'Red October' plant – three workshops. The fires took on a wide scale because the city is mostly wooden and has very crowded buildings. Due to the capture on 23 August of the village of Rynok (2 km north of Stalingrad), where the main water intake takes place, the city was left without a main source of water supply.

Malenkov and Vasilevsky asked Stalin for permission to evacuate the most valuable equipment from large enterprises and create a special commission to assist the affected population. In addition, on the same evening, a belated decision was made to remove all women and children from Stalingrad to the eastern bank of the Volga. But a state of siege was introduced in the city only a day later.

Richthofen flew over Stalingrad on the morning of 25 August to see the results of the raids. 'The city is destroyed and stands without any further targets for bombing,' he summed up in his diary. Nevertheless, the raids on Stalingrad continued from dawn until late in the evening. The bombers operated in groups of 15–30 aircraft at an altitude of 4,000–5,000m and under the cover of fighters.

In total, as a result of the air attacks on 24–26 August, about 2,000 residential buildings were destroyed in Stalingrad, the water supply system, the electricity grid and the city telephone network failed, and all train stations and piers were destroyed. According to the Russian Rescue Service (MPVO), 1,017 people were killed and 1,281 were injured and concussed. Later calculations (there was no column for 'missing persons' in the Soviet reports) showed that from 23 August to 29 August, 1,816 corpses were buried by funeral teams and 2,698 wounded were picked up. Most likely, the number of victims was about 2,000 people. The troops defending the city themselves suffered heavy losses. The artillery of the 62nd Army alone from 21 to 29 August lost 45 guns, 16 vehicles and 40 tractors due to bombing.

Despite the fact that in the northern sector the Germans managed to quickly break through to the Volga and gain a foothold there, in the south the Soviets (despite the panic that gripped many) were able to prevent the rapid capture of Stalingrad, principally by delaying the advance of the German 4th Panzer Army from the south. By 28 August, the Germans had managed to capture Zety, Kosh and Tebektenerovo, but they were still 25–27km from the southern outskirts of Stalingrad.

Interestingly, on the morning of 28 August, Soviet reconnaissance planes reported large clouds of dust in the steppe to the east of Lake Tsatsa. Eremenko's headquarters immediately concluded that the Germans were moving towards the Volga and would soon reach the river in the area of Solodovniki–Cherny Yar. There was, it seemed, the threat of an enemy breakthrough to Stalingrad from the east and even the encirclement of the city! The Volga military flotilla was ordered to form detachments to counter amphibious assaults and prepare to fire on the Germans as soon as they reach the shore.

However, the alarm turned out to be false, the Russian pilots having seen reconnaissance groups raiding the Soviet rear. At that time, the Soviets were most afraid of a German breakthrough to the Volga in the area between Astrakhan and Stalingrad and their crossing to the eastern bank. Moreover, there was practically no one to defend this huge space. At the ferry crossings in the area of Cherny Yar, Nikolsky and others it was possible to place only small units of sailors and rear-echelon soldiers.

On 30 August, after massive air attacks by the Luftwaffe, the 4th Panzer Army managed to force the Chervlennaya River and seize a bridgehead on the north-eastern bank near Gavrilovka. This success caused optimism among the German command, and Field Marshal von Weichs, despite the objections and doubts of his subordinates, ordered the 6th Army to forget about the threat from the north and immediately advance south to join the 4th Panzer Army. The 14th Panzer Corps, which barely held the extended positions, had to continue to hold them and somehow also launch an offensive to the south. However, this plan, clearly drawn up under the influence and pressure of Hitler, tired of waiting for the 'Volga stronghold' to fall, already resembled not a bold operation, but an outright adventure. 'Everything is going well,' Richthofen wrote in his diary on the evening of 30 August. He insisted that the 6th Army could and should capture Stalingrad right now, while the defenders were discouraged and demoralised by the bombing. The losses, he believed, would be high, but in the current circumstances, acceptable.

In reality, the Battle for Stalingrad was only beginning then! It was at the end of August that the 'unstoppable Wehrmacht offensive' actually stalled. Although the 6th Army reached the Volga, the 4th Panzer Army advancing from the south was still far from the city and had to literally gnaw through the stubborn Russian defence. At the same time, in the Caucasus, German tanks stopped on the banks of the Terek River due to lack of fuel, and mountain battalions and units of the 17th German Army were stuck in the passes of the Caucasus, left without the support of the Luftwaffe.

In addition, the excessively sprawling northern flank along the Don caused more and more concern. The weakened divisions of the 6th Army were never able to completely push the Soviet divisions to the north bank of the river, and the command actually had to put up with the presence of several dangerous bridgeheads at once. The allied troops, who gradually replaced the Germans in the area from Voronezh to Kletskaya, did not inspire much confidence even then. No sooner had the Italians properly settled in their sector, than panicked reports about real and imaginary Soviet attacks and landings began to arrive at the headquarters of Army Group '. On 21 August, 'information' was received, as if the Russians were preparing to force the Don on the section between Vyoshenskaya and Krutovsky on numerous ferries prepared in the cover of the overgrown northern bank.

Due to the fact that most of the aviation units were occupied near Stalingrad, I./KG27, which was based in the rear – at Kharkov and Kursk – was assigned to conduct reconnaissance and attack the detected targets. The pilots were surprised by what they saw. Bomber navigator Hans Reif wrote: 'In the area of reconnaissance, we could not find either ferries or Russians, because they have always been masters of disguise! On the other hand, the Italians looked like a disorderly flight: the devastation in the villages, abandoned trucks and other vehicles, fleeing people. We were content to drop our bombs on the supposed concentration sites of ferries.'

Reif and his comrades received even more facts about what the allied troops were like when they temporarily relocated to the airfield at Rossosh. It was under the jurisdiction of the Italians and, accordingly, was covered by Italian air defences. To the surprise of the Germans, during the raids of Soviet ground-attack planes and bombers, Italian anti-aircraft gunners, instead of shooting at them, hid under the guns, shouted 'Oh, mia madre' and loudly prayed to the Madonna!

By the way, the Italians achieved a significant success only once during the Stalingrad military campaign. On the morning of 24 August, in the battle for the Izbushensky farm (near the village of Ust-Khoperskaya), the Savoia Cavalry Regiment (3rd Rgt 'Savoia Cavalleria') from the 3rd Mobile Division 'Amadeo Duke D'Acosta' defeated the 812th Rifle Regiment of the 304th Rifle Division. This battle went down in history as 'the last horse sabre attack at the gallop'. The 812th Regiment was defeated, 150 men were killed, and the remaining 900 surrendered. However, due to the disorganisation of the Italians, 300 men later simply fled, and only 600 were captured as a result. The trophies of the 'macaronis' were four regimental guns, 10 mortars and 40 machine guns and light machine guns. They themselves lost 40 killed, 79 wounded and 108 horses.

Chapter 5

'NOT A STEP BACK'

'We need to die, but not to shame ourselves . . .'
The situation of the Red Army by the beginning of autumn looked desperate. 'The troops of the Front have been fighting continuously for the last month in conditions of continuous mass attacks from the air, tank attacks on the march, fighting in a semi-circle and encirclement by superior enemy forces, which has extremely depleted the material resources and forces of the troops of the 62nd, 64th, 51st Armies,' the combat magazine of the South-eastern Front reported. For example, in the 126th Rifle Division there were only 100 soldiers and not a single artillery piece, in the already-mentioned 38th Rifle Division – 1,000 soldiers and 16 guns, in the 138th Rifle Division – 550 soldiers and 12 guns, in the 29th Rifle Division and the 154th Marine Brigade – 400 soldiers without artillery, mortars and machine guns. In the ten tank brigades that were part of the South-eastern Front, 146 tanks remained, including 66 T-34s, 42 T-70s, 21 T-60s and 17 KV-1s. 'There are no reserves. There is nothing to defend the city of Stalingrad,' Yeremenko and Khrushchev stated.

On 1 September, the Germans captured Basargino, located 20km from the southern outskirts of Stalingrad. Due to the current situation (the threat of a German breakthrough to Pitomnik and further north), the Soviet command was forced to order the 62nd Army to leave its positions along the Rossoshka River and withdraw to the Rynok line– Hills 144,2, 143,6–Gonchara-Alekseevka farm. This withdrawal not only avoided another encirclement, but also allowed the creation of small reserves by reducing the length of the front.

Nevertheless, no one was going to surrender the city. 'All commanders and fighters should remember that the Motherland has entrusted us with a responsible task – to defend the city of Stalin. Not a single step back from their positions. We will not surrender the city of Stalin to the enemy,' said Yeremenko's order of 2 September. A similar appeal was distributed by the commander of the 8th Air Army, General Timofey Khryukin: 'We need to die, but not to shame ourselves in the face of the ground troops and, most importantly, shoot down German aces more. At any cost, up to the battering ram.'

At the new front line, the Soviet troops could not resist either. By the evening of 3 September, the Germans had captured Voroponovo and Elkhi, coming very close to the city. At 07.00 on 4 September, the leading units of the 295th Infantry Division broke into Gumrak, while to the south, the vanguard of the 24th Panzer Division was able to break through along the valley of the Tsaritsa River to the western outskirts of Stalingrad near the brick factory. The captured territory cost the Germans a lot of blood. Over two days (4 and 5 September), the 295th Infantry Division lost 37 men killed and 226 wounded, the 71st Infantry Division lost 308 soldiers and officers killed and wounded, and several more were missing. By German standards, these losses were heavy!

On 5 September, the 389th Infantry Division broke through to the heights to the west and north-west of Gorodische, capturing the village of Kamenny Buerak. At the same time, 16 dug-in tanks were destroyed. The next day, units of the 51st Army Corps broke through the defence of the 62nd Army to a depth of 7km and reached the Central Airfield. 'The enemy fought hard and fiercely, there was a struggle for every house and every trench. The Experimental Station has 200 dead Russians left,' the corps headquarters reported. At the same time, an unusual tactical technique was noted. A group of 15 Red Army soldiers with their hands raised moved towards the Germans, as if surrendering, and then pulled out pistols hidden in their tunics and opened fire.

On the morning of 7 September, the units of the Russian 23rd Tank Corps found themselves in a critical situation, in connection with which the commander of the 62nd Army, Lieutenant General Lopatin, authorised the withdrawal of two tank brigades several kilometres to the east. This gave rise to the removal of Lopatin from his position with the words 'for failure to comply with the order not to leave the occupied line a step'. Major General Krylov was appointed the new commander of the army. But a few days later he was replaced by Lieutenant General Vasily Chuikov.

The 62nd Army itself continued to melt away. As of 7 September, 50 to 200 soldiers remained in four rifle divisions, and the 35th and 126th Rifle Divisions numbered about 1,000 men each. There were five tanks left in the 189th Tank Brigade, and none in the 99th Tank

Brigade. The Germans continued to crawl towards the Volga. On 8 September, the 48th Panzer Corps advancing south of the Tsaritsa River captured the Sadovaya railway station (the last suburban station on the Stalingrad–Morozovskaya line) and reached the 'suburb of Minin' residential district. On the night of 8/9 September, Yeremenko and Khrushchev left Stalingrad, crossing with the headquarters to the eastern bank of the river.

But by that time, the German 6th Army was already only a shadow of what it started Operation Blau as. For example, in the 51st Army Corps, eight out of 22 infantry battalions were considered 'exhausted' and nine 'weak'. And in the 8th Army Corps, which numbered 24 infantry battalions, 17 were considered 'exhausted', two 'weak' and one 'very weak'. But these soldiers had to 'inhale and exhale' for a long time: the 51st Army Corps was to attack the centre of Stalingrad, and the 8th Army Corps was to defend the small bend of the Don against endless Soviet attacks!

Of course, there was 'encouraging news'. By this time, He 111-bombers had dropped 53.5 million propaganda leaflets on Stalingrad. Moreover, these 'paper attacks', according to the headquarters of the 6th Army, 'led to good results'. These conclusions were made on the basis of a survey of surrendered Red Army soldiers and the number of prisoners: from 21 August to 7 September, there were more than 25,000 of them. Interestingly, the main 'theme' of the leaflets was a visual image of the 'Stalingrad pocket', in which the Russian 62nd Army turned out to be! This drawing was destined to become a prophecy.

By the evening of 9 September, the Germans had captured Gorodishche, Uvarovo and Alexandrovka, continuing to consistently drive wedges into the stretched and weakened front of the 62nd Army. The next morning, the Luftwaffe heavily bombed the positions of the Russian 138th, 204th and 126th Rifle Divisions defending the southern approaches to Stalingrad. Werner Halle of the 29th Motorised Division recalled: 'At exactly 9 o'clock there was a hum in the air, Stukas circling above us, and it began. With sirens wailing, Stukas drop bomb after bomb on the enemy right in front of us. At the same time, we ourselves bury our heads in the mud. So, they pave the way for us to the Volga. There is only smoke and gunpowder smoke in front of us.' Following the Ju 87s, He 111 bombers appeared, also bombarding Russian positions with hundreds of small fragmentation bombs.

When the smoke and dust cleared, the German motorised infantry slowly went on the offensive. At lunchtime, the Germans captured Zelenaya Polyana and the southern part of Kuporosnoye. Three rifle regiments and two anti-tank regiments of the 64th Army were almost entirely wiped out. 'Finally, we, the first German soldiers, see south of Stalingrad, from a steep bank, a mighty river, which here has a width of perhaps more than 1,000 meters. How proud we are to have accomplished this task!' Werner Halle continued.

Thus, 18 days after Wietersheim's tanks reached the Volga north of the city, Kempf's motorised infantry also reached the river – 30km downstream. From the high bank, there was a beautiful view of the steppe beyond the Volga, the Akhtuba floodplain and the shining ribbon of the Volga, which stretched to the south-east – to the Caspian Sea. Once again it seemed to the German command that the long-awaited turning point had come in the battle. On this day, Paulus got his hands on Stalin's order, obtained somewhere, to defend the city by all possible means to the last man, since its fall would lead to serious consequences. From this piece of paper, the narrow-minded Field Marshal von Weichs once again concluded that the capture of Stalingrad was supposedly of the greatest strategic importance. Therefore, victory in the war was closer than ever! 'The troops of the 4th Panzer and 6th Armies have been fighting for Stalingrad for the past three weeks, showing excellent training and a rush to attack, despite the difficult combat conditions. I offer my gratitude for their exceptional services. Ahead of us lies the successful capture of Stalingrad and the defeat of the enemy,' Weichs said in a pathetic order.

The Russians, at the headquarters of the South-eastern Front, were in a panic. Yeremenko ordered the urgent organisation of a defence the eastern bank of the Volga in the area from Sredne-Pogromny to Raigorod. But the next day (11 September), the situation stabilised. The 126th Rifle Division, together with the remnants of the 131st Rifle Division, desperately managed to dislodge the Germans from Kuporosnoye and push the Germans away from the riverbank. At the same time, the vanguard of the 29th Motorised Infantry Division, which had recently been proud of itself, was almost completely destroyed in close combat. Infantryman Werner Halle was among the few survivors and broke through to his own lines.

From 5 to 12 September, Luftflotte 4 carried out 7,507 sorties (mainly in the Stalingrad area). During 11 weeks of continuous offensive, the number of aircraft decreased by 40 per cent to 950, of which, due to a shortage of spare parts, only 550 were in combat-ready condition. But the Luftwaffe still had enough strength to break a path for its ground troops.

On 13 September, German aircraft in groups of 15–20 Ju 87s, Hs 123s, Ju 88s and He 111s attacked the northern and southern parts of Stalingrad and the Volga River ferry crossings. When the smoke and dust from the explosions dissipated, the 51st Army Corps launched a decisive offensive, the purpose of which was to break through to the Volga. 'Everything for Germany! Therefore, we must take Stalingrad!' said a pathetic appeal to the soldiers, distributed before the attack. The offensive was carried out mainly by 'depleted' and 'weak' infantry battalions, whose combat strength was far from what it should have been. For example, in the 71st Infantry Division, the shortage of personnel before the attack was 170 officers and 4,657 men, and in the neighbouring 295th Infantry Division – 194 officers and 5,508 men. The situation of the 389th Infantry Division was slightly better; it had a shortfall of 'only' 155 officers and 3,275 men and most of the battalions were considered 'average'. The 6th Army at that time had 140 tanks and 26 self-propelled artillery pieces (mainly StuG IIIs). In general, the 6th Army could not be called 'the most powerful unit of the Nazi army', as stated in Soviet newspapers and leaflets!

In the evening, having broken through the stretched defences of the 399th Rifle Division and the 272nd Rifle Regiment, the Germans reached the railway line running through the whole of Stalingrad from south to north. The vanguard of the 71st Infantry Division broke into the central part of the city. Having moved through the streets by rushes, right past the frightened residents and the fleeing men of the Russian rear units, the Germans captured several high-rise buildings.

On the morning of 14 September, Paulus flew to the headquarters of the 51st Army Corps, located in Gumrak. Then he drove in an armoured car to the forward command post located on a hill in the vicinity of this Settlement. From there, Paulus saw Stalingrad for the first time, the Volga lying behind it and the boundless steppe stretching far to the east. Everywhere in the vast space, columns of explosions and flames of fires were visible, as well as German planes bombing the central and southern parts of the city. Paulus was deeply impressed by what he saw, because the Volga was the final line of occupation in the plan of Operation Barbarossa, in the development of which he had been directly involved. And now it was he who led the offensive against this city, which was the last Russian outpost on the way to Asia.

At noon, the command post received a message that the vanguard of the 71st Infantry Division had captured the railway station, and three hours later that they had reached the Volga embankment near the piers. To the north, units of the 295th Infantry Division also reached the shore and Hill 102.0 (the Mamayev Kurgan). Paulus was pleased. Returning to his headquarters, located in the village of Golubinskaya, he ordered the 51st Army Corps to take full control of the central part of the city, and then prepare for an offensive to the north-east – to the 'Red October' factory – to link up with the 14th Panzer Corps. Yeremenko reported to Stalin that the Germans were 'climbing to the Volga through mountains of corpses of their soldiers'. In fact, the 51st Army Corps lost only 48 dead and 195 wounded that day.

When the Germans broke through to the Volga embankment in the centre of Stalingrad, the only unit that could be thrown into battle was the 13th Guards Rifle Division. It was by no means 'elite'; on the contrary, it was a typical Russian division hastily recruited from poorly-trained recruits from Central Asia. Moreover, the soldiers even arrived at the front without weapons. Initially, Eremenko planned to send the division to the northern part of the city – to defend the area between the Mamayev Kurgan and the 'Red October' plant. However, the situation made its own adjustments and before crossing by ferry to the west bank on the night of 13/14 September, the Guards received a new mission: to occupy a bridgehead near the embankment, counter-attack the enemy in the sector between the central ferry crossing and the train station, knock the Germans out of large buildings.

In the southern sector, the 48th Panzer Corps launched an offensive deep into the Voroshilovsky district on 14 September. On the very first day, the Germans managed to break through the Russian defences, and the headquarters of the 29th Motorised Infantry Division even had to cancel the massive Stuka airstrike planned for 05.30 on the northern part of Kuporosnoye at the last moment so that they would not hit their own soldiers. Soon the infantrymen again occupied this locality, for the second time gaining a foothold on the bank of the Volga. The next day, the 24th Panzer Division captured the Stalingrad II railway station and then broke through to the bank at Tsaritsa. At the same time, the huge grain elevator, located near the railway, was not occupied by anyone and was captured by a detachment of German infantry without a fight. However, it was not possible to quickly occupy and take control of a fairly long urban area, divided into two parts by a railway embankment and intersected by numerous ravines and narrow streets. The Germans simply did not have enough men to quickly occupy such a large territory.

Meanwhile, the battle was taking an increasingly dramatic turn. Having delivered significant reinforcements to the city, the new commander of the 62nd Army, Vasily Chuikov, managed not only to strengthen the defence on the stretched front winding along the city outskirts, streets, ravines and numerous industrial zones, but also to organise several counter-attacks at once. By the middle of the day on 16 September, the Red Army had recaptured part of the Mamayev Kurgan and the railway station. The next day, the Germans managed to break into Saratov, Communist, Artemovskaya and Republicanskaya Streets and again seize the station building. Then this important stronghold changed hands several times. The headquarters of the 6th Army was forced to state that the 51st Army Corps not only had not taken control of the central part of the city, but also lost some of the buildings it had previously captured, and its combat potential was significantly 'depleted'. During the three days of fighting, the losses of three infantry divisions amounted to about 1,500 killed and wounded.

Similar things were going on in the southern sector, which was defended by the remnants of two rifle divisions, one rifle brigade and one tank brigade (with three KV-1 tanks). On the evening of 16 September, the fighters of the consolidated battalion of the 10th Separate Rifle Brigade (recruited from sailors) launched a surprise attack on the grain elevator, managed to kill the small German garrison and occupied this huge building that dominated the entire surrounding area.

The next day, the commander of the 48th Panzer Corps, General Kempf, ordered the 'concrete colossus' to be recaptured immediately. The assault groups of the 94th Infantry Division managed to break into the first floor, but there they were met by heavy fire from the second floor and found the stairs were barricaded. After the attack failed, at 15.05 Kempf personally called Richthofen and asked him to drop high-power bombs on the grain elevator. He accepted the request with his usual enthusiasm and passion for destruction, and asked for their own troops to withdraw to a safe distance. At 17.00, several Stukas from StG2 appeared overhead, which alternately dropped bombs weighing one ton (SC1000s) on the building. However, the powerful explosions, to the surprise of the soldiers watching from a safe distance, did not lead to any serious damage. The prolonged shelling of the grain elevator from 88mm anti-aircraft guns and 105mm howitzers also had no effect.

The assault was eventually thwarted by a sudden attack by Russian sailors from the 92nd Separate Rifle Brigade, who attacked the Stalingrad II railway station and other strongholds in the Voroshilov district. Separate groups of soldiers even managed to break through to the grain elevator and strengthen its garrison. As a result, instead of a decisive assault, the Germans had to fight for every quarter again. The commander of the 29th Motorised Infantry Division stated that his units, after endless attacks and counter-attacks by the enemy, were no longer able to advance. With the 'motorisation' itself, it was also bad, after the battles in the city, only eight serviceable tanks remained in the division, five Panzer IIIs and three Panzer IIs. The losses of the Soviet troops, as usual, were much greater. For example, the 36th Guards

Rifle Division, which fought fierce battles on the southern outskirts of Stalingrad, suffered 1,500 casualties from 15 to 18 September, including 553 killed and missing.

However, the Soviets quickly replenished their troops. The Volga ferry crossing, despite constant shelling and bombing, continued to function. New units were constantly arriving in the city to replace the broken and destroyed ones. On the night of 16/17 September, the minesweepers of the Volga Military Flotilla delivered 1,054 soldiers to the west bank and almost 400 wounded were taken out of the city on return journeys. The following night, despite heavy shelling from the shore, the aforementioned 92nd Rifle Brigade of Marines and the 137th Tank Brigade managed to be transported to Stalingrad. On the night of 18/19 September, most of the 95th Rifle Division crossed to the west bank. On the night of 20/21 September, two batteries of the 57th Artillery Regiment and one regiment from the newly-arrived 284th Rifle Division crossed to the bridgehead. This division had been completely defeated near Voronezh, then withdrawn to the rear – to Krasnoufimsk, where it was replenished with a rather motley cadre of personnel from the NKVD, officer schools, sailors of the Pacific Fleet and ground personnel of the Air Force. It was as part of this division that an unknown 27-year-old sailor of the Pacific Fleet Vasily Zaitsev (a future sniper) crossed to Stalingrad at that time.

The Luftwaffe conducted a merciless hunt for Soviet ships and vessels in the Stalingrad area. They were constantly fired at by German artillery, which hit targets both with direct fire and with the help of observers located on the upper floors of buildings, as well as spotter aircraft. For example, on 13 September, German gunners sank the tugboat *Trawler*, the river vessels *1-KP* and *G-71*, and the river passenger vessel *Thirteenth*. On 14 September the tugboat *Aitodor* was sunk by aircraft at Kapustin Yar, and the next day the vessels *G-16* and *G-99* were destroyed. On 17 September, as a result of artillery shelling, the tugboat *15 years of the Komsomol* sank near the city. The next day, the tugboat *Pozharsky* was also sunk by artillery. On 20 September, the railway ferry *Stalin* (length 95m, width 20m), the railway ferry *Pereprava Vtoraya*, and the tugboats *Stakhanovets* and *Kurzukh* were sunk. On 24 September, the tugboat *Nabludatel* was destroyed in Stalingrad as a result of an air attack by Ju 87s. On 29 September, as a result of a Stuka raid, the rescue service steamer *Gasitel*, and the vessels *G-10*, *G-46* and *G-109* were sunk.

The Luftwaffe also continued to regularly mine the river on the approaches to Stalingrad. But it was not possible to completely paralyze river transportation. In the Stalingrad area, there were many islands, channels, bays and backwaters on the river, and the Volga itself was duplicated in this place by the Akhtuba River flowing parallel to it, which also had numerous branches and channels. At the end of the month, the 39th Guards Rifle Division and eight marching companies were transferred to the west bank, which, despite the shelling from the shore, successfully crossed the river and took the places of the broken and thinned units.

'It is not yet time for the troops to go on vacation'

By 21 September, only three isolated strongholds remained in the hands of the Russians in the southern part of Stalingrad: a fortified area at the mouth of the Tsaritsa, a cannery factory on the banks of the Volga and the grain elevator. At 05.30, after several powerful air attacks by Stukas against the factory, the 48th Panzer Corps began storming this 'bastion'. At the same time, the 29th Motorised Infantry Division attacked the ruins of the cannery factory from the south, and the 94th Infantry Division from the north, towards the first. According to Soviet information, the Luftwaffe changed tactics and acted step by step. Ju 87s and other ground-attack planes consistently 'processed' block by block, building by building, gradually going deeper into Soviet positions. At the same time, the bombing was combined with shelling from six-barrelled rocket launchers and howitzers in the same places. As a result, already at 11.45, the assault groups captured the entire cannery and joined up east of the grain elevator.

According to the plan, at this very time the Luftwaffe were to make a second raid on the grain elevator, dropping high-power bombs on it. However, at the last moment, the Stukas were withdrawn, as the German infantry was near the building and could have been hit. The raid was postponed for three hours. At 14.00, a large group of Ju 87s reached the target and made a circle, after which the bombers one by one began to dive down. From numerous explosions, the grain elevator building was enveloped in a solid cloud of dust and smoke, pieces of concrete and bricks scattered over a radius of 500m. However, when the dust cleared, the Germans were surprised to find that the building was still standing and practically intact. But no one fired from there.

As soon as it got dark, the grain elevator garrison tried to break out towards the Volga, but was stopped by German infantry fire. Most of the Red Army soldiers surrendered, the rest went back to the building and only a few soldiers managed to break through to the bank of the Volga. At 21.15 (Berlin time), units of the 29th Motorised Infantry Division came close to the building. However, after negotiations between the headquarters, the 94th Infantry Division was given the honour of carrying out the last assault and plant a flag with a swastika over the 'Bolshevik stronghold'. At 04.00, the assault group reported the completion of the sweep and the capture of the grain elevator.

Meanwhile, on 22 September, the 6th Army went on the offensive in the central part of Stalingrad. At 05.00, Stukas struck the vicinity of the Mamayev Kurgan and the bank of the Volga, at 05.30 He 111s bombed the same targets from a great height, then artillery shelling was carried out on the same targets. At 06.20, the 295th Infantry Division launched an offensive in the direction of the oil storage facility located on the river bank. The assault groups of the 517th and 518th Infantry Regiments managed to break through to the coastal road. However, the Germans again failed. The 6th Army's war diary reported:

> The powerful artillery preparation and Luftwaffe raids did not lead to the expected decrease in Russian morale in front of the 295th Infantry Division. Due to the most stubborn resistance in barricaded houses, earthen bunkers, a bloody battle with the use of flamethrowers and concentrated explosive charges, with the support of assault guns and sappers, did not give any result. The weakened infantry had only a slight advance.

Having lost 50 men killed and 170 wounded, the 295th Division was forced to stop its attacks.

The Soviets also experienced incredible difficulties. After the bombs hit the oil tanks, several of them exploded, and a huge column of fire and smoke rose into the sky. Then there were extensive fires, in one of which the infantry of the 284th Rifle Division, which had recently crossed to the west bank, landed. Some of the panicking fighters, engulfed in flames, ran towards the German positions, terrifying the enemy. But most of the division could not break through the flames and smoke to the rescue of the 13th Guards Rifle Division, the remnants of which fought fierce battles in the city centre. During this day alone, the division lost 2,000 killed and wounded and barely held its positions.

On 26 September, units of the 71st Infantry Division, four battalions of which, according to the German classification, were 'weak', the remaining three 'exhausted', seized the last administrative buildings in the city centre. At noon, the commanders of the 191st and 211st Infantry Regiments hoisted a banner with a swastika over the department store and the city theatre. 'In the afternoon, the German military flag flies over the buildings of the Bolshevik Party. Half of the city is in the hands of the Germans,' wrote Richthofen in his diary. At the same time, the capture of the mouth of the Tsaritsa River was coming to an end, where the remnants of several Soviet units were still defending themselves. On the night of 27 September, the remnants of the 92nd Separate Rifle Brigade sailed to Golodny Island. The brigade commander, Lieutenant Colonel Tarasov, and the senior battalion Commissar Andreev were the very first to evacuate, actually abandoning their men. Then they were mercilessly shot for not following the order 'Not a step back'.

Now the Germans had captured the entire bank of the Volga from Kuporosny to the 'January 9' Square, finally gained a foothold on the Volga embankment, keeping all three piers of the central ferry crossing under fire. But these victories came at a very high price. For example, the average strength of infantry companies in the 94th Infantry Division by the end of the battle for the southern part of the city was reduced to one officer, two NCOs and 18 privates. But the young soldiers, intoxicated by Nazi propaganda, believed that these sacrifices were not in vain, the 'spirit of the fallen comrades' remained with them, and the exit to the Volga seemed to them a kind of 'happy moment' for the Wehrmacht! 'It is not yet time for the troops to go on vacation. Stalingrad, which has become a symbol for the enemy, continues to be a key point of the battle,' said the commander of the 94th Infantry Division.

Meanwhile, the 6th Army finally prepared to storm the northern industrial part of Stalingrad. All the divisions that Paulus had at his disposal were seriously short of personnel, and the meagre replacements in the form of marching battalions did not cover the losses. Therefore, he could create assault groups only by deep regrouping and replacing some units with others. The 389th Infantry Division and the 100th Jäger Division, transferred from the southern bank of the Don, and the 24th Panzer Division, recently withdrawn from the southern part of the city, were concentrated in the area between Gorodische and the Mamayev Kurgan. In fact, the only source of reserves for the 6th Army was its own left flank, which was gradually handed over to the Romanians. The only reinforcements that arrived from the deep rear were the 71st Sapper Battalion (Pi.Btl.71) of the 50th Motorised Infantry Division. This was urgently transferred by Ju 52 transport planes from the Crimea.

On the morning of 27 September, the 51st Army Corps went on the offensive. The Germans and Croats (a Croatian battalion and two Croatian artillery batteries operated as part of the 100th Jäger Division) managed to push aside the infantry of the 62nd Army, make their way to the outskirts of the 'Red October'. residential district and immediately capture Hill 107.5. Having drained their divisions of blood not only by exhausting defensive battles, but also by constant counter-attacks, Yeremenko and Khrushchev once again reported to headquarters that it was impossible to restore the situation with the forces remaining, asking them to urgently allocate at least 50,000 soldiers and 250 tanks.

On 28 September, the Luftwaffe attacked the positions of the 62nd Army in the northern part of Stalingrad as well as the Volga River ferry crossings from 06.00. After that, units of the 24th Panzer Division broke into the western part of the 'Barricades' residential district, coming close to the factory of the same name. And the 100th Jäger Division managed to advance along the northern slopes of the Mamayev Kurgan to the western edge of the 'Tennis Racket' (railway loop) and capture most of the meat-processing plant located there. At the same time, the Germans for the first time recorded the use of dogs with mines that ran towards tanks, but were shot and exploded prematurely.

On 29 September, the fighting continued. At 10.25 the Luftwaffe made a massive raid on Orlovka, the last stronghold of the 62nd Army located outside the city. 'Stukas! The fountains from the explosions reach the heavens,' the war diary of the 16th Panzer Division enthusiastically reported. At 11.05 the Germans went on the offensive in this area, delivering converging blows simultaneously from Gorodische and from Latoshinka. The next day Orlovka was surrounded. Another success for the Germans was the capture of the 'Barricades' residential district. The Soviet 23rd Tank Corps defending in this area suffered heavy losses, including in tank battles. In the 138th Tank Brigade, only two T-60 tanks and 60 soldiers remained in service, in the 6th Guards Tank Brigade – three T-34s and 38 soldiers. The Soviet infantry also suffered heavy losses, 563 soldiers remaining in the 112th Rifle Division, 230 soldiers in the 95th Rifle Division. The remnants of brigades and regiments retreated to Goncharnaya, Kazachya, Sculpturnaya and Aeroflotskaya Streets.

On this day, the battle was personally observed from the forward command post by the commander of Army Group B von Weichs, who saw Stalingrad for the first time with his own eyes and simultaneously held a meeting with the commanders of the army corps. The small successes achieved again cost the Germans great sacrifices. The 100th Jäger Division operating on the slopes of the Mamayev Kurgan hill suffered especially, taking 500 casualties on the first day of the offensive alone, and on the second day the 'hunters' lost 70 soldiers and officers killed and 276 wounded.

At the end of September, it seemed to the German command and the Führer that the battle for the 'fortress' of Stalingrad was going according to the Sevastopol scenario and was nearing its end. But it seemed real only on the map. In fact, the 6th Army was sinking more and more into the swamp into which Hitler had driven it. Due to the great remoteness of the combat area and the underdeveloped railway and road network in this desert area, the Germans never managed to establish normal supplies for the 6th Army. The battles had to be fought with a constant shortage of ammunition, and the 75mm shells most needed to fight Soviet tanks were still having to be brought in by air. Transport planes were loaded with them at distant rear bases, and then delivered them to an improvised airfield near Peskovatka.

The shortage of troops and shells was compensated of by the fanatical activity of the Luftwaffe. The pilots of Stukas literally did not get out of their cockpits, making three or four sorties a day. 'This meant that we needed no more than 45 minutes for each departure for everything about everything, including taxiing to the start, take off, flight to the target, climbing to an altitude of 4,000m, target detection, diving for a bomb strike, flying at low altitude, landing, taxiing to the parking lot. Then a new load, a short technical repair – another 15 minutes,' recalled Major Paul-Werner Hozzel, commander of StG2 Immelmann. The crews of twin-engined bombers fought with the same zeal. For example, the commander of 1./KG100, Hauptmann Hans Batcher, made 45 sorties during the month, dropping 52.6 tons of bombs on various targets in the Stalingrad area. On some days his He 111 appeared two or three times over Stalingrad. Amazing efficiency for a single bomber!

No less self-sacrifice was shown by the pilots of German fighters. For example, 21-year-old Lieutenant Wilhelm Crinius from I./JG53 in the period from 1 to 22 September alone won 46 aerial victories, and his friend and peer Oberleutnant Wolfgang Tonne – 31 aerial victories. On some days, they shot down three or four Soviet aircraft, becoming unsurpassed record holders in Luftflotte 4. Both aces flew literally to exhaustion, fighting at the limit of human capabilities. As a result, by mid-September, Crinius was in a feverish state, his body temperature was kept at 38–39°, and lost up to 53.5kg in weight. Often during air battles, Crinius lost consciousness and orientation, and because of constant nausea, he had to use his own cap lined with paper to vomit in! But fanaticism and a sense of duty to the Führer again and again forced him, like other I./JG53 pilots, to fly to complete exhaustion. The chiefs appreciated this loyalty to Germany, and on 23 September, Crinius and Tonne were awarded the Oakleaves to the Knight's Cross, despite the fact that Crinius has not yet managed to receive the usual Knight's Cross.

In general, Luftflotte 4 carried out 9,746 sorties from 16 to 25 September. Even with a small number of combat-ready aircraft, the Luftwaffe constantly hung in the air over the Volga. Instead of bombs (which were not enough), propaganda leaflets were generously loaded into bomb bays. In the period from 23 August to 23 September, 100 million leaflets with 70 different texts were already scattered in front of the front of the 6th Army! The whole 'collection of works' turned out by German propaganda. . .

Russian aviation could not compete with the Luftwaffe. But 'Stalin's falcons' took revenge on the enemy at night! As the battle for Stalingrad dragged on, Soviet night bombers caused more and more concern to the Germans. U-2 biplanes constantly bombed the positions of German troops in the occupied part of the city from low level, preventing the Germans from sleeping and causing serious losses to rear units. Long-range bombers raided targets in the deep rear: pontoon crossings, bridges, railway stations, headquarters and supply bases. For example, in the 51st Army Corps, 600 horses were killed and wounded as a result of night bombardments in just 10 days in September, and many motor vehicles were damaged. 'All night long, continuous raids by enemy aircraft on the city and the rear, especially heavy bombardments with heavy bombs in the area south of Tsaritsa, Hill 102, positions at the airfield and Tatarsky Val,' stated the corps' summary for 23 September. The next night, the Germans recorded the dropping of 950 bombs on the parts of Stalingrad they occupied.

At the end of the month, Soviet bombers conducted several successful raids on the 6th Army's lines of communication. During two nights – 26/27 September and 27/28 September – air attacks were carried out against the railway stations at Chir and Surovikino. In Chir, 28 wagons, 435 76.2mm anti-tank shells (for PaK.36 (rus) guns), 3,013 charges for light howitzers, 926 150mm high-explosive shells and about 5 tons of food were destroyed. At Surovikino station, a train with fuel was destroyed by direct hits. The unloaded ammunition nearby also blew up, then the train with shells for heavy howitzers exploded. At the same time, Soviet saboteurs set fire to the railway bridge near Likhaya station. As a result of these operations, the already poorly organised supply of troops storming Stalingrad faced even greater interruptions.

On 29 September, Soviet bombers carried out another successful raid on the supply base of the 6th Army in Nizhny Alekseevka, destroying 428 280mm shells, 276 37mm shells, 2,173 charges for light howitzers and 1,698 152mm shells.

Chapter 6

'NORTHERN BARRIER'

'The dropping of pieces of rail from aircraft was noted'
While the Germans stormed the ruins of Stalingrad, the Soviets made a second attempt to crush the stretched northern flank of the 6th Army between the Don and the Volga. By early September, the Soviet command had concentrated General Moskalenko's 1st Guards Army on the front of the German 14th Panzer Corps between the Don and the Volga. Initially, it was intended for a counter-attack against the 6th Army on the bank of the Don, but when the Germans broke through to the Volga, a force consisting of six rifle divisions, three tank corps, six regiments of Katyusha rocket launchers and other combat units was transferred through ravines and wastelands to the Kotluban-Yerzovka sector. In addition, General Malinovsky's new 66th Army was concentrated in the same sector, consisting of six rifle divisions and four tank brigades.

If we consider that the 4th Tank Army was still in the same sector (although there were practically no tanks left in it), and the 24th Army was formed up there (on 1 September there were five rifle divisions in it), it turns out that four Russian armies were concentrated against one German tank corps! They consisted of 22 rifle divisions, three tank corps and seven separate tank brigades! In this group there were 2200,000 men, 748 tanks (including 430 serviceable), 1,900 guns, 3,500 mortars, 27,345 horses and 4,600 motor vehicles.

The Soviets were confident that with these huge forces they would be able to easily crush the enemy's 'northern barrier' and disrupt the storming of the city. Initially, Eremenko wanted to launch an offensive on the morning of 5 September, when most of the new units would finish concentrating. However, Stalin intervened in the preparation of the operation. The leader was very nervous and feared that Stalingrad would be captured in the coming days. On the night of 2/3 September, he called his representative on the Stalingrad Front, Georgy Zhukov, and demanded that the attack begin immediately. And then he called again. As a result, instead of a powerful attack with all available forces, a series of consecutive strikes by different combat groups occurred.

The headquarters of the German 14th Panzer Corps learned about the upcoming offensive and the directions of attacks in advance, from defectors. At the same time, the Russians were sure that after the fierce battles that had taken place at the end of August, the German divisions were significantly weakened. In reality, there were 134 tanks in the 16th Panzer, 3rd and 60th Motorised Infantry Divisions by this time, including 90 Panzer IIIs, 27 Panzer IVs and 17 Panzer IIs.

The 1st Guards Army was the first to go on the offensive at 05.30 on 3 September. The attack was preceded by powerful rocket-launcher volleys, from which parts of the 3rd Motorised Infantry Division suffered serious damage. 'As soon as the morning of September 3 is engaged – at 3.00 o'clock – as "witchcraft" begins anew. It's unbelievable, where does the enemy get this "human material" from,' recalled Oberleutnant Sittig from the 7th company of the 8th Grenadier Motorised Regiment (7./Gr.Rgt.8.(mot.)). The regiment's positions were first fired on by 'Stalin organs', then the Soviet infantry went on the attack under the cover of a smokescreen. However, at the crucial moment, the cloud was blown away by the wind, and just at that time a pair of Bf 109 fighters appeared over the battlefield. 'Fortunately, the pilots immediately understand what is happening and fall on the crowds of Russians, firing from onboard cannons and machine guns,' continued Sittig.

Although German ground-attack planes appeared over the front line in the early morning, at 09.30 the headquarters of the 6th Army asked Fliegerkorps VIII to send another group of Stukas to this sector. And two hours later, the headquarters of the 14th Panzer Corps reported that the breakthrough at Point 416 and Hill 111.1 had been successfully liquidated with 'very good support from the Luftwaffe'. Richthofen flew to this sector twice in his 'Storch' and personally observed the air attacks of his subordinates.

At dawn on 4 September, German artillery opened heavy fire on Soviet troops preparing to continue the offensive. The shelling continued until 07.00, at the same time the front line was bombed and shelled by ground-attack planes and bombers. As a result, the Russian attack failed again.

On the morning of 5 September, Zhukov struck what was intended to be the decisive blow, throwing four armies into the offensive at the same time. Several times tanks and infantry rolled in waves on German positions in several places at once. In the first half of the day, the Soviet troops managed to break through the defence in six places at once, which was literally bursting at the seams. The decisive role was again played by the powerful support of aviation. Throughout the day, bombers and ground-attack planes continuously attacked the advancing tanks. 'Throughout the day, our advancing troops were exposed to enemy aircraft in groups of 20–40. At the same time, the bombing was carried out by them methodically, aiming each bomb. Some groups of bombers were over the troops for more than an hour. The dropping of pieces of rails and empty barrels from aeroplanes was noted,' the headquarters of the Stalingrad Front complained.

According to German information, 112 Russian tanks were destroyed during the day, of which 20 were due to anti-aircraft artillery and about 40 to the Luftwaffe. At the same time, German fighters continuously patrolled over the front line, preventing Soviet aircraft from approaching the battlefield. 'With the strong tension of all the forces weakened in the battles of recent days, with significant losses in men and weapons, having brought the last reserves into battle and having spent a large amount of ammunition, it was generally possible to hold the line of defence. The powerful strikes of ground-attack planes and bombers of the Fliegerkorps VIII had a special impact,' Wietersheim's headquarters reported on the evening of 5 September. 'During September 5, the Russians also remained active. But they are being smashed by our air raids,' stated Oberleutnant Sittig from 7./ Gr.Rgt.8.(mot).

The next day, the attack on the 'northern barrier' of the 6th Army resumed. At the same time, fog descended on German airfields, making it impossible for the Stukas and fighters to take off. The absence of their planes in the sky immediately caused panic among the German soldiers. Wietersheim had to throw into battle his last reserves, consisting already of individual tanks. And not until the afternoon did Stukas, Hs 123s and Hs 129s again fall on the positions of the Russian armies.

Meanwhile, German reconnaissance planes flew over the vast expanse north of Stalingrad and saw everything that was happening there. Numerous columns of infantry and trucks were moving along the river to the south, and several Volga ferry crossings were operating in the Verchniy Balykley area (90km north of Stalingrad). It was there that reinforcements moving from Central Asia to the Stalingrad Front sailed from the eastern shore. '40 per cent are young, 60 per cent are national minorities (Tatars and Uzbeks). In companies of 120 men,'

German intelligence of the 207th Rifle Division reported. 'The division was formed in March 1942 In Krasnoufimsk, at the beginning of June was in Samara, 4.9 arrived near Kotluban. 25 per cent Russians, 75 per cent national minorities (Uzbeks, Kazakhs, Kirghiz).' And it was true. More than half of the Russian troops operating near Stalingrad were from Central Asia. The Germans called them 'Mongols' for their pronounced Asian features.

Wietersheim dreaded the continuation of the attacks, but in reality, after two days of fighting, the Soviets had suffered huge losses. They were no longer capable of advancing with the same ferocity. German losses remained at a minimum level. By 7 September, 125 tanks remained in the 14th Panzer Corps (at the beginning of the Soviet offensive there were 134).

After the failure of the general offensive, Zhukov and Eremenko tried to set limited tasks for the troops (to continue attacks in certain areas). But they completely failed, and already on 9 September, the war diary of the Stalingrad Front stated that 'none of the advancing armies has fulfilled its task'. Among the reasons for this latest failure, the Russians indicated 'false reports of units about the successes achieved', 'an offensive without a shock fist', 'poor interaction of artillery with tanks and infantry', and 'the dominance of enemy aviation'.

Nevertheless, on 9 September, the defence of the 14th Panzer Corps was cracking again. General Wietersheim, during another tantrum, demanded that the next day the entire Fliegerkorps VIII act in his support, claiming that otherwise the front could collapse. However, Richthofen had already received a request from the 4th Panzer Army for maximum support of the 48th Panzer Corps. As a result, he decided not to disperse his forces, but to act differently. From 09.00 all Stukas, ground-attack planes and bombers bombed the southern part of Stalingrad, and then at 13.00 switched to the 'northern barrier'. During this 'aviation pause', the defence of the 14th Panzer Corps again 'trembled', and only with the introduction of a few reserve groups into battle were the Germans again able to repel attacks and restore the situation.

Under constant pressure from Stalin, Soviet commanders continued to drive their divisions to the slaughter. And they regularly reported the lack of success and the all-crushing blows of the Luftwaffe. 'Aviation in groups of 15–25 planes systematically bombed the army's battle formations,' the headquarters of the 24th Army reported on 11 September. On this day, the Stukas struck the initial positions of the Soviet troops in the morning. At 11:00, they accurately hit the units of the 24th Army preparing for the attack. As a result, they were only able to launch an offensive three hours later. But after 30 minutes, a second Ju 87 raid followed, again sowing chaos and confusion in the ranks of the attackers and forcing them to lie down. Captured Russian soldiers honestly told that the raids of German ground-attack planes, especially the Ju 87s, made a strong moral impression. And besides them, the soldiers were very afraid of the Fw 189 'Frame' reconnaissance planes, since their appearance in the sky was soon followed by an artillery strike.

As a result, Zhukov ordered the attacks to stop, and the 1st Guards Army, which did not meet expectations and suffered heavy losses, was temporarily withdrawn to the rear. However, after the bloody battles some of the Russians 'retreated' in the other direction. On 13 September, a whole company of the 173rd Rifle Division, two officers and 41 men, defected to the Germans south of Kotluban. And in the area of Yerzovka, 72 soldiers from the 99th Rifle Division ran away to the enemy. They explained that they were sent by their commanders into a suicidal attack, then they spent a long time holed up in no man's land. The soldiers were afraid to go back because of the blocking detachments and executions, so then decided to crawl to the Germans. The defectors spoke about the effectiveness of Luftwaffe air attacks, as a result of which many infantry companies lost more than half of their personnel.

After taking a little rest and receiving reinforcements at dawn on 18 September, the Soviets again went on the offensive in the general direction of Gumrak. At 05.45, the headquarters of the German 6th Army began receiving numerous reports from the headquarters of the 14th Panzer Corps and the 8th Army Corps about masses of Soviet ground-attack planes, as well as heavy artillery fire in the Kotluban area. Paulus immediately called Richthofen. During the day, Fliegerkorps VIII carried out 875 sorties, bombers and ground-attack planes dropping 395 tons of bombs of all sizes on the positions of the advancing Soviet troops and their rear positions.

Several times during the day, crisis situations arose in this sector, the German defence was bursting at the seams again, and T-34 tanks were able to break into the German rear in several places and even reach their communications. But by the evening the situation had been stabilised.

On 19 September, the Luftwaffe continued massive raids on the initial positions of the Soviet troops and their rear facilities. At dawn, He 111 bombers appeared, dropping 250kg fragmentation bombs. They were replaced by the Bf 110 Zerstörers, which dropped high-explosive bombs and strafed the Russian infantry with cannon fire. Then Hs 123 biplanes flew in at low level, attacking point targets (artillery positions, tanks and trucks). Then it was the turn of the Stukas. As a result, another Russian attack was nipped in the bud.

Having failed in a large-scale offensive, the Soviets launched daily attacks involving tanks and infantry in various sectors, trying to exhaust the Germans and simply 'move' the front line as far as possible. A typical entry in the combat log of the 8th Army Corps reported:

> From 04.30, the Russians launched an offensive with the forces of one fresh rifle division with a tank brigade east of point 413, managed to break through the defence of the 203rd Infantry Regiment and along the Thin ravine reached the second line, defeating the command post of the 230th Infantry Regiment and the command post of the 3rd Company of the 176th Artillery Regiment. The counter-attack was carried out by the forces of a sapper company, a battery of assault guns and an anti-tank company PanzerJag.Abt.521. After a heavy battle, the enemy who broke through was thrown back and destroyed, the gap in the front was eliminated.

To the east, on the front of the 14th Panzer Corps there were fierce battles for several days for Hill 111.1 and neighbouring hills, which changed hands several times.

Shortly before dawn on 24 September, a Soviet assault group consisting of 30 tanks, accompanied by infantry, managed to approach the advanced German positions south of Kotluban unnoticed and make a breakthrough to an area 5km north of Bolshaya Rososhka. Having reached the enemy's communications, the Red Army soldiers quickly dug in and took up a circular defence. However, the promised reinforcements never arrived, and at lunchtime the group was first heavily bombarded and shelled, and then attacked and defeated by German mobile detachments. At the same time, the offensive of the 66th Army, which began at 16.00 in the area of Yerzovka, was disrupted due to pre-emptive artillery shelling of the initial positions.

'The freedom-loving Russian people will never give up Stalingrad'

As a result of continuous fighting and bombing, Soviet units had been thinned out considerably. For example, the 233rd Rifle Division of the 24th Army lost 5,367 men from 17 to 22 September, including 1,470 killed. The 260th Rifle Division of the 1st Guards Army lost 5,861 soldiers, including 1,447 killed and 517 missing. Approximately the same losses were suffered by other advancing divisions. The 16th Tank

Corps lost 51 tanks in just one day of fighting for Hill 130.4, a third due to air attacks. A second lieutenant from the 217th Tank Brigade, who surrendered, said that his unit was completely destroyed, only one T-34 remaining. In addition, the prisoner complained to the enemy about the poor quality of tanks produced at the 'Krasnoe Sormovo' plant in the city of Gorky.[1] Not only did they not have oil and fuel gauges, but even gunsights! However, these facts did not prevent Eremenko from declaring that 'the enemy is exhausted' and 'hardly holds positions', and only 'unsatisfactory management' hinders success. Because of this, he ordered on the morning of 26 September to launch another offensive, already the fourth from the north, against the 'northern barrier' of the 6th Army.

But this time the operation ended in complete failure. On 30 September, the 66th Army, after a powerful raid by Il-2 ground-attack planes, launched another desperate attack south of Yerzovka. It was accompanied by 90 Stuart, Lee and Valentine tanks from the 285th, 167th and 241st Tank Brigades. They were formed in August in the cities of Gorky and Dzerzhinsk, arrived at the Ilovlya railway station at the end of September, and then immediately thrown into battle. As usual, the assault group managed to break through the stretched positions of the Germans, but in the depths of the defence it was left without support and was then shot up by German ground-attack planes and anti-aircraft guns, and then finished off by a tank counter-attack. According to German data, 71 tanks were destroyed and 800 men from the accompanying infantry were captured. 'The bulk gets stuck under the fire of our anti-aircraft guns and tanks and replenish the tank cemetery. Our soldiers are amazed to note that American tanks are knocked out at a greater distance than the Russians, and when hit, they explode while the Russians are just burning out,' wrote Oberleutnant Sittig from 7./Gr.Rgt.8.(mot.). The 'hero of the day' was the Panzer IV commander Feldwebel Zeisig of the 3rd Motorised Infantry Division, who in one engagement disabled 18 Russian tanks.

The headquarters of the 1st Guards Army reported: 'Army units as a result of nine-day battles (from 18.9) severely drained of blood. Some divisions do not even represent any real force, although they continue to receive a combat mission. For example, the 292nd Rifle Division has 89 active soldiers in its composition, the 24th Rifle Division has 83 active soldiers, the 16th Tank Corps has 6 tanks in service, the 4th Tank Corps has 21 tanks.' In general, during the month of fighting, this army suffered 53,688 casualties, including 14,323 killed and missing (at the

---

1 Now Nizhny Novgorod.

beginning of the operation, it had 75,000 soldiers). The neighbouring 24th Army lost 41,198 men including 14,500 killed and missing (at the beginning of the operation it had 54,000 people). German losses in were about 40 (!!!) times less, in tanks also minimal (a little more than 40). At the end of the month, all three 'exhausted' divisions of the 14th Panzer Corps were still considered 'suitable for offensive tasks'.

The representative of the headquarters of the Main Command, Georgy Malenkov, blamed the failure of the operation on Eremenko's deputy (assistant) on the Stalingrad Front, General Gordov. 'Gordov does not bring a fresh stream, rather we can say that he himself belongs to the category of generals who are accustomed to retreat. Gordov needs to be replaced. The headquarters of the Stalingrad Front must be seriously refreshed with new workers from other Fronts,' he wrote in a memo to Stalin on 27 September. Along the way, Malenkov also touched upon Marshal Tymoshenko, who inherited a 'rotten headquarters', and turned out to be a 'slacker', indifferent to the fate of the Soviet government and the motherland.

The leader eventually listened to his messenger and really 'refreshed' the headquarters. On 28 September, the Stalingrad Front was renamed the Don Front, and a young Lieutenant General, Konstantin Rokossovsky, was appointed its commander. The South-eastern Front was renamed the Stalingrad Front, and Colonel-General Yeremenko remained its commander.

However, all this does not mean that the desperate and bloody Russian offensive did not yield any results. Since the last days of August, Paulus had been constantly putting pressure on the headquarters of the 14th Panzer Corps, trying to force it not only to hold the northern flank, but also to take part in the attack on Stalingrad. Compromise decisions were made several times. But Wietersheim, who saw what powerful forces were concentrating in the wasteland before his stretched front, stubbornly ignored both polite hints and direct instructions. It was even planned to reassign the 60th Motorised Division to von Seydlitz's 51st Army Corps. But the attacks that followed from the north eventually proved Wietersheim right. In addition, the general reasonably believed that panzer corps did not exist in order to conduct gruelling positional struggles with the greatly superior forces of the attacking enemy. He was sceptical of the ambitious plans of the command and doubted the possibility of quickly capturing a huge city stretching along a riverbank. As a result, Wietersheim annoyed Paulus and von Weichs, and the Führer. On 15 September, this 'eternal alarmist' was replaced by Hitler's favourite General Hans Hube.

In addition, the German command had to postpone until better times (which never came) the planned offensive to the north in order to encircle the Soviet troops located between the Don and the Volga and the subsequent construction of winter positions along the line of Yerzovka–Pichuga ravine–Hill 139.1–Karkagon ravine–the southern bank of the Panshinka River. The plan of this operation was code-named Herbtzaitlose ('Autumn Time') and it was approved by the Führer in early September. The Germans also had to constantly postpone Operation Wintermorchen ('Winter Tales') to eliminate the Soviet bridgehead in the Serafimovichi area and the offensive of the 4th Panzer Army on Beketovka and Krasnoarmeysk.

And at the end of September, due to constant attacks and lack of forces, the 6th Army was forced to leave the bend of the Don River south of Ilovlya, which had been so triumphantly occupied in August. The 384th Infantry Division that occupied it (three 'exhausted' and three 'weak' battalions) retreated to a straightened 'chord' position. The Luftwaffe also did not have time to fulfil all the numerous requests of army commanders for air support, and sometimes simply ignored them. The success of aviation in one sector had to be paid for by delays and difficulties in another.

After the victorious August for the Wehrmacht, which revived the general 'atmosphere of the summer of 1941', September did not bring any major successes for the Third Reich, except for the capture of the Taman Peninsula and Novorossiysk. Whilst in the northern and central sectors of the front, the Germans repelled the constant attacks of the Red Army, in the south they themselves were hopelessly bogged down in the Soviet defence.

A Soviet leaflet in German, dropped over the positions of the 6th Army at the end of the month, said:

> You have been at Stalingrad for about a month. What have you achieved? Tens of thousands of Germans died at Stalingrad, and it remains and will remain Soviet. And this is not accidental, because Stalingrad is a Soviet city. Stalingrad is the Volga. And the Volga is Russia. The freedom-loving Russian people will never give up Stalingrad, nor will they give up the Volga, nor will they kneel before the invaders.

In addition, the leaflet threatened German soldiers with the ever-increasing power of the Red Army and the approaching winter, as well as with analogies with 1918. They said that the Kaiser's Germany collapsed after four years of war, although before that it had constantly won victories. The Third Reich will also collapse. 'The year 1942 will be fatal for fascist Germany, like 1918 for Kaiser Wilhelm's Germany,' the leaflet said. By the way, this 'prophecy' reflected the mood in the Soviet elite in the autumn of 1942. If last winter comparisons with Napoleon were in fashion, now ones with the Kaiser were!

Meanwhile, at the end of September, the first night frosts occurred near Stalingrad, which clearly showed the Germans that they were not in Africa after all (as it might have seemed during the August sandstorms), but still in Russia. The last day with summer weather was 29 September, when the sun was still hot, and the air temperature was +24 – +26°. But already on 30 September, a sharp cold snap began. The daytime temperature dropped to +15°, and at night it reached almost zero. The soldiers had to think about heating their dugouts and bunkers. 'Since there is nothing to get hold of in the steppe, except a meagre juniper, we are heated with gasoline. Soldiers make stoves from canisters on which shell casings are mounted as a pipe,' wrote Oberleutnant Sittig from the 3rd Motorised Infantry Division.

Chapter 7

THE 'DECISIVE' ASSAULT

The Hozzels breakthrough

By the beginning of October, both the German and the Soviet troops in the Stalingrad area were largely exhausted by endless fighting. Most of the German divisions, infantry companies and battalions were able to conduct an offensive only after long pauses for rest. And by that time the battle itself had finally disintegrated into a series of small fights, local attacks and counter-attacks that took place at different times and in different sectors.

At the beginning of October, the headquarters of the 6th Army had the first serious concerns about the storming of the remaining part of Stalingrad, and about holding the stretched front. 'If the Russians make a strong blow, which is quite possible, then the weakened front, left without reserves, will simply collapse,' Chief of Staff of the 6th Army Schmidt warned the higher command.

On 3 October, Richthofen, accompanied by the Luftwaffe Chief of the General Staff, General Hans Jeschonnek (who was conducting an inspection trip to the front), arrived at the headquarters of the 51st Army Corps. There they met with its commander, Major General Seydlitz-Kurzbach, and Paulus. After a heated discussion of the situation, the high-ranking 'quartet' came to the conclusion that 'success is guaranteed, but only with the arrival of reinforcements'. Then, in private, Richthofen told Jeschonnek that it was all about the lack of a clear goal of the offensive. He said that Luftflotte 4 could continuously bomb the ruins of Stalingrad, while some units constantly have to be diverted to the Caucasus to support the 17th Army and the 1st Panzer Army. 'We just can't go on the offensive everywhere at the same time,' he said. Richthofen insisted that the operations should be carried out consistently. Jeschonnek agreed with these arguments, noting that 'first of all we must finish what we started, especially in Stalingrad and Tuapse'.

On the morning of 4 October, German bombers carried out raids on the northern part of Stalingrad, dropping fragmentation bombs weighing 500kg and 1,400kg on the Russian positions. Avoiding hitting their own troops was a difficult mission for twin-engined bombers. Hans Berhrens from 6./KG27 recalled:

> As a flight mechanic, I flew from Kursk to the first bombing of Stalingrad in the crew of Oberleutnant Peter Laas. We attacked the Russian bridgehead on the west bank. When approaching the Stalingrad area, we were informed by radio about the location of our target, which was not previously known for sure. When approaching the target, we were led by a leader code-named 'Father' for accurate targeting. Accordingly, we dropped our bombs, knowing the exact 'address'. When leaving after the bombing, the 'Father' thanked us and announced that the bombs had hit the target exactly.

After the bombing, the Germans resumed the offensive in the area of the Mechetka River – the 'Barricades' residential district. Within an hour they managed to break through the front, after which the tanks and the infantrymen of the 24th Panzer and 389th Infantry Divisions following them reached Nogina, Verkhneudinskaya and Deputatskaya Streets, as well as the stadium and Sculpture Park.

After a two-day pause, at dawn on 7 October, the sky over Stalingrad was again filled with the terrifying howl of the Stukas, who for four hours bombed the positions of the 37th Guards and 112th Rifle Divisions on the approaches to the Tractor Plant. In total, Russian observers counted about 900 flights of German aircraft in the sky over the city. At 10.30, the assault groups of the 389th Infantry Division, supported by tanks, again launched an attack and by evening reached Vosduchoplavatelnaya, Vozovaya, Topogradskaya, Shtepenko and Surkova Streets, as well as the mouth of the river Orlovka, coming close to the complex of buildings of the Tractor Plant. At the same time, the 141st Marine Infantry Company and the remnants of the 282nd NKVD Regiment were surrounded. The next night, a group of nine men broke through to their own lines.

The Luftwaffe once again ensured success. But the battle for the 'Barricades' district again led to huge losses on both sides. Thus, the 295th Infantry Division lost 24 men killed and 115 wounded in three days of fighting. Only 535 officers and men remained in the

94th Infantry Division, which had not received any reinforcements for a long time. 'The successful capture of Stalingrad is hindered by the extreme weakness of the infantry units stationed there, despite all possible efforts. The supply of new forces is needed,' the headquarters of the 6th Army reported to Army Group B. It was during these days that the optimistic mood that the German commanders tried to maintain in September was replaced by a pessimistic and anxious one. If earlier Paulus's staff was almost sure of the final success, then at the beginning of October the possibility of capturing the remaining part of Stalingrad was already openly questioned.

Things were no better on the other side of the street. For example, by the morning of 4 October, only 17 soldiers remained in the 42nd Rifle Brigade, 48 in the 92nd Rifle Brigade, and 36 in the 351st Rifle Regiment. In each regiment of the 138th Rifle Division, only 70–80 soldiers remained. The 95th Rifle Division (which had arrived in the city on the night of 18/19 September) had lost 80 per cent of its personnel in 10 days, mainly from air attacks, artillery and mortar fire.

But the Russians' broken units were gradually replaced by new ones. Despite the constant shelling and bombing of the Volga ferry crossings, they continued to work smoothly. This was facilitated by the gradual reduction of daylight hours. At the beginning of October, the 39th Guards Rifle Division and the 308th Rifle Division were transferred to the west bank. On the night of 3/4 October, the 84th Tank Brigade, consisting of 24 T-34s, 20 T-70s and five KV-1s, began crossing into the city. Tanks came to the bank one by one, after which they carefully camouflaged themselves. At night they were loaded onto special ferries and pontoons and transported across the river. These tanks were no longer intended for manoeuvre battles: pits were dug for them in advance, and after the crossing, special guides accompanied the crews to their positions. The tankers had to take a position in the ground, camouflage it, and then fight to the last shell and cartridge.

Between 27 September and 6 October, 7,023 men, 45 tanks, many guns and 270 tons of cargo were transported to Stalingrad. The Russians took out 630 wounded on the return trips. The Volga military flotilla at that time, despite heavy losses, was still a significant force. As of 5 October, there were 30 ships in it, including 12 armoured boats, eight minesweepers, seven gunboats and three floating artillery batteries. Damaged vessels were repaired in numerous backwater locations on the eastern shore of the Volga, and put back into service.

The Germans were much worse off for reinforcements. On 5 October, it was decided to replenish and replace the weakened combat groups with personnel from supply units. At the same time, the Führer's instruction on the possibility of mass use of prisoners of war for auxiliary work was transmitted to the headquarters of the army corps. Later, the reduction of the manpower of artillery batteries also began.

In order to strengthen the assault group of the 51st Army Corps, Paulus decided to perform another permutation. The 'depleted' 76th Infantry Division was sent to the left flank of the 'northern barrier' (west of Kotluban), and the 'exhausted' but more combat-ready 305th Infantry Division went to Stalingrad. The 14th Panzer Division, which had been withdrawn from the city earlier (it was planned to use it in Operation Heron – the offensive on Astrakhan), also returned. The next released units were supposed to arrive from the Don after the Romanians changed their positions. German troops were so in need of reinforcements that they were often airlifted. For example, the marching battalion of the 389th Infantry Division that arrived at Millerovo station and a company of recovering soldiers were transported from there by Ju 52 aircraft to the Peskovatka forward airfield.

With the decrease in daylight, Russian night bombers began to play an increasingly important role. It turned out that the Luftwaffe completely dominated the sky during the day, so the Russians did not particularly interfere with them. But after sunset, on the contrary, Soviet aviation revived, which was also not opposed by anyone. For example, on the night of 1/2 October, Russian bombers carried out a successful raid on the supply base of the 6th Army in Nizhne-Alekseevsky. As a result, the warehouses located there were completely destroyed, and 400 tons of food burned. The camp for Soviet prisoners of war there was also damaged. On the night of 4/5 October, Russian bombers carried out a series of attacks against the positions and rear of the 6th Army. The pilots observed many explosions and fires, some of which were visible from 100km away. Four Li-2s raided the Likhaya railway junction and 10 more bombed the line between Likhaya and Morozovskaya. The rest attacked the Salsk railway junction and the line between it and Kotelnikovo. In total, Russian long-range bombers carried out 113 sorties, and the crews reported numerous fires in the target area.

According to German data, the ammunition warehouse in Chir suffered the most, where about 7,500 37mm, 75mm and 76.2mm shells were destroyed. On the night of 6/7 October, a raid was carried out on Surovikino, which also caused significant damage. The headquarters of the 6th Army stated: 'The nighttime dominance of Russian aviation in the air has significant consequences. The troops are never left alone, their forces are constantly strained. There are losses in people and property.'

Despite all these difficulties, on 8 October, Paulus received a categorical order from von Weichs to launch a powerful new offensive no later than the 14th, throwing all combat-ready units into battle. On the same day, the headquarters of the 6th Army received a message from weather forecasters that the good weather was ending and that they should expect the beginning of a period of bad weather.

The Soviets knew about the enemy's plans and felt that a threat was looming over the northern part of Stalingrad. Yeremenko and Khrushchev were afraid that after the seizure of the factories, the Germans would force the Volga and move further towards Kazakhstan. In addition, the Russians were seriously afraid that the Wehrmacht would launch ships and start sailing on the river! Therefore, work was intensified on equipping positions on the eastern shore, as well as on numerous islands. On 8 October, the headquarters of the Stalingrad Front issued an order: 'Create three barrage lines. Front line: the Volga riverbed. The task is to prohibit the sailing of enemy ships. Second line: exits to the islands. The task is to prevent the enemy from crossing the river.' The villages of Sredne-Pogromnoye, Nizhne-Pogromnoye and Verkhnyaya Akhtuba were to be turned into strongpoints protected by minefields and anti-tank ditches. In Moscow, too, it was feared that after the capture of Stalingrad, the Wehrmacht could launch an offensive to the east and north – towards Kamyshin and Saratov. Therefore, on 10 October, the headquarters of the Don Front received an order to prepare defensive lines in the area of Gornaya Proleika – the valley of the Berdiya River and on the eastern bank of the Volga to Lugovaya Proleika.

For the 'decisive blow', the Jaenecke assault group (under General Erwin Jaenecke, commander of the 389th Infantry Division) was assembled, which included the 305th and 389th Infantry Divisions and the 14th Panzer Division. Of the 14 infantry battalions that Jaenecke had, nine were considered 'exhausted', four 'very weak' and one 'weak'. Of the two attached sapper battalions, one was 'strong', the other 'exhausted'. The 14th Panzer Division consisted of 52 tanks, including 34 Panzer IIIs, 15 Panzer IVs and three Panzer IIs. The main blow was to be delivered in the direction of the 'Dzerzhinsky' Tractor Plant. On the very first day of the attack (or at the latest on the second), the assault group had to reach the Volga east of this point. After that, the Germans wanted to turn south along the bank and seize the 'Barricades' plant. After that, the 295th Infantry Division and the 100th Jäger Division were to go on the offensive. The ultimate goal of the operation was to capture the entire industrial zone of Stalingrad.

Apparently, to raise the morale of the commanders of exhausted divisions before the next battle, several of them were awarded the Knight's Cross at once. Among the 'cavaliers' were Jaenecke, the commander of the 71st Infantry Division General von Hartmann, and the commander of the 76th Infantry Division General Rodenburg.

The attack itself, as usual, was planned in the spirit of adventurism. For example, part of the ammunition for the 389th Infantry Division was planned to be delivered not on the eve of the operation, but during the first day. However, on the night of 13 October, an accident occurred on the railway between Tatsinskaya and Morozovskaya (trains collided), as a result of which, less than a day before the attack, the rear services had to collect shells from the warehouses of other divisions and deliver them to the Gumrak railway station. There they were hurriedly loaded onto cars and taken to their consumers.

The 62nd Army seemed well prepared to defend the rest of the city. Two hundred and fifty buildings were adapted to all-around defence, and a total of 8,000 anti-personnel and 3,300 anti-tank mines were laid on the approaches to them. All the streets on the way to the Volga were blocked by barricades and trenches, covered by numerous artillery positions and dug-in tanks. In the area of the Tractor Plant, two continuous strips of anti-tank mines were laid, all stone buildings were turned into fortresses, and communication passages and strong dugouts were excavated: the infantry 'dug deep into the ground'. The Russian defence in this sector was built in two lines. The first line was occupied by the 109th and 114th Rifle Regiments of the 37th Rifle Division, the 117th Rifle Regiment of the 39th Guards Rifle Division and the 90th Rifle Regiment of the 95th Rifle Division. The second line was occupied by the 524th, 112th and 118th Rifle Regiments of the 37th Guards Rifle Division and the 84th Tank Brigade. This line of defence, created in a dense urban environment, might seem impregnable to infantry and tanks. But could it resist the might of the Luftwaffe?

On 14 October, at 09.00, a powerful artillery bombardment began, then the familiar howl of sirens was heard in the sky. This time the Stukas acted like a 'string of pearls'. One by one, they approached the target, then dived, fell vertically down and dropped bombs on pre-determined targets. While one Ju 87 was approaching the city, the second was already approaching the target, the third was diving, the fourth was already going up, having just dropped a bomb, the fifth was gaining altitude, and the sixth was already moving away to base. After hitting targets directly in front of the front line, the following Stukas struck at strongpoints located 100–150m deep in the Soviet positions, 'processing' the entire area of the offensive step by step.

At 09.30, the German assault troops slowly went on the attack, gradually advancing through the newly-bombed neighbourhoods. The commander of StG2, Major Werner Hozzel, recalled: 'Richthofen made us understand that our Geschwader must conduct bombing with extreme precision in order to avoid danger to our troops close to the target. We could have avoided the risk and bomb from a height of 4,000m because of the wide area of the objective. However, we had to dive to the minimum height, dropping bombs directly over the roofs.'

One of the soldiers of the German 389th Infantry Division, waiting for the order to attack, wrote: 'The whole sky is filled with planes, artillery is firing, bombs are falling from the sky, sirens are blaring. Now we will rise from the trenches and take part in this monstrous performance.' The commander of the 62nd Army, General Chuikov, who was on the other side of the front line, described this October morning as follows:

> What I saw on the street, especially in the direction of the Tractor Plant, is difficult to describe with a pen. Dive-bombers roared overhead, falling bombs howled, anti-aircraft shells exploded, and their tracer trajectories traced the sky with a red dotted line. Everything was buzzing, groaning and tearing. In the distance, the walls of houses were collapsing, the buildings of the workshops of the Tractor Plant were burning.

In total, 600 tons of high-explosive and fragmentation bombs were dropped on the Tractor Plant and strongpoints around it. In fact, the Luftwaffe cut a strip in the Soviet defence 2.5km wide and 1–2km long! And in all this space, almost all strongpoints and dugouts were destroyed and 80 per cent of the minefields were blown up. Both lines of defence of the 62nd Army were subjected to uniform impact. As a result, all units suffered huge losses and were demoralised. All day long huge clouds of dust and smoke rose over the Traktorozavodsky district, which did not allow the Russians to use divisional artillery, as well as adjust howitzer fire from the eastern shore. Perhaps, it was one of the most effective (both in terms of entertainment and damage) Stuka raids of the entire Second World War!

At noon, the Jaenecke assault group captured the Six-Coal Quarter, then the ring of streets surrounding it and the southern part of the Tractor Plant. After lunch, Paulus arrived at the forward command post of Fliegerkorps VIII, located east of the Razgulyevka railway station. There he discussed with Richthofen, who was pleased with his subordinates, plans for the use of aviation the next day. At 13.45, Paulus visited observation posts west of the 'Red October' residential district. From there, he observed the strikes of Stukas and the artillery shelling of the Tractor Factory, in the western part of which the remnants of Soviet troops were still holding out.

The 6th Army headquarters believed that the objectives of the first day of the offensive had not been fully achieved. In fact, already in the evening, the 2nd Battalion of the 103rd Panzergrenadier Regiment (II./PanzerGren.Rgt.103) reached the Volga in the area of the oil tanks, where it took up an all-round defence. This became known only the next morning. The communication of the Stalingrad Front headquarters with the units of the 62nd Army was disrupted, and Eremenko learned that the Germans had reached the shore from tank crews stationed on Zaitsevsky Island. It was located directly opposite the Tractor Factory.

At night, Eremenko arrived at Chuikov's headquarters on an armoured boat to assess the situation. 'My conclusion is that the enemy was successful only thanks to the dominant position in the air and the massive use of bomber aircraft,' he said in his report on the results of the trip. The headquarters of the 62nd Army reported on the huge losses inflicted on the enemy, but in fact, the breakthrough to the Volga cost the Jaenecke assault group relatively few casualties. For example, the 305th Infantry Division, with the 389th Infantry Division sub-units attached to it, lost 102 dead and missing and 293 wounded.

'The enemy is fighting hard and with ferocity'

On the morning of 15 October, Ju 87s from StG2 attacked the northern part of Stalingrad again. The main targets were the 'Barricades' plant, the village of Rynok and Soviet artillery positions on the eastern bank of the Volga. 'Fliegerkorps VIII with all its forces continuously supported and ensured today's success of the offensive in the north part of Stalingrad,' it was reported in the war diary of the 6th Army. Meanwhile, the Germans separated the remnants of the 37th Guards Rifle Division into parts, and then reached the river in the district of Pribaltiyskaya Street, capturing the pier of the Tractor Plant and the brick factory. The width of the breakthrough to the Volga reached 2km. At the same time, the 16th Panzer Division and the 94th Infantry Division went on the offensive in the northern suburbs. They managed to reach the outskirts of the villages of Rynok and Spartanovka, but there the assault groups encountered unexpectedly fierce resistance. 'Unusually heavy losses (up to 30 per cent) have been suffered,' the headquarters of the 14th Panzer Corps reported. This small bridgehead was defended by the remnants of the 124th and 149th Rifle Brigades, as well as the survivors of the 115th Rifle Brigade and the 2nd Marine Infantry Brigade, who had previously managed to break through from Orlovka – only about 2,000 men.

German troops moving towards Stalingrad.

Sd.Kfz. 231 armoured car from the 16th Panzer Division at the Volga River.

He 111 bomber from KG27 drops bombs on Stalingrad. (*Boelcke Archiv*)

Bombing of the southern part of Stalingrad.

Russian anti-aircraft gunners in position.

Stalingrad after the bombing attack.

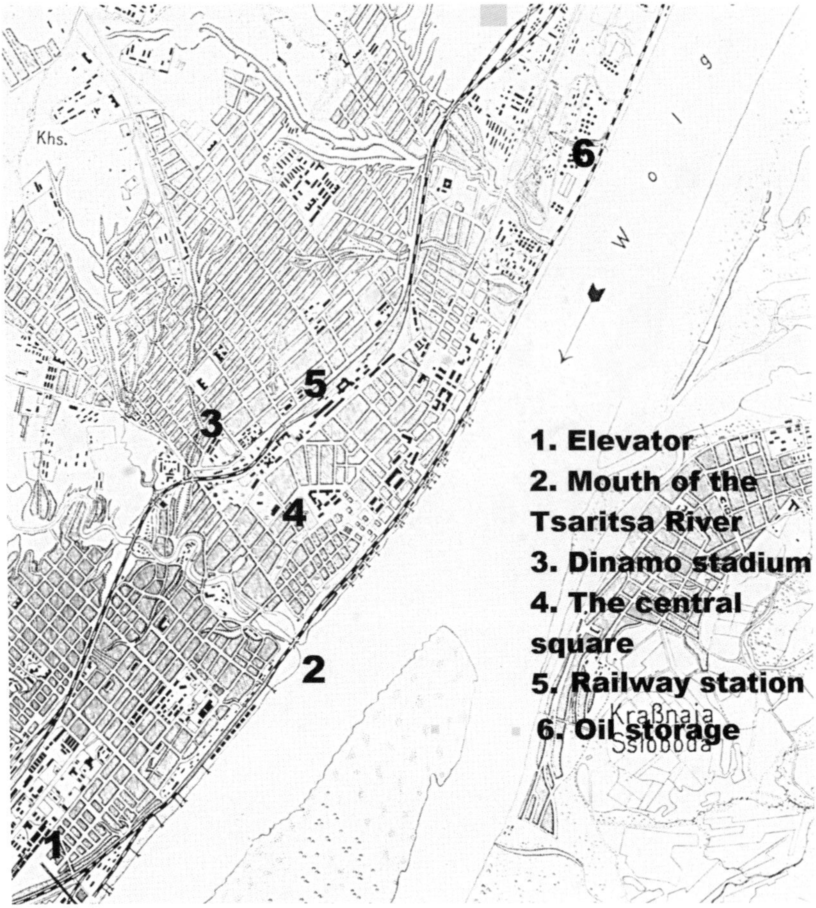

1. Elevator
2. Mouth of the Tsaritsa River
3. Dinamo stadium
4. The central square
5. Railway station
6. Oil storage

Khs.

W o l g a

Kraßnaja Ssloboda

Plan of the central part of Stalingrad.

Tanks of the 24th Panzer Division enter the southern part of the city.

Marder III self-propelled gun in the vicinity of Stalingrad.

StuG III assault gun in Stalingrad.

Ju 87 dive-bomber over Stalingrad.

Hill 102.0 (the Mamayev Kurgan).

Russian infantry in Stalingrad.

German gunners change position.

Soviet KV-1 heavy tank among the ruins.

German infantrymen in the entrance of a house.

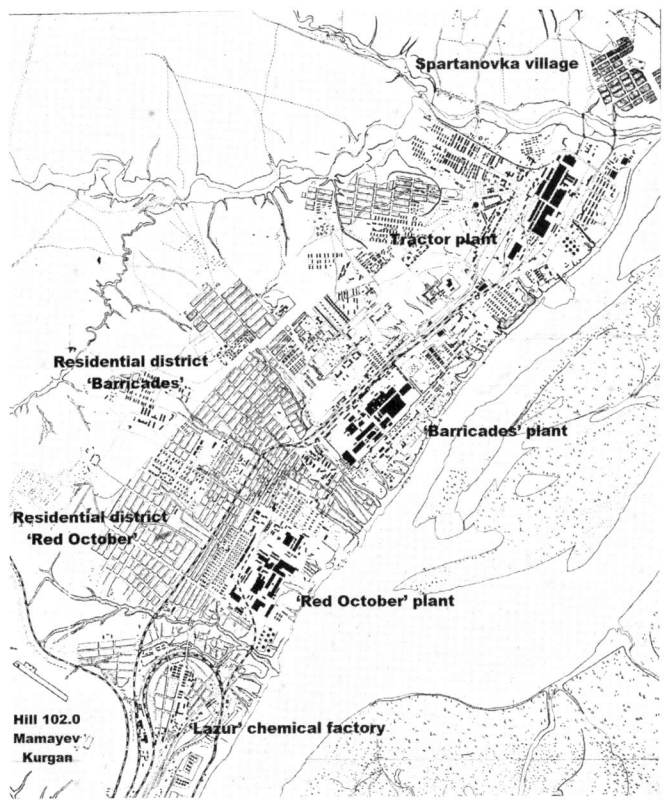

The northern part of Stalingrad.

Russian infantry moving through the ruins.

A StuG III firing.

German assault groups attack the Tractor Factory.

Soldiers of the 45th Rifle Division at the 'Red October' factory.

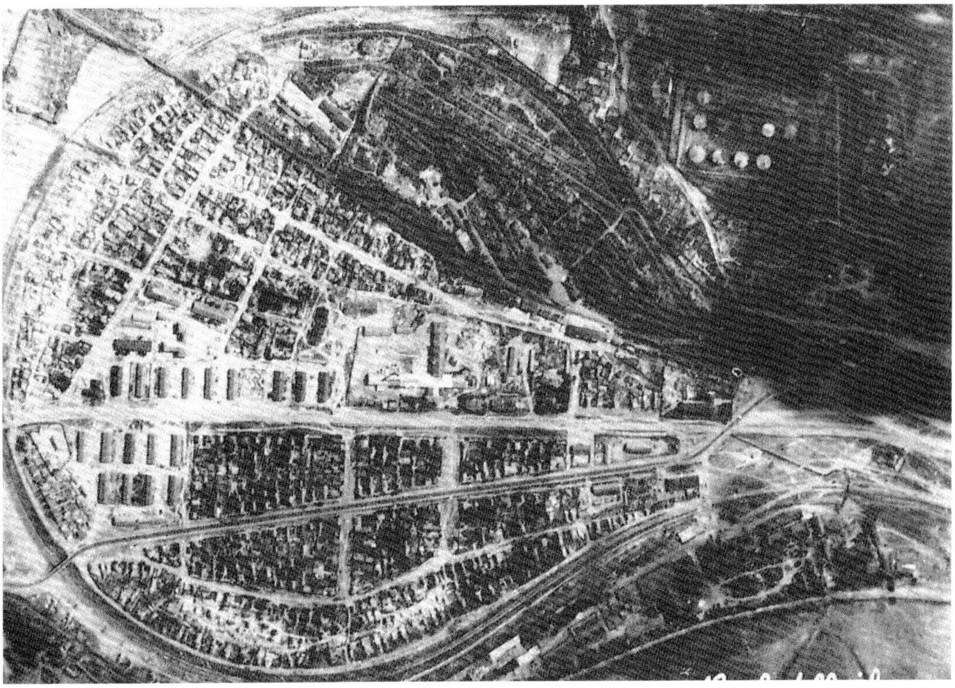

The 'Tennis Racket' (the 'Lazur' chemical factory) before the battle.

The 'Tennis Racket' after the battle.

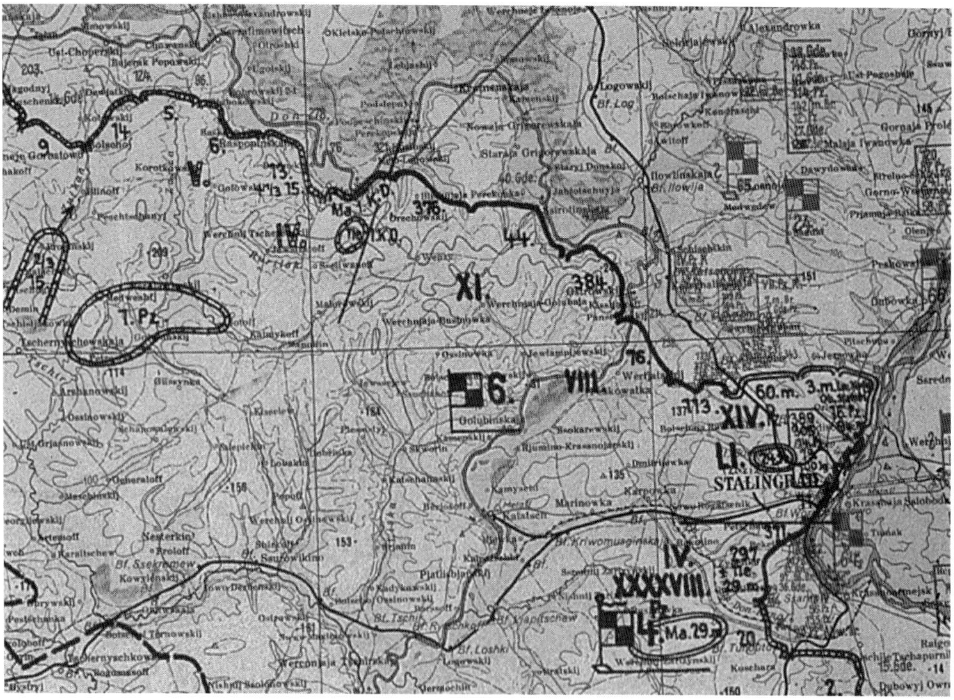

Wehrmacht map showing the situation near Stalingrad on 31 October.

One of the streets of the city after the battle.

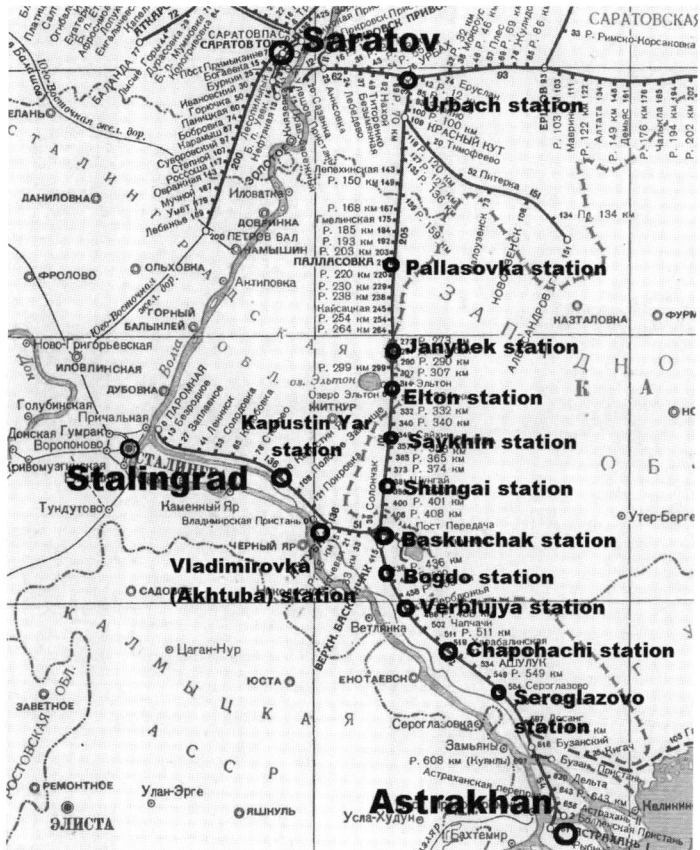

Map of the Saratov–Urbach–Astrakhan railway.

Loading cargo containers into an He 111 bomber. (*Boelcke Archiv*)

He 111 bomber from KG27 before another mission to supply the 6th Army. (*Boelcke Archiv*)

He 111 during a flight to Pitomnik. (*Boelcke Archiv*)

The grain elevator after the battle.

Paulus poses for a Russian cameraman.

German tanks abandoned in the Stalingrad area . . .

In the late afternoon, Paulus arrived at the command post of the 103rd Panzergrenadier Regiment, located in the western part of the 'Barricades' residential district. So, the commander of the 6th Army was in the city for the first time, having examined the numerous ruins and traces of recent battles. After the meeting, it was decided to continue the offensive from the Tractor Plant to the south, along the railway, while striking from the west in the direction of the 'Barricades' plant. 'Good progress has been achieved in Stalingrad, the Russians were clearly caught off guard. We reached the Volga on a three-kilometre front,' Richthofen wrote in his diary that night.

The next day, the commander of Luftflotte 4 flew to Hitler's 'Werwolf' headquarters, where he showed him photographs of the destroyed Stalingrad and devastated suburbs, and at the same time complained about Paulus, Hoth and others. 'He was especially kind to me,' Richthofen wrote in his diary. The Führer listened attentively and approved his operational plans, as well as his assessment of the situation. On the same day, Richthofen also met with Göring. The Reichsmarschall was delighted with the work of the Luftwaffe and promised him a field marshal's baton as soon as Stalingrad fell.

On 16 October, the Luftwaffe again subjected Russian positions to large-calibre bombs (SC1800s and SC2500s). The powerful explosions of such weapons not only led to massive destruction, but also had a strong moral impact on the defenders. They caused real earthquakes. And a pair of Ju 88s from III./KG6 carried out a mission to destroy an underground fortified shelter in Stalingrad. Judging by the Soviet data, they completed it successfully! Bombs fell on the command post of the 62nd Army, as a result of which several dugouts were destroyed and collapsed. The exact location of the Russian headquarters had been established by German intelligence during the interrogation of a commissar, who had been captured the day before.

However, numerous dug-in KV-1 and T-34 tanks were not damaged during the bombing. They became a serious obstacle in the way of the assault groups of the 305th Infantry and 14th Panzer Divisions. According to German information, 16 tanks were destroyed during the protracted battle, but their own losses amounted to 17 tanks. Nevertheless, by the evening, the Germans managed to break through to the northern part of the 'Barricades' factory and occupy the adjacent group of houses.[1]

---

1 From 21 August to 17 October, the total casualties of the 6th Army amounted to 40,000, including 8,830 killed and missing and 31,181 wounded. During the same period, 57,800 Soviet prisoners were taken.

On 17 October, the Luftwaffe again bombed the 'Barricades' and 'Red October' factories and the islands of Zaitsevsky and Golodny, as well as the eastern shore of the Volga. About 4,000 bombs were dropped for these purposes, including several weighing 2.5 tons. By evening, the 51st Army Corps reported the capture of most of the gun factory ('Barricades'), but the buildings in its south-eastern part were still held by the remnants of the 308th Rifle Division. Anti-aircraft units of the Luftwaffe played an important role. 88mm guns punched massive holes in the concrete and brick walls of factory buildings and suppressed machine-gun nests with fire. 'It's a fantastic sight. Absolutely nothing in the suburbs escaped destruction. We fired several thousand rounds there, including many anti-tank shells used against the strongest buildings,' wrote Generalmajor Pickert, commander of the 9th Anti-aircraft Division, on 17 October.

The Soviet troops suffered very heavy losses, and the resulting gaps were plugged only thanks to the arrival of the 138th Rifle Division, which managed to cross into the city over two nights. On the night of 17/18 October, young soldiers penetrated the buildings in the northern part of the 'Barricades' factory in several places, driving out the Germans from there, and then managed to recapture several ruined houses near the plant in a desperate attack. For the Germans, this sortie was a complete surprise. Communication with the groups of the 305th Infantry Division at the factory was lost and for a long time Paulus' headquarters did not know what was going on there at all. Meanwhile, the thinned units of the 37th Guards Rifle Division retreated to the 'Red October' plant and the bank of the Volga, while the remnants of the almost completely destroyed 95th Rifle Division had to be evacuated to the eastern shore.

Night ferry crossings, despite the loss of part of the berths (piers) and increased artillery shelling, still worked smoothly. For example, on the night of 16/17 October, 393 soldiers, five tanks, 77 tons of food and 53.5 tons of ammunition were delivered to the west bank. Another 62 bags of cargo were dropped from planes. The following night, the minesweepers transported another 560 soldiers and 32 tons of cargo to Stalingrad. On the night of 18/19 October, 491 wounded people were taken out of the city, although the minesweeper *No. 337* was sunk by a direct hit. Ten crew members and 75 wounded died on the ship, only two people escaped. On the night of 20/21 October, 711 people and 3.5 tons of cargo were delivered to the city, and 723 wounded were evacuated in the return trips.

On 19 October, it turned sharply colder in the Stalingrad area, heavy rain fell, and in some places even the first snowfalls. Cloud cover limited the actions of the Luftwaffe, which immediately affected the pace of the offensive. As a result, the Germans could not capture the 'Barricades' plant quickly. Hand-to-hand fights were constantly taking place inside the workshops and outbuildings, several German flamethrower tanks entered the territory of the plant, spraying the buildings with jets of flame. By nightfall, the 305th Infantry Division managed to retake Workshops No. 5 and 5A. During 20–21 October, fierce battles were fought for Shop No. 4 and the northern part of Shop No. 6. In just one day, the Russians lost 700 soldiers killed and wounded at the factory.

On the morning of 23 October, it warmed up again in Stalingrad, and the skies over the Volga were cloudy. Visibility was 10–15km, and the air temperature was +9 – +18°. German artillery opened heavy fire on the positions of the 138th, 308th and 193rd Rifle Divisions. Then the hum of aircraft engines was heard in the sky. The Luftwaffe tried to repeat the success of nine days ago, once again paving the way for ground troops to the Volga. Stukas from StG2 again used the tactics of the 'pearl necklace'. They approached the city in a long, sprawling formation, and then alternately dived for various targets and gradually moved strikes deeper into the Soviet defence. The main targets of the bombing were the south-eastern part of the 'Barricades' plant, the 'Red October' plant, the Banny ravine and Zaitsevsky Island (from there Russian artillery fired on German positions). In some periods, 40–50 German planes in total 'hung' in the sky at the same time. During the day, Soviet observers recorded the fall of about 4,000 high-explosive and fragmentation bombs! The Ju 87s were able to achieve direct hits on the command post of the 308th Rifle Division and the command post of the 62nd Army headquarters. Four bunkers collapsed, all radios were destroyed, and 15 people were killed and injured. Many barricades and minefields were blown up.

At noon, the assault groups of the newly-arrived 79th Infantry Division launched an offensive in the direction of the 'Red October' plant. An hour later, the leading units reached the railway running along the western fence of the enterprise. However, at that moment the sky became overcast, and aviation support ceased. At 14.00 the attacks resumed, and at 14.30 the Germans captured Shop No. 4 and part of Shop No. 5. By the evening, the battle had taken on a fierce character and often turned into hand-to-hand fighting. By nightfall one assault group had made its way to the Volga, occupying the river bank for about 400m. This success cost the 79th Infantry Division heavy casualties: 400 dead and wounded. At the same time, the 14th Panzer Division was fighting for a bakery located between the 'Barricades' and 'Red October' factories. Eremenko again remained in the dark about this latest breakthrough of the enemy to the Volga, the summary of the Stalingrad Front reporting only that the Germans had reached the 'Red October' plant. It happened a few hundred metres from the command post of the 62nd Army.

On 24 October, German aircraft continued to bomb Russian positions in the industrial zone of Stalingrad, carrying out about 1,000 sorties. At the same time, Stukas again achieved success in attacking Soviet command posts. This time, the headquarters of the 1045th Rifle Regiment was destroyed by a direct hit and its commander, Lieutenant Colonel Timoshin, was killed.

Paulus, who now visited Stalingrad almost daily, driving between the ruins in an armoured personnel carrier, visited the forward command posts of the 14th Panzer Division and the 305th Infantry Division that day. Then he went to the command post of the 51st Army Corps. From there, he watched the Ju 87s dive on the 'Red October' factory, over which huge columns of smoke and dust rose. However, the offensive itself once again was prematurely exhausted due to heavy losses and stubborn resistance of the Russians.

The next day, the Luftwaffe, taking advantage of the clear weather, went on the rampage again. The bombers dropped about 4,000 bombs on various targets. Using air support, the German assault groups managed to advance another 300m between the 'Barricades' and 'Red October' factories, gradually encircling the first of them. However, it was not possible to occupy the vast territory of the destroyed enterprises. For this, the German infantry simply did not have enough strength. Russian assault groups began to actively use underground communications and sewers, through which they unexpectedly penetrated into the basements of several workshops occupied by the Germans. They literally rose up out of the ground, striking terror among their enemies.

On 26 October, units of the 14th Panzer Division broke through the positions of the 193rd Rifle Division and reached Mashinnaya and Gazovaya Streets. Assault groups of the 79th Infantry Division captured the southern part of Shop No. 5, the end parts of Shop No. 1 and the north-western part of Shop No. 9.

But the Russians still held out. Thanks to the fact that two battalions of the 45th Rifle Division (1,588 men) were able to be transported to the west bank on the previous nights, the Soviets again managed to plug the gaps in the defence, which ran in winding lines between the ruins of factory buildings and houses. However, over the next day, the new battalions lost 70 per cent of their personnel. The Germans managed to capture the northern part of the 'Red October' plant and once again reach the Volga River in the area of the oil tanks.

On 28 October, the Germans advanced another 100–200m and captured several factory buildings, pushing the Red Army soldiers even closer to the bank. The headquarters of the 6th Army reported: 'The enemy is fighting hard and with ferocity, every house is prepared for defence.' Nevertheless, at the end of the month, it seemed to Paulus, von Weichs and Hitler that the battle, albeit with great delay, was coming to an end. The length of the Russian bridgehead had been reduced to 5.5km. The German military leaders believed that after the full occupation of the industrial zone in the northern part of the city, it would become almost impossible for ferries to cross the Volga, and only a small bridgehead east of the Mamayev Kurgan would remain in the hands of the Soviets. On 29 October, for the first time, an offensive plan was announced for the 'Tennis Racket' (the 'Lazur' chemical factory) and then for a link-up with the 71st Infantry Division in the city centre.

During 29 October, the 138th and 308th Rifle Divisions, still defending the 'Barricades' factory, lost 260 men, and only 33 soldiers remained in the ranks. However, the Soviets again managed to reinforce their broken units. The 45th Rifle Division and several marching companies were urgently transferred to the city. Despite the constant shelling, the ferry crossing of the Volga River still worked smoothly. For example, on the night of 28/29 October, 1,769 people and 70 tons of cargo were transported to the west bank. From 7 October to 28 October, the 44th Separate Pontoon-Bridge Battalion, which served the Volga River ferry crossings in the Stalingrad area, lost nine steamships, seven barge ferries and 35 half-pontoons. However, the Germans could not interrupt this communication. 'The crossing is carried out all day on steamers, boats and rafts, it goes on all day, although it is fired from all types of weapons,' the headquarters of the 6th Army reported.

At 06.00 on 1 November, after a short artillery shelling and bombing, German assault groups launched another attack in the area of the 'Barricades' factory. However, already at 10.00 the Soviet artillery opened a powerful fire from the eastern bank of the Volga. And half an hour later, the ruins were shaken by shouts of 'Hurrah', and crowds of Red Army soldiers rushed to the attack. It turned out to be completely unexpected by the Germans, as a result of which the 39th Guards Rifle Division was able to recapture the open-hearth, varietal and gauge workshops, as well as the finished-goods warehouse. A significant part of the important stronghold was again in the hands of the Soviets.

On 2 November, 1,300 flights of German aircraft were recorded over Stalingrad. After the bombing, the entire Russian bridgehead was engulfed in fires and smoke. However, the successes of the German infantry again turned out to be modest. The 305th Infantry Division captured one block of houses north of the oil tanks, and the assault group of the 389th Infantry Division was able to capture a 200m-long stretch of shore south of the brick factory. The commander of the 89th Artillery Regiment, who conducted shelling of the sectors of the factories 'Barricades' and 'Red October' occupied by Soviet troops, complained to Paulus that the infantry forces were so weakened that even the most powerful artillery rounds and bombardments could no longer ensure the success of the attack.

On 4 November, over 1,000 flights of German aircraft were recorded, and 2,400 bombs were dropped. However, the infantry again could not advance further. This meant that the Wehrmacht could not take Stalingrad before the beginning of winter (in Russia, stable winter weather usually begins in November).

For the Germans themselves, the most unpleasant hours began with the onset of darkness. Infantrymen, gunners and tankers hiding in the ruins and crevices watched with horror as huge TB-3 bombers appeared overhead, which slowly flew in circles over the city, dropped high-explosive and incendiary bombs on them. German anti-aircraft gunners mainly aimed at the sound of engines and periodically streaked the sky with tracer fire. But this did not even frighten the Russian pilots, and the hum of the planes did not subside during almost the entire night. With these actions, the Soviet pilots took revenge on the enemy for the daytime domination of the Luftwaffe. For example, on the night of 3/4 November, Russian night bombers carried out 477 sorties. The Germans recorded the flight of 165 bombers over the positions of the 24th Panzer Division alone.

In response to these raids, the Germans began using their Hs 126, Ar 66 and Go 145 light night bombers from Behelfskampfstaffel 4. This squadron, equipped with old biplanes, was formed in the autumn, and the tactics of its crews copied the actions of Russian Polikarpov U-2 light bombers. Flying at low altitude, they dropped small high-explosive and fragmentation bombs on suitable targets in the Soviet rear.

***

The battles on the northern flank of the 6th Army between the Don and the Volga in October took on a positional character. The Germans repeatedly and unsuccessfully attacked Spartanovka. The situation in this village, spread out among ravines with its old houses stretching directly to the bank of the Volga, swung like a pendulum depending on the situation in the air. For example, on 28 October, before dawn, the Red Army launched a desperate attack from the north-eastern part of Spartanovka and recaptured one block of houses. At 07.00 sirens were heard howling over the Volga, after which a group of Stukas struck the eastern part of the central street of the village. After the smoke and dust settled, the 267th Grenadier Regiment went onto the attack and captured several houses on the south-eastern edge of this street. But the Germans did not have time to gain a foothold properly, as artillery shelling began from the eastern shore, supplemented by volleys of Katyusha rockets. After that, at 11.00, shouts of 'Hurrah' were heard, heralding a counter-attack from the ruins of the school. After lunch, the ruins captured by the Germans were again taken from them. But at 14.00 Stukas appeared in the sky again, which, despite the frenzied firing of anti-aircraft guns from the eastern shore, struck at the north-eastern part of Spartanovka. Columns of explosions rose into the air again, throwing pieces of logs, bricks and rebar into the air, which fell with a crash on the positions of the Red Army. Then the grenadiers again ran to the attack and captured several ruins . . . And so it went on every day.

The Soviets also tried to attack the 'northern barrier' from the north, but these efforts turned out to be much weaker than in September. On the German side, the area between the bend of the Don and Yerzovka was occupied by six divisions: the 384th, 305th and 113th Infantry, 60th and 3rd Motorised Infantry and the 16th Panzer Division. They were opposed by four Armies of the Don Front (4th Tank, 1st Guards, 24th and 66th) consisting of 24 rifle divisions, 10 tank brigades, three tank corps and many other units. Three Russian armies numbering about 200,000 men and 300 tanks each occupied fronts of only 17km, and each of them was opposed by only one German division!

The Russians tried to tie the enemy down, preventing them from relaxing and transferring reserves to Stalingrad. On 6 October, attacks were carried out in the 1st Guards Army's sector, while on the 9th and 10th, the 1st Guards, 24th and 66th Armies tested the strength of the German defences. Then, after a three-day pause, the 1st Guards Army again launched a local sortie, and on 20 October, the 24th and 66th Armies attacked. Finally, on 23–26 October, the 66th Army again attacked the German positions south of Yerzovka in order to help the 62nd Army in the defence of the city. At the same time, organisational changes took place. On 15 October, the 1st Guards Army went into reserve, and on 22 October, the 4th Tank Army, which had not had a single tank for a long time, was renamed the 65th Army.

The only significant success of the Red Army in this sector was the capture of Hill 112.7 (2.5km north-west of Kuzmichi), and the recapture of 158 of their damaged tanks lost in the September battles. Of these, 33 later turned out to be useable and were evacuated from the 'tank cemetery' to the rear . . .

In addition, at the end of October, the Russians conducted a river landing operation! On the night of 30/31 October, a reinforced battalion of the 300th Rifle Division numbering 600 men was landed from armoured boats on the bank of the Volga near Latoshinka. The purpose of the operation, which looked more like an outright adventure, was to capture a bridgehead and connect with the units cut off in the area of Rynok and Spartanovka (Gorokhov's group). At 00.30, landing craft moored to the shore in different places under fire, and the soldiers rushed up the hill as fast as they could to get out of the open space, leaving no guards at the water. Climbing the slope, one of the rifle companies managed to break through to Latoshinka and capture several houses there. The rest of the troops scattered chaotically across the plateau. Of the convoy of 14 boats with food and ammunition sent to the western shore, only two returned. Some of the Russian armoured boats supporting the landing were hit by cannon and machine-gun fire. By the morning of 1 November, the Germans completely surrounded the Russians, and then destroyed and captured them in detail. Five hundred and twenty-one men (almost the entire reinforced battalion) were captured.

Interestingly, a very scandalous incident occurred on the northern flank of the 6th Army in October. The headquarters of the 3rd Motorised Infantry Division reported that its positions were attacked with a new type of bombs. The explosion scattered a lot of small black insects. They immediately attacked the German infantrymen and started biting them! In this regard, the headquarters of the 6th Army received a panicked message about the use of biological weapons by the Russians! 'The insect bombs dropped yesterday at the positions of the 14th Tank Corps are being studied by the army sanitary and hygienic service. A large number of these insects were found at the site of the bomb explosions,' a report two days after the incident said.

Chapter 8

THE DEADLY RAILWAY

When the Wehrmacht reached the Volga near Stalingrad, the Luftwaffe had a new target. It was the Saratov-Urbach–Astrakhan railway, which ran from north to south along the eastern bank of the Volga. This huge 600km logistics route was of crucial importance for the Soviets. Trains with Caucasian oil and with American and British military equipment, supplied under the Lend-Lease programme through Iran, moved along it. Troops from the northern and eastern regions of the Soviet Union were transferred to Stalingrad by the same railway. The line was single-track, passed through the uninhabited steppe and partially crossed the western regions of Kazakhstan.

The first air attacks against this route were recorded on 25–28 August. From the beginning of September, German bombers began to carry out almost continuous attacks. Already on 8 September, the order of the Stalingrad Front headquarters stated: 'On the section of the Krasny Kut–Astrakhan–Verkhny Baskunchak–Stalingrad railway, enemy aircraft continuously keeps trains with troops and military cargo going for the Stalingrad Front under their influence, disrupting the planning of operational transportation and inflicting heavy losses in manpower and material resources.'

Before the start of the bombing, the movement of trains was carried out in a relay-race way for 80–100km, the distance that a steam locomotive could cover without refuelling with water and coal. Then, at the relay station, the locomotive was unhooked from the train and switched to another track, and the baton was taken by a refuelled locomotive. The first locomotive, having replenished supplies, hooked up another train going in the same direction, and drove it to the next precinct station. Constant bombing had disrupted this system. Precinct stations were destroyed, water tanks were smashed, coal stocks burned. In these conditions, the Russians had to include two or three, and sometimes five fully-fuelled locomotives in the train! These almost non-stop trains ran from Astrakhan to Urbach station (near Saratov). In addition, coal wagons were attached, as well as flatcars with anti-aircraft guns. All this has significantly increased the size of the trains, turning them into huge railway caravans.

The speed of movement had been significantly reduced. In September, and then in October, the section from Astrakhan to Saratov trains travelled no more than 30–40km per day, and even less on the Baskunchak–Elton section. At the same time, downtime at the junction stations, despite the desperate efforts of railway workers, reached up to seven days. In the area of Saratov, Engels and Atkarsk, 5,124 cars had accumulated by 22 September, and another 2,700 cars were in motion, crawling from station to station at a snail's pace. On 30 September, the headquarters of the Stalingrad Front was forced to issue the following order on the timely delivery of ammunition trains and their withdrawal from enemy air raids. 'All trains with ammunition should be allowed to pass only at night and out of any queue. The ammunition trains should be brought to the unloading stations in such a way that they were all loaded before dawn,' it said.

The chronicle of the events of October shows how intense the German air raids were.

On 1 October, German bombers made four raids on Elton station and two raids on Baskunchak station.

On 3 October, two stations were simultaneously attacked – Elton and Pallasovka.

On 5 October, a group of German bombers, accompanied by a pair of Bf 109s, raided Janybek station.

On 7 October, the Luftwaffe, in groups of 10–12 bombers, again carried out raids on the stations at Shungai, Saykhin, Elton and Bengilevka.

On 8 October at 06.40 11 He 111s bombed Elton station from a height of 3,000m. At 10.30 another group of bombers attacked trains on the Janybek–Elton and Baskunchak–Seroglazovo sections At 14.12, five He 111s bombed Elton station. The 6th Army's war diary for that day says: 'Defectors claim that although there is still movement on the railway to Stalingrad, there is no movement in the opposite direction.'

On 9 October, the Luftwaffe carried out raids on the Janybek, Seroglazovka stations, bombed and shelled several trains on the Janybek–Elton and Baskunchak–Seroglazovka stages. For the first time, a specialised aviation group III./KG6 under the command of the famous pilot Major Hermann Hogeback took part in the mission. It was formed on the basis of the former III./LG1 and equipped with Ju 88A dive-bombers. All the crews recruited into the group were top-level specialists in point-target attacks. They acted only singly or in pairs. The first target of III,/KG6 was the Kaisatskoye railway station (200km north-east of Stalingrad).

On 11 October, German planes bombed stations and sidings on the Janybek–Batkul Lake section.

On 12 October, 10 Ju 88As from III./KG6 raided the station at Vladimirovka (Akhtuba).

On 13 October, the Germans bombed trains on the Elton–Baskunchak section. As a result, 26 wagons with shells and mines exploded and burned. There was a huge traffic jam on the railway, and traffic was completely paralyzed until the evening of 14 October.

On 14 October, between 15.05 and 15.55, four bombers raided Shungai station, where at that moment several trains were at the same time.

On 15 October, the Luftwaffe attacked the stations at Janybek and Seroglazovo and junction No. 365. Four Ju 88A from III./KG6 bombed Chapchachi and Verblujya stations. As a result, 25 freight cars, four flatcars and one tanker wagon with fuel were destroyed. The explosions destroyed 320m of rail.

On 18 October, at 10.00, nine Ju 88s carried out a raid on Chapchachi station, dropping 90 high-explosive and fragmentation bombs on it. As a result, three buildings, a water tank for steam locomotives, and 20 rail sections were destroyed, electricity and telephone lines were cut, and twenty-two tanker wagons and two platforms burned down. The fire continued for a day. In addition, Baskunchak, Kochevaya and Bogdo stations were raided.

On 19 October, single 'railway hunters' appeared several times from behind the clouds in different places, dropping bombs and firing at several trains and way-stations.

On 20 October, the Luftwaffe bombed Baskunchak and Bogdo stations.

On 21 October, Elton and Verblujya stations were attacked.

On 22 October, a train was attacked near Shungai station. As a result, the cars derailed, and two platforms and two fuel-tanker wagons burned.

German bombers operating over the western regions of Kazakhstan were rarely attacked by Russian interceptors. Their main opponent was the 102nd Fighter Aviation Division of the Air Defence, which in October was concentrated in this sector. The Russians were equipped with 52 fighters, including 19 British Hurricane Mk IIs.

On 24 October, the Luftwaffe carried out their next missions and this time met with 'Stalin's falcons'. V. Hartl, the radio operator of a

German bomber from the 8th Staffel of KG27 recalled: 'On this day, the 8th Squadron took off led by the He 111 "1G+LS" of squadron commander Hauptmann Quednau to attack trains near Lake Elton. The Russians used this railway to deliver reinforcements and supplies to Stalingrad. This raid on railway stations and trains was carried out at a relatively high altitude by seven planes.'

According to Soviet sources, the strike was carried out at the Pallasovka and Shungai stations, junction No. 365, Verblujya station (32 high-explosive and fragmentation bombs were dropped) and Dosang station (36 bombs were dropped). Not long before the raid, a pair of Hurricanes from the 629th IAP were on patrol in the Pallasovka area. The pilots received an order by radio to attack a single enemy reconnaissance aircraft. However, when the fighters made visual contact with the target, it turned out to be a Russian Pe-2 bomber. And just at that moment, a message came about the bombing of the Pallasovka station.

The Hurricanes could not catch up with the enemy, but a group consisting of one LaGG-3 and two Yak-1s, which took off from the Baskunchak air base, managed to intercept German bombers in the Shungai area. These were He 111s of 8./KG27. However, the attack ended fatally for the Russians. Hartl continued his story:

On the way back, we were attacked by three fighters. One of them attacked our commander's plane and immediately fell into the zone of barrage of other He 111. After my entire crew began shouting with all their might: "Shoot! Shoot! Shoot!", I let the interceptor get to a range of about 50m, and then fired the entire drum into the MiG's engine. Suddenly, a black plume of smoke burst out of it, and it flew among us.

In fact, a LaGG-3 from the 572nd IAP was shot down. The pilot was killed. In addition to He 111s from KG27, Ju 88s from 8./KG6 also participated in the raid on Shungai. As a result of the bomb attacks, railway traffic was completely halted for eight hours.

On 27 October, the Shungai–Baskunchak stage was attacked. As a result, a train was damaged 10km north of Baskunchak: movement was paralyzed for 2.5 hours.

In the early morning of 28 October, Ju 88s bombed railway trains on the Baskunchak–Leninsk–Stalingrad line, as well as Shungai station.

On 29 October, at 00.45 on the Zaplavnoye–Leninsk section a German plane dropped two bombs on an ammunition train that was unloading. As a result, 20,000 shells exploded, 25 wagons burned and 150m of track were destroyed. At 07.15, a raid was made on Kapustin

Yar station. Bombs hit freight train No. 904 and train A88096, as a result of which 19 tanker wagons with gasoline and kerosene, two wagons of mustard, a refrigerated wagon with cheese, three passenger carriages, seven freight wagons and 28 platforms burned down. There were many causalities. In addition, the rails at railway junction No. 332 and No. 254 were destroyed at night. Traffic was paralyzed for 5 hours. At 07.55, seven Ju 88s attacked trains near Shungai station. A second raid on the same target was carried out in the afternoon.

On 30 October, the Luftwaffe bombed Baskunchak and Kapustin Yar stations.

In total, during September and October, the Luftwaffe carried out 226 air attacks against this logistics route (according to Soviet information), which affected 25 railway stations, destroyed 1,419 track sections, 1,026 spans of wire, 105 buildings, eight water towers, four depots and two power plants. On Baskunchak station alone in October, German planes dropped 1,374 bombs of various types: 1,195 units of rolling stock were destroyed from military trains (this is not counting ordinary civilian trains), including 261 ammunition wagons, 198 fuel-tanker wagons, 101 wagons with fodder, 54 locomotives and 581 other wagons.

In early November, air attacks against Russian railway communications continued. For example, on the 4th, the Luftwaffe bombed Chapchachi, Verblujya and Shungai stations. The most effective was the raid on Shungai, in which 20 ammunition wagons and 150m of rail track were destroyed. Train traffic was paralyzed for 15 hours.

On 6 November, the attack against Shungai was repeated, and as a result, 13 ammunition wagons burned and 110m of rail was destroyed.

On 8 November, four He 111s raided Bogdo station, dropping 50 bombs on it. As a result, 600m of rail track were destroyed, and 28 petroleum-tanker burned.

On 15 November, four Ju 88s attacked the Vladimirovka station, achieving direct hits on a train with ammunition. A huge fire broke out, burning until the next night, and some time-bombs exploded the next day.

The Luftwaffe gradually changed tactics. Instead of air attacks by groups of bombers, they increasingly began to send single 'hunter planes' against Russian railway lines. These were experienced crews who operated singly and at night. This method was quickly successful, and on 10 December, based on the Night Fighter Link of the 4th Air Fleet (Nachtjagdschwarm der Luftflotte 4), a long-range Night Fighter Link (Fernnachtjagdschwarm – FNJS) was formed under the command of Oberleutnant Krems. Initially, it consisted of only three He 111s from the Boelcke bomber Geschwader (KG27). Later FNJS became the basis for the formation of the first specialised railway Staffel (Eis-Staffel) – 14.(Eis)/KG27. This was the beginning of the creation of the famous 'Eis-squadrons'.

These bombings caused numerous problems for the Soviets. For example, at the beginning of October, the 61st Cavalry Division was supposed to arrive to join the 28th Army (which occupied the front in the Astrakhan region). However, due to traffic jams (congestion), it was not possible to take it to its destination. During the delay, the horses ate all the harvested forage and began to starve, and the soldiers who found themselves in the middle of the steppe suffered from thirst. On 13 October, the division was unloaded at the Elton station, after which the cavalry moved to the Volga ferry crossing and from there, after numerous adventures and a long delay, arrived at the front.

The 93rd Rifle Brigade moved in a similar way. On 13 October, the first train with soldiers reached Elton station. There it was unloaded, as it was impossible to proceed further to Stalingrad. Then the soldiers had to march 160km across the open steppe. At the same time, the last train with this brigade was still near Urbach (near Saratov). The units of the 97th Rifle Brigade, moving to Astrakhan, stretched along the entire length of the railway from Urbach to Bogdo! This unit was unlucky. Instead of a relatively calm front in Kalmykia, the brigade was eventually transferred to Stalingrad . . .

Trains carrying the 123rd Artillery Regiment left Saratov on 15 October. Five days later, the wagons stretched out on the Elton–Saykhin railway stretch, and the unit arrived at Kapustin Yar station only on the 26th.

On 19 October, the lead train with equipment and personnel of the 235th Tank Brigade reached Urbach station. Three days later, the trains stretched along the Saykhin–Baskunchak section. It was not until 29 October that most of the brigade reached the Bright Yar, where they prepared to cross the Volga. The average speed of transportation of reserves by rail had fallen to 30km per day. Many units, without waiting for transport by rail, travelled tens and hundreds of kilometres on foot.

It should be noted that it was by this railway that the transfer of troops intended for the upcoming Operation Uranus began in mid-October. First of all, for the southern assault group (fist). Most of the units were unloaded at Zaplavnoye and Kapustin Yar stations, then they crossed the Volga in the area of Kamenny Yar and Svetly Yar (respectively 25km and 75km south-east of Stalingrad). In order to hide the concentration of assault groups from the ubiquitous reconnaissance aircraft, movement from stations to destinations was carried out only at night. Day movements were strictly prohibited, and from dawn to dusk, the army had to disperse on the ground and all equipment was carefully camouflaged. Due to the constant congestion on the railway, this whole long process was delayed, and the left 'fist' turned out to be much weaker than the right one. Interruptions in the work of the railways led to the fact that by mid-November, 76mm, 122mm and 152mm shells, grenades, 12.7mm cartridges and even cartridges for TT pistols began to run out in the warehouses of the Stalingrad Front. In addition, the stocks of biscuit, canned meat and fish, concentrates and vodka had almost been exhausted.

In addition, by October, an acute shortage of petroleum products began to be felt in the Soviet Union. The oil refineries in Ufa, Syzran, Gorky and Konstantinov were the first to sound the alarm. Plans for the delivery of raw materials were not carried out, and it seemed that the flow of oil would soon stop altogether. In September, 30–40 per cent of the required amount for refining arrived, but in October only 25 per cent. Electric power stations and boiler houses were hastily transferred from fuel oil to cheaper fuel, mainly peat. Thousands of peasants were forcibly sent to peat bogs and swamps to harvest this cheap fuel.

Thus, the efforts of the Luftwaffe brought a tangible effect. But they could not completely paralyze and weaken the Red Army. The protracted operation against the Astrakhan–Saratov railway and communications of the Stalingrad Front ultimately failed to achieve its goal. Firstly, the Luftwaffe simply did not have the strength to maintain the momentum and strength of air attacks for a long time. The longer the battle for Stalingrad dragged on, the more the available forces were dispersed over a vast area from the Don to the Caucasus. Secondly, by the end of autumn, Soviet railway workers had finally learned to live and work in conditions of regular bombing, to quickly eliminate their effects and ensure relatively stable train traffic.

Chapter 9

THE 'RED BARRICADES'

Hitler sends sappers

This time, unlike in 1941, Hitler began to prepare for winter in advance! Back on 14 October, when the battle for Stalingrad seemed to be coming to an end, he issued an order to switch to strategic defence on the Eastern Front, with the exception of certain 'not yet completed' operations. 'This year, the summer-autumn campaign is over, with the exception of operations currently underway and still planned,' the Führer wrote. In fact, he admitted that the ultimate goal of the offensive had not been achieved and decided to 'settle for less'. One area of oil fields – Maykop – had been captured, the Kuban and Donbass were also in his hands, and the Soviet fleet had been driven into the south-eastern corner of the Black Sea. Although the Wehrmacht did not reach Baku's oil, it cut off Stalin from it. German troops are standing on the Volga, and the railway in the Kazakh steppe is paralyzed by the blows of the Luftwaffe. In general, it's not so bad! Now the main thing is to keep it all, simultaneously continuing the offensive in several areas. Hitler's order stated:

> An assessment of the enemy's condition and his plans gives reason to believe that the Russians currently generally do not have the strength to carry out major offensives with far-reaching goals. The only means of countering such tactics of the enemy is a fierce defence of the troops in their positions to the last cartridge and immediate counter-attacks by local reserves . . . Every commander and subordinate officer must be convinced of the sacred duty to stand to the last. Even if the enemy has bypassed it from the right and left, even if its unit is cut off, surrounded by tanks and shrouded in smoke.

Later, the Führer's order 'On integrity and honesty in the management of troops' was also issued to the troops. In pursuance of these directives, the 6th Army was actively preparing to winter on the Volga, equipping positions and making plans for the future. 'There is an assumption that Russian aviation will focus its efforts in the area between the Volga and the Don in the winter. The main targets will be railways, bridges, communications and bridges,' Paulus' headquarters reported on 1 November. In this regard, he asked that additional anti-aircraft units be sent.

Interestingly, at the beginning of November, Hitler seriously instructed Paulus to study the question of possibly putting the Tractor Plant back into operation and establishing the production of German tanks there! And this was at a time when the city had not yet been captured, and the territory occupied by the Germans was daily subjected to shelling from the eastern shore and bombing at night. Nevertheless, the obedient general visited the enterprise on the morning of 9 November, inspecting the workshops and the surviving equipment. 'The plant, in general, is one of the most modern in the world. Although a large number of factory buildings and machinery have been destroyed, there is still a lot of suitable equipment, including those evacuated from Kharkov last year. There are wagons with 300 tons of loaded rolled metal on the rails,' the corresponding report read.

On the eve of the next battles and with the effective absence of reinforcements, the Germans continued to search for internal reserves. In early October, the process of replacing German soldiers with Russian volunteers-collaborationists was started. Such people were widely accepted for the positions of drivers, assistant drivers, auxiliary workers, and in construction and supply divisions. In addition, 'Hiwis' also served in front-line units as ammunition carriers, cable carriers, 5th and 6th calculation numbers in divisional and field artillery batteries, sappers, etc. In addition, Paulus ordered the withdrawal of their crews from tank regiments (except drivers and commanders) and to form battle groups from them, armed with light and heavy machine guns, and then send them to quiet areas of the defences. The infantry thus released could be used in assault operations.

Another event was the inclusion of one Turkestani battalion in each division of the 6th Army. Their formation and initial training were carried out in the rear area of Army Group B on the basis of the 162nd Infantry Division. It was expected that the Turkestanis would arrive at their duty stations by 18–19 November , but fortunately for the latter, there were some delays. Given that policing in the occupied areas of the city was carried out by the 'hundred' of the 6th Ukrainian battalion in addition to the 1st Company of the 541st Motorised Battalion of the Feldgendarmerie (Feldgend.Abt.541(mot)),it can be stated that the 6th Army was increasingly turning into an international military gathering.

On 1 November, a meeting was held at the forward command post of Fliegerkorps VIII, located in a brick factory in the village of Razgulyevka. Paulus, the commander of the 51st Army Corps, Seydlitz-Kurzbach, Fibig and Richthofen took part in it. Angry and annoyed, Richthofen said that further aviation support for the 6th Army was pointless. Firstly, the troops were still unable to use it, and secondly, the bridgehead held by the Soviet troops has shrunk so much that it was easier to throw hand grenades than to waste bombs. The generals tried to justify themselves and gave a lot of 'objective' reasons, but they did not satisfy Richthofen. 'I heard old and stupid excuses from them. Which are only partly true: lack of troops, lack of professional training in this type of fighting and lack of ammunition,' he wrote in his diary.

Of the eight divisions that were part of the 51st Army Corps at that time, only one (the 100th Jäger Division) was considered as suitable for the offensive. The rest, according to the German classification, were considered suitable only for defence. Considering that serious reinforcements were still not expected, the headquarters of the 6th Army decided to carry out another 'castling' of its forces: to withdraw the 'exhausted' 305th Infantry Division from the city, sending it to the 'northern barrier' instead of the 60th Motorised Division. And the 60th, after eight days of rest, on the contrary, would be sent to Stalingrad to attack on the 'Lazur' chemical factory. It was the last industrial facility that the Germans had not yet reached. This operation was supposed to start no earlier than 15 November.

However, then another option was proposed: to urgently transfer five sapper battalions to Stalingrad. The 50th Panzer Engineer Battalion (PanzerPi.Btl.50) and the 45th Motorised Engineer Battalion (Pi. Btl.(mot).45) went to Stalingrad on their own, the 162nd Motorised Battalion was transported by Italians, and the 294th and 336th Battalions were airlifted.

There were some disagreements between the headquarters of the 6th Army and the High Command of the Amy (OKH) in the use of these units. The command demanded first to capture the 'Tennis Racket', and only then to occupy the riverbank. The headquarters of the 6th Army believed that the condition for the attack on the 'Lazur' factory had to be the complete elimination of the bridgehead near the 'Red October' and 'Barricades' factories. This dispute was eventually put to Hitler himself, who sided with Paulus: before attacking the chemical factory, it was first necessary to capture the area east of the metallurgical and gun factories.

The 294th Pioneer Battalion was the first to be transferred to Pitomnik airfield at 11:00 on 4 November, and in the evening the 336th Battalion arrived after him. The total number of combat personnel of the five sapper battalions, on which high hopes were pinned (although mainly by the Führer, and not by the headquarters of the 6th Army), was 1,753.

At the same time, the Soviets, taking advantage of the respite, strenuously strengthened their last positions, preparing to desperately defend the last bridgehead. In the first days of November, the weather was warm in the Stalingrad area, during the day the thermometer showed +12 – +15°, at night +3 – +5°. It should be noted that during the Second World War in Germany, the transition to winter time was carried out, so on 1 November, the hands of the clock were moved forward an hour. Accordingly, the difference with Moscow time in winter was not two hours, but one.

'The main factory bastion'

On 7 November, the headquarters of the 6th Army approved the final date of the new offensive – 11 November. Three assault groups were formed to attack. The first consisted of two sapper battalions, three StuIG 33B assault guns, a heavy mortar division and two light mortar divisions. Its main goal was to capture the open-hearth shop of the 'Barricades' plant. The second assault group included the 305th Infantry Division, reinforced by an assault company of the 44th Infantry Division, two sapper battalions, a battalion of assault guns (six StuIG 33Bs), a tank company of the 14th Panzer Division, two platoons of heavy infantry guns, and six heavy mortars. The third assault group consisted of a part of the 389th Infantry Division, reinforced by a sapper battalion, three StuIG 33Bs and an assault company of the 24th Panzer Division. These group were to capture the bank of the Volga east of the 'Barricades' plant. After reaching the first objective of the offensive, it was necessary to regroup and, no later than 15 November, launch an offensive along the bank to the south.

The Germans had high hopes for the aforementioned latest StuIG 33B assault guns. They were self-propelled guns based on the StuG III with a 150mm sIG-33 heavy infantry gun mounted in a high rectangular casemate superstructure. At the same time, the frontal armour of the hull and conning tower was 80mm, and the side armour was 50mm.

This gave good protection from artillery and grenades even in close combat and allowed the use of these 'StuGs' to attack buildings and factories. In October, the 'Alkett' company produced 24 StuIG 33Bs, and the first batch was immediately sent to Stalingrad. There they became part of the 244th and 245th Assault Gun Battalions (StugG. Abt.244, StugG.Abt.245).

On 11 November, at 05.00, shelling of Russian positions began, then at 07.00, Stukas appeared, which, with sirens wailing, dived on the buildings of the 'Barricades' and 'Red October' factories occupied by Soviet troops, artillery positions on the eastern shore of the Volga and the islands.

When the entire bank of the Volga was enveloped in clouds of smoke and dust, the assault groups, accompanied by 'StuGs', slowly moved forward, making their way through the dilapidated and burnt-out workshops with flamethrowers and explosive charges. By the end of the day, the 1st and 241st Rifle Regiments of the 95th Rifle Division were completely destroyed, and other Russian units suffered heavy losses. As a result, the German assault groups managed to advance 200–300m, at the same time destroying several dug-in tanks. The 305th Infantry Division reached the cliff above the Volga east of the oil tanks and broke through to the ravine to the north. The neighbouring 389th Infantry Division also occupied about 500m of the Volga coast north-east of the Barricade plant.

On 12 November, after another Stuka strike from StG2, the offensive continued. The Germans broke through to the oil tanks, cutting off the remnants of the 138th Rifle Division from the rest of the Russian units.

The next day, Ju 87s continued to bomb Soviet artillery positions on the islands and the eastern bank. And by the evening, the 305th Infantry Division, after persistent fighting, captured the 'house of commissars' and another 70m-long stretch of bank (north-east of the oil tanks). Soviet troops suffered heavy losses, but did not retreat. By evening, only 220 men remained in the 138th Rifle Division. 'For three days, day and night, the troops of the 62nd Army fought fierce battles, reaching mass hand-to-hand fights. 'The enemy is suffering huge losses. Piles of enemy corpses are piled up on the site of the 138th Rifle Division (the area of the 'Red October' plant),' the Stalingrad Front's war diary reported. The Russians estimated the losses of the 6th Army during the last assault at 6,000 officers and men killed. And although these figures were again a considerable exaggeration, the attack really cost the 6th Army a lot of casualties. The sapper battalions were particularly affected, having lost 440 men on the first day alone, including 109 killed and missing.[1] But the Luftwaffe again acted without opposition from Russian aviation, and did not suffer any losses. During two days, only one Hs 129B-1 armoured ground-attack plane of 6./Sch.G1 was damaged.

Already on 13 November, it became clear that the assault had not achieved its goals. The headquarters of the 51st Army Corps admitted that it was unlikely to be possible to capture the 'main factory bastion' (the open-hearth shop) in the near future. The attack on the 'Tennis Racket' was postponed until 25–30 November, and the capture of the last Russian strongholds (parts of the 'Red October' plant and the oil storage facility opposite the Mamayev Kurgan) was postponed entirely until December . . .

By 16 November, the Germans managed to capture most of the 'Barricades' plant, seize the treatment facilities and once again reach the Volga. The bridgehead, still defended by the remnants of the 138th Rifle Division (called 'Ludnikov Island') was reduced to the size of 400m x 900m.

But Hitler would not accept failure. On 16 November, he signed another order No. 4640/42 'On the breakthrough to the Volga in Stalingrad', addressed to the command of the 6th Army, which said:

> I am aware of the difficulties of the battle for Stalingrad and the decrease in the combat strength of the troops. However, the difficulties of the Russians due to the ice drift on the Volga are even greater. If we use this time, we will save a lot of blood in the future. I expect that the command once again with all the energy that it has repeatedly demonstrated, and the troops with the skill that they have often shown, will do everything to break through to the Volga, at least at the artillery factory and metallurgical factory and capture these parts of the city.

The Luftwaffe had to once again 'exert all its forces' to support this offensive. Paulus, in his characteristic spirit, immediately replied that 'the Führer's order gave the troops a new impetus', although in reality all the senior officers of the 6th Army already understood that it was impossible to fulfil it.

In the following days, the 'creeping offensive' continued. On 18 November, the Germans managed to further reduce the bridgehead of the 138th Rifle Division by capturing three buildings on its left flank.

---

1 The total casualties of the 6th Army during the storming of Stalingrad from 13 September to 15 November amounted to 26,675 men, including 5,675 killed and missing. At the same time, about half of this number was lost during October. Another 12,039 officers and men (2,879 dead and missing) became casualties on the 'northern barrier'.

Along the way, another operation was carried out against another bridgehead at Spartanovka and Rynok. But even there, the Germans failed to achieve decisive success, despite strong air support. On 17 November, several tanks broke through to the central streets of the village of Rynok, fighting was going on in the very centre of the village, but the Wehrmacht could not reoccupy it (the first time it succeeded was at the end of August).

The supply of the 62nd Army functioned successfully despite all difficulties and obstacles. For example, on the night of 4/5 November, four armoured boats delivered 1,059 men, 17 tons of food and 3.5 tons of ammunition to the west bank. The Germans managed to damage one of the boats with mortar fire. The next night, 478 soldiers and 11 tons of cargo were delivered to Stalingrad in difficult weather conditions, and 511 wounded were evacuated to the eastern bank. On the night of 7/8 November, armoured boats transported 611 people, 13.5 tons of gasoline for tanks of the 84th Tank Brigade and 13 tons of food. On the night of 9/10 November, five armoured boats under fire transported 2,603 people, 20.5 tons of ammunition and 21.5 tons of food to the right bank. Two hundred and three wounded were evacuated on the return trip. Over the next two nights, another 2,500 soldiers and a large amount of cargo were transported to the bridgehead.

On 14 November, drifting ice appeared on the Volga, which hindered communication between the banks. Nevertheless, over the next two nights, another 1,500 soldiers managed to be transported to the bridgehead.

On the night of 17/18 November, four armoured boats broke through the fog to the west bank, delivering 140 men 17 tons of cargo and taking out 183 wounded. The next night, 488 soldiers crossed to Stalingrad, and another 452 were delivered by the tugboat *Pugachev* under the cover of fog. The supply of a small bridgehead of the 138th Rifle Division was carried out by boats and U-2 biplanes. Although the volume of supplies was significantly reduced, and delivery was partially carried out by air, the Germans did not manage to completely paralyze the work of the ferry crossings until the very beginning of Operation Uranus. As of 19 November, the 62nd Army (on both sides of the Volga) had 40,000 men, 468 guns, 723 mortars and 17 tanks.

Chapter 10

URANUS RINGS AND CONTAINER MATHEMATICS

The Russian Plan against the Hubertus Plan

The Soviet command began to develop a plan for Operation Uranus around the beginning of October, when the latest attempts of the Don Front to break through the 'northern barrier' of the 6th Army failed. The exact date has not yet been established, since many different variants are mentioned in Soviet documents. Historians usually rely on information from the memoirs of Soviet military leaders, but they do not inspire confidence. The 'Uranus' plans provided for a breakthrough of the defences of the Romanian troops on very narrow fronts, and then a rapid dash deep into German territory in the general direction of Kalach-on-Don. For the headquarters of the South-western Front under the command of Colonel General Nikolai Vatutin, the task was formulated as follows:

1. Destroy the main forces of the 4th Romanian Army defending in the Rybny–Kletskaya sector;

2. By the end of the third day of the offensive, cut the communications of the Stalingrad grouping of enemy troops, for which, by the end of the second day, move mobile units to the lower reaches of the Chir River and the Don River, seize crossings and create bridgeheads on the left bank of the Don River on the section of the Nizne-Chirskaya–Kalach. To get in touch with the troops of the Stalingrad Front and complete the encirclement of the Stalingrad enemy group;

3. In cooperation with the troops of the Stalingrad and Don fronts, destroy the Stalingrad grouping of the enemy.

The task of the Stalingrad Front sounded about the same. The troops of the 51st and 57th Armies were to launch an attack a day later, and then reach Kalach-on-Don within two days.

The Soviet command managed to concentrate large masses of troops secretly from German intelligence and especially from the ubiquitous reconnaissance aircraft. All movements, crossings and marches were carried out only at night, in small columns. The concentration was carried out far from the front line, and tanks, guns and personnel were carefully camouflaged in ravines. Almost 50,000 local residents were evicted from the settlements located in the area of the starting positions.

The right shock 'fist' (5th Tank Army and 21st Army) consisted of 12 rifle divisions, six cavalry divisions, 10 tank brigades, three motorised rifle brigades and other sub-units. They numbered 179,500 men, 1,683 guns, 2,764 mortars, 280 anti-aircraft guns and 576 tanks. However, this group could not be called very powerful. Half of the rifle divisions had been formed during the autumn of 1942 and had no combat experience. Of the 378 tanks that were part of the 5th Tank Army of General Prokofy Romanenko, only 70 were heavy KV tanks and 153 T-34s. The rest of the armoured vehicles were T-60 and T-70 light tanks, which had questionable combat value.

The left shock 'fist' (64th, 51st and 57th Armies) numbered 106,000 men, 933 guns, 1,697 mortars and 374 tanks. Thus, the left-flank assault group of the Russians was significantly weaker than the right. This was a consequence of the Luftwaffe's constant air attacks against the Saratov–Astrakhan railway line and the Volga ferry crossings. The Russians simply did not have time to transport all the troops and combat supplies to the concentration areas.

The popular claim that the Soviets assembled a huge amount of artillery for Operation Uranus is wrong. In many books it is reported that 20,000 guns were involved in the offensive. Therefore, in the Soviet Union, 19 November (the beginning of the offensive at Stalingrad) was even declared Artillery Day. In fact, there were only 2,500 guns in the shock groups of the South-western and Stalingrad Fronts, of which only 400 were howitzers. At the same time, 270 howitzers were assigned to the right assault group and only 130 to the left assault group. Only in some areas (against the 3rd Romanian Army) did the Russians manage to achieve a high density of artillery fire – up to 150 guns per kilometre of the front. On the left flank, the density of artillery did not exceed 10–20 guns per kilometre.

Unlike previous operations, when divisional guns and howitzers simply fired at general areas, wasting ammunition, this time a detailed plan was developed. The first bombardment was to cover the enemy defences to their full depth in order to demoralise the defenders and create panic. The projectile fuses were set to fragmentation action in order to hit the Romanian infantry. Then the artillery systematically destroyed the enemy defences for half an hour, each battery being employed for one specific purpose. Then the suppression phase began. The fire first fell on the front edge, then moved to the depth of the defence for ten minutes and again was transferred to the front edge for five minutes. In the last artillery strike, the shell fuses were put on high-explosive (delayed) action to destroy enemy fortifications. After the start of the attack, the guns had to gradually creep the barrage into the depth in bounds of 100m. The instructions distributed on the eve of the attack said: 'Two minutes before the first fire raid, the guns are loaded, and the gunners take up the lanyards, at a signal, by phone and radio (in no case do not install light signals), "promptly, fire" simultaneously produce a shot, after which they conduct a cursory fire according to the calculation.'

Initially, Operation Uranus was scheduled for 10 November. However, the Soviets had to postpone it for ten days. The first reason was the unavailability of the left-flank assault group. Due to air attacks against their communications, the Russians could not concentrate the minimum necessary number of troops on time. The second reason was the unsuitable weather (it allowed the Stukas to operate). In addition to surprise and powerful artillery preparation, weather conditions were considered the most important condition for success. The experience of previous unsuccessful battles showed that even the most carefully planned operation often quickly fell apart due to massive German air strikes. And the best defence against them were not anti-aircraft guns and fighters, but clouds and fog!

On 12 November, the Main Directorate of the Hydrometeorological Service of the Red Army (GUMS KA) informed the Headquarters that cloudy weather with fog, rain and short-term snowfalls would arrive in the Don region in the near future. As a result, the next day Stalin ordered the offensive to begin on the morning of 19 November. The crucial forecast turned out to be correct. By 17 November, it had warmed up to +5° near Stalingrad and heavy fog had set in, seriously reducing visibility. 'Cloudy, rains, poor visibility, heavy icing,' the 6th Army's war diary said the next day. The weather was about the same on the 19th.

Soviet intelligence made serious mistakes and did not have a complete picture of the enemy, his formations and reserves. The headquarters of the South-western Front, until the very beginning of the offensive, was sure that the positions of the 4th Romanian Army were in front of it, although in reality they were on the opposite flank. A week before the planned offensive, Vatutin did not have an accurate idea of where the front line of the Romanian defence was located. The dugouts and trenches were so carefully camouflaged that Russian observers could not spot them on the ground.

As a result, Vatutin had to conduct a major reconnaissance by combat. On 13 November, the 21st Army launched strong attacks in the area of the village of Kletskaya. This hit the positions of the 4th Romanian Army Corps, and was accompanied by bombing of several strongholds and villages, as well as numerous flights of reconnaissance aircraft. In response, Romanian aviation (FARR) carried out airstrikes on the villages of Tarashchinsky and Kletskaya in the morning. Then at 11.15–11.30 the Romanians bombed the village of Nizhne-Zatonsky, ravines to the west and north of Staro-Kletskaya and the forest to the north of Staro-Kletskaya, as well as clusters of Soviet troops on Hills 115.2 and to the south. At 11.45, German Ju 87s appeared overhead, which struck the positions of Soviet troops west of Kletskaya. At 14.15, a new airstrike was carried out on the same targets. By evening, the entire southern bank of the Don was shrouded in clouds of smoke. At the same time, the Romanian troops suffered minimal losses, captured 87 prisoners and were pleased with themselves. On 17 November, four rifle divisions of the 5th Tank Army launched an attack. The Romanian infantry put up unexpectedly effective resistance and the assigned missions were only partially completed. And in some places the Romanians even counter-attacked. As a result, even by the morning of 19 November, Vatutin had not received accurate data on the enemy's defences. Many targets for artillery shelling had to be determined at random. Soviet intelligence also made other gross mistakes. For example, the strength of Paulus's 6th Army was estimated at approximately 90,000, although in fact it was more than one and a half times more.

The Soviets failed to completely hide from the Germans the concentration of new troops on the Don bridgeheads and in the area of the Sarpin Lakes. Therefore, both the headquarters of the 6th Army and the headquarters of the Army Group B guessed about the planned large-scale offensive of the Red Army. In addition, at the end of October–beginning of November, many captured Soviet soldiers began to tell that the Red Army command was preparing a general offensive on the anniversary of the 'Russian revolution' – either on 7 November or a few days later. In this regard, Hitler issued another order requiring officers and soldiers to bravely stand to the death, 'not sparing their own lives'.

However, contrary to the alarming expectations, no serious attacks followed and the Germans, taking a deep breath, continued to prepare for the next 'decisive offensive' in Stalingrad. When the Soviets attacked the positions of the 3rd Romanian Army on 14–17 November, the Germans initially took it for the beginning of the Russian offensive. But on 18 November, the headquarters of the 4th Romanian Corps noticed that for some reason the attacks were carried out without the support of heavy artillery, tanks and aircraft. 'The tasks of these attacks have the character of reconnaissance by combat,' the Romanians reported to the headquarters of the 6th Army.

All this time, the Germans were trying to prepare for the threat as much as the situation in Stalingrad allowed. At the end of October, the Hubertus plan was developed, which assumed the early deployment of German units, primarily anti-tank units, in the rear areas, as well as directly behind the Romanian positions. As part of this event, by 11 November, several German units were concentrated behind the left flank of the 3rd Romanian Army: the 376th Sapper Battalion, the 614th Anti-Aircraft Battalion, the 670th Tank Destroyer Battalion, an anti-tank company of the 376th Infantry Division, an anti-aircraft combat group and a number of other units. In addition, the plan assumed the concentration of reserve units in the Kalach area (a tank-fighter detachment, a battalion of assault guns, the 80th Sapper Battalion, a reserve battalion of the 384th Infantry Division, and one regiment of the 44th Infantry Division), ready to move to the critical section of the front at any moment.

In cities, towns and rear bases, several alarm-battalions, companies and teams were formed, provided with vehicles and armoured vehicles. In the event of a serious threat of a breakthrough of the front, the second phase of the plan – Hubertus-Jagd – came into effect. It provided that within 24–36 hours after receiving the corresponding code signal, reserve units and alarm-teams would arrive in the specified area and engage the enemy, as well as provide protection for rear communications and facilities. In the future, during November, it was supposed to withdraw the 14th and 24th Panzer Divisions, as well as the 29th Motorised Infantry Division, to the rear.

However, the Germans failed to fully complete the Hubertus plan. Instead of 100 planned alarm-teams with a total of 11,131 men, only 6–7 teams could be formed. The developed measures, as history has shown, were not enough because of the underestimation of the threat. After all the Soviet attacks on the 'northern barrier' were successfully repelled in September, the German command assured itself that the Soviets were not capable of conducting offensive operations to a greater depth. And most importantly, it was convinced that if anything happened, the Luftwaffe would be able to parry any blow and stop any offensive of the 'Bolshevik hordes'.

But Fliegerkorps VIII had been seriously weakened by the beginning of November. Several units had left for other sectors of the front. For example, on 22 October, the specialised air group I./KG100 relocated from the Morozovskaya airbase to Armavir, 350km to the south. Two days later, KG76 also went there, and on 25 October, Ju 88s from II./KG51 landed at Armavir. The main objective of the bombers was to support the offensive of the 1st Panzer Army on Ordzhonikidze, and the secondary one was to attack oil tankers in the Caspian Sea. Another air group, III./KG55, was relocated to the Crimea for raids on the Black Sea ports of Tuapse, Poti and Sukhumi, and the specialised air group III./KG6 was ordered to begin relocating to northern France in order to then participate in raids on England.

As a result, by mid-November, Fliegerkorps VIII was only a shadow of what it had been at the start of Operation Blau. Losses in equipment due to wear, accidents and enemy action had not been properly replenished for a long time, and trained and experienced crews were becoming fewer. The nine bomber groups (I. and III./KG1, I. and part II./KG51, I. and II./KG55, I., II. and III./KG27) had a total of 127 combat-ready bombers. Air groups II./StG1, I. and II./StG2, Sch. G1 were also 'worn out'. They had only 67 serviceable ground-attack planes left. The only fighter squadron remaining in the Stalingrad area, JG3 Udet, had 64 Bf 109s, and the three long-range reconnaissance squadrons (3.(F)/Aufkl.Gr.10, 3.(F)/Aufkl.Gr.121 and 4.(F)/Aufkl.Gr.122) had only 14 serviceable Ju 88D. There could be no more talk of any massive air support.

'The Romanian soldier defends himself stubbornly'

On the night of 18/19 November, soldiers of the 1st Romanian Cavalry Division captured a Soviet officer. He said that soon – at 05.00 – a big offensive would begin. The following hours were a turning point for the Wehrmacht and the entire Third Reich . . .

This is how the beginning of Operation Uranus was described in the war diary of the 5th Tank Army:

> During the night, the troops were preparing for the task, before the attack, all the fighters were fed, familiarized with the upcoming task. Short rallies were held in the subdivisions, the fighters got acquainted with the appeal of the Military Council of the Front and the Military Council of the Army, demanding a decisive transition to the offensive

and the destruction of the fascist occupiers and their lackeys. By 7.00, the units occupied the starting position for the attack. At 7.30, a powerful artillery bombardment of the enemy's defence area began. At 7.40 a.m., the methodical destruction of enemy firing points began, alternating with powerful artillery shelling. Under the cover of this fire, the fighters approached the front edge of the defence at 200–300m. Volleys of Katyusha rocket mortars and heavy divisional howitzers M-30 were especially strong. At 8.50 the fire was transferred to the depth of the enemy's defence and the units went on the attack.

However, the Russians did not succeed immediately. Artillery fire destroyed only the front line of the Romanian defence, while in the depth their defensive positions survived. The Soviet troops were experiencing serious difficulties. Some of them arrived very late at their starting positions. Communication with the advancing units was maintained only by radio. At the same time, the Russians were very fond of coded signals and coded maps of the area. The result was confusion and chaos. For example, at the time of the Romanian infantry counter-attack near the village of Korotkovsky, the commander of the 119th Rifle Division, Colonel Kulagin, panicked and mistakenly reported to the command that his division was surrounded. On the same evening, Kulagin was removed from his post for alarmism. Some tank units got lost, lost contact with the accompanying infantry and came under fire from their own artillery. At the same time, the Front headquarters constantly harried subordinates, demanding they move forward faster and not look back. Meanwhile, some Russian units were counter-attacked by the Romanians and suffered serious losses. Some divisions were unable to advance at all. A quarter of the Russian tanks got stuck in the mud or broke down for technical reasons.

The headquarters of the 6th Army learned that a major offensive had begun against the 3rd Romanian Army only at 09.45 (Berlin time). That is, two hours late. After that, only intermittent contradictory messages were received. It was not possible to conduct high-quality aerial reconnaissance due to poor visibility.

In the morning, at Millerovo airfield, Unteroffizier Ludwig Denz of KG27 received an order, despite bad weather conditions, to fly towards the Don and establish what was happening in the Romanian positions. Soon, the He 111 bomber was rolling down the runway, mixing the mud left over from the snow that had just melted with its wheels. Having risen into the sky, the plane headed for the Don through solid clouds. Nothing was visible through the glass of the cockpit, and the pilot was guided only by instruments. Then the clouds began to disperse, the brown steppe appeared below. And then a frightening sight appeared before the eyes of the pilots. They saw huge columns of Soviet troops: tanks, infantry and armoured vehicles were moving south and south-east in many places. The radio operator immediately reported what he saw to the Kampfgeschwader headquarters. It was obvious that the Russians had launched a large-scale offensive. Soon the bomber returned to Millerovo, where the crew verbally reported on the results of the reconnaissance. KG27's commander Baron Oberst von Beust reacted immediately. Half an hour later, II./KG27's planes took to the air to attack the Soviet troops that had broken through. Due to poor visibility, the He 111s were forced to drop bombs from low altitude, actually playing the role of ground-attack aircraft.

Meanwhile, the Russians continued to attack. Here is how the 5th Tank Army war diary described the events of the afternoon:

> In the depth of the defence and especially on the right flank, in the area of Hill 228, there were unsuppressed firing points that opened fire on our advancing units. The resistance of the enemy was especially strong in the area of Hill 228, south of the farms of Bolshoy, Klinovy, Hill 223, Verkhne-Fomikhinsky farm. The 14th Guards Rifle Division met the strongest resistance in front of it and advanced only with its left flank during the day of the battle ... the 437th and 570th Rifle Regiments were stopped by strong enemy resistance in the area of the Ust-Medveditsky farm, where they fought all night together with units of the 1st Tank Corps and 8th Cavalry Corps.

The 21st Army, advancing on the left flank, also met stubborn resistance from the Romanian troops. The breakthrough of the first line of defence lasted until lunchtime, and the 4th Tank Corps of General Andrei Kravchenko did not move to the attack until 12.00. At that time, it was composed of 133 tanks. The right column of the corps managed to slip through the Romanian strongpoints and by the evening reached the farm of Manolin (35km south of Kletskaya). However, the left column in the area of the Vlasov Farm came across the positions of Romanian guns, got involved in a heavy battle and got stuck. As a result, Kravchenko's corps lost 27 tanks (19 T-34s, five KV-1s and three T-70s), and the same number broke down due to technical reasons. The infantry, which had no trucks, lagged behind the tanks. As a result, a quick breakthrough failed, and the 4th Tank Corps was stuck at Manolin for two days.

The Soviets had high hopes for their cavalry, primarily the 3rd Guards Cavalry Corps of General Issa Pliev. At that time, it consisted of three cavalry divisions. According to the plan, the cavalry had to quickly break through the Romanian defences, and then smash the headquarters and bases in the enemy's rear. However, Pliev's unit crossed the Don very slowly, was late in concentrating on its starting positions and was ready for battle only in the evening. And when trying to break through the Romanian defences in the area of Platonov farm, the Russian cavalry came under heavy artillery and machine-gun fire. As a result, they suffered heavy losses and was unable to fulfil their mission.

Because of all these problems, the Russians failed to fulfil the mission of the first day of the offensive. The situation was saved by the 26th Tank Corps of General Alexei Rodin. He managed to quickly bypass the Romanian strongpoints and advance deep into the rear of their positions.

Thus, the beginning of Operation Uranus was different from the previous Russian offensives against the 'northern barrier' of the 6th Army. The Red Army still suffered from poor discipline, poorly-trained commanders and junior officers, poor communications and poor quality of equipment. The stories that the Romanian troops 'were weak', 'had poor weapons' and 'fled after powerful enemy attacks' are lies. The Romanian infantry was quite capable of resisting Russian tank and infantry attacks, and defended itself fiercely and inflicted great damage on the enemy.

Meanwhile, life in Stalingrad was still going on as usual! German assault groups captured several more buildings to the east of the 'Barricades' factory and were preparing for new attacks. During the day, the Russian 95th Rifle Division lost 260 killed and wounded in the fighting, despite the fact that in the morning it had only 700 soldiers.

Not until the evening did the headquarters of the Army Group B realise the scale of the threat. At 22.00, Paulus' headquarters received a radio message with an order to immediately halt all offensive operations, urgently withdraw the 14th and 24th Panzer Divisions from the city and send them to the west. At the same time, the headquarters of the 4th Panzer Army reported that active movements of Soviet tanks had been spotted in the Sarpin Lakes area, which probably indicates preparations for an offensive against the 4th Romanian Army.

The events of 19 November did not necessarily portend a catastrophe at all. If the Romanians and Germans had quickly brought reserves into battle and requested Luftwaffe support, the crisis that had arisen could have been easily eliminated. But neither was at the disposal of the 3rd Romanian Army! The reserves were very small and there were not enough of them for a huge front, and German aviation could not operate effectively because of the bad weather.

On 20 November, the Russians continued to advance in several areas at once. And the Germans brought their main reserve into battle – the 22nd Panzer Division. Acting in separate mobile groups, this unit was able to slow down the advance of the 5th Tank Army and create several crisis situations for the Russians. Several tank battles took place in the area of Perelazovsky and Ust-Medveditsky, during which German tankers inflicted significant damage on the enemy. From the air they were supported by He 111 bombers, which dropped high-explosive and fragmentation bombs on Russian columns from low level. At one point, it seemed to the Soviet command that the offensive was slowing down. The angry commander of the 5th Tank Army, General Romanenko, even issued an order in which he scolded his subordinates for poor leadership of the troops.

However, one German panzer division could not close all the gaps in the defence, and full-fledged air support was impossible. If the Germans had at least one more panzer division in reserve, and the troops were commanded by the resolute Walter Model, probably the Russian offensive could have been stopped. However, this division was not there, and the troops were commanded by the confused Paulus and Weichs, who were waiting for instructions from Hitler. The inconsistency of actions between the German and Romanian troops also had an effect. Due to bad weather, the Luftwaffe's 'all-seeing' aerial reconnaissance could not monitor the movements of Soviet troops, so the objective of the offensive and the direction of the main strikes remained unclear for a long time.

By the evening of 20 November, the vanguard units of the 26th Tank Corps broke into Perelazovsky. This success cost the unit 30 tanks and 260 men killed and wounded. Among the dead was the commander of the 157th Tank Brigade, Senior Battalion Commissar Ivanov. He burned in his T-34 during a battle with German tanks.

The breakthrough of the Russians to Perelazovsky caused panic in the headquarters of the 6th Army. This farm was located just 70km west of the headquarters dugout in Golubinskaya, and 60km north of Oblivskaya, where the headquarters of Fliegerkorps VIII was located. An even greater shock was caused by the news that the armies of the Stalingrad Front, striking from the area of Sarpa and Tsatsa lakes, had attacked the positions of the 4th Romanian Army. At 06.30, the 51st Army went on the offensive, and the 57th Army was the last to join the operation two hours later. On the first day of the operation, this army lost 1,340 men and 34 tanks, that is, the Romanians still showed some resistance. But then they were still completely crushed and scattered. There were no German reserves behind the positions of the 4th Romanian Army!

On 21 November, the Soviets continued to advance to the south and south-east. Between the Lipovsky farm and Surovikino, a tank battle again took place between the Russian 1st Tank Corps and the German 22nd Panzer Division. 'Enemy tanks (40 units) launched counter-attacks several times and inflicted losses on the corps. Enemy aircraft continuously bombed the combat formations of the corps. During the day of the battle, the corps suffered heavy losses,' the 5th Tank Army's war diary reported. The successful actions of the 22nd Panzer Division and German bombers made it possible to stop the Russian offensive to the south (to Oblivskaya and Nizhnechirskaya). The 1st Tank Corps of General Vasily Butkov lost 100 tanks out of 136 available and by the end of the third day of the offensive had actually lost all combat capability.

The Russian 21st Army continued to slowly gnaw through the Romanian defences south of Kletskaya, while suffering serious losses. For example, the 76th Rifle Division lost 350 men during the battle for the Vlasov farm. Kravchenko's 4th Tank Corps advanced from Manojlin to the east – to the Mayorsky farm. There was another tank battle, which cost the Russians another 16 burned tanks. However, the Red Army was again rescued by Alexey Rodin's 26th Tank Corps. The vanguard, consisting of two motorised rifle companies of the 14th Motorised Rifle Brigade, five tanks of the 157th Tank Brigade and armoured vehicles of the 15th Separate Reconnaissance Battalion, launched a breakthrough to Kalach-on-Don. At night, with the headlights on, the force went to the bridge over the Don. The bridge guards mistook the armoured vehicles for their own, as a result of which the Russians managed to capture the crossing intact.

Soon this became known at the headquarters of the 6th Army. The situation was changing so rapidly that all measures taken by the German command were too late. While the units of the 14th Panzer Division advanced to the Don were still going to counter-attack in accordance with the Führer's order to the north-west, in the direction of Manolin, the Soviet 57th Army had already reached the vicinity of Karpovka (east of Kalach). The German command had no idea at all about what was happening in the vast areas south of Manojlin and south of the Likhaya–Stalingrad railway. Left without their 'eyes' in the form of reconnaissance aircraft, trusting the Führer's assurances that 'the Russians are no longer capable of major offensives', the German generals suddenly found themselves in a fog, like the one that enveloped the Don steppes on those days. They didn't understand what was going on (maybe it's a bad dream?) and they were amazed at how huge territories, conquered with such difficulty, kilometre after kilometre last summer, suddenly turned out to be in the hands of a 'half-broken' and 'exhausted' enemy in three days . . .

For three days the Romanian troops fought bravely and desperately with the Red Army, inflicting heavy losses on it. No mass flight of the Romanians from their positions, which was written about in many post-war books, has not been documented. On the contrary, Soviet combat logs indicate that the enemy fought skilfully, and put up fierce resistance. However, the Romanians could not resist the vastly superior enemy alone for long. The Germans could not support them in time, and the forces of the single 22nd Panzer Division were not enough. By the evening of 22 November, the defeat of the 3rd Romanian Army became obvious, and the Russian right and left shock 'pincers' meanwhile met up in the Kalach-on-Don area. 'The Romanian soldier is on the defensive stubbornly, but as soon as this defence was breached, the fear of encirclement, the inept organisation of the battle management in the depth of the positions violated the entire defence system and forced the Romanian units to begin an immediate withdrawal,' a report of the 4th Tank Corps said. According to the Russians, the strength of the Romanian defence was reliable camouflage and good equipment of the front line of defence. It could only be broken through by large forces and at the cost of significant losses. But at the same time, the Romanians did not know how to build a layered defence. When the troops began to withdraw to the rear, there were no trenches or equipped strongpoints for them to fall back to.

The time of 'fatal decisions'

At 19.00 (Berlin time), Paulus' headquarters reported to the headquarters of Army Group B that the 6th Army was surrounded. 'Despite the fierce resistance in the hands of the Russians are: the entire valley of the Tsaritsa, the railway from Sovetsky to Kalach, the bridge over the Don located there, the hills along the western bank of the Don to Golubinskaya, Oskinsky and Krainy,' the message said. It shocked first von Weichs and his subordinates, and then Hitler's entourage. At the same time, the question of the possibility of a breakout from the pocket was raised for the first time and the only possible direction was determined – to the south-west. At this time, the headquarters of the 6th Army itself had already been evacuated from the village of Golubinskaya to the east – to Gumrak. At night, the depressed Paulus spoke to Hitler for the last time by direct telephone (the line that ran along the railway had not yet been cut). The Führer tried to cheer up his protege, and said that all positions should be held, despite the 'threat of encirclement'. They spoke sincerely and frankly, but no final decisions were made!

Despite the fact that the Soviets seemed to have achieved stunning successes, at that moment the crisis could have been easily averted. Not all the plans of the Soviet command had been implemented. For example, the 64th Army was supposed to advance through Basargino to Karpovka, but in fact all its attacks stalled to the west of Beketovka. And the 62nd Army was faced with the task of 'clearing Stalingrad from the enemy' with a quick blow. On 21 November, Red Army soldiers managed to recapture a part of the Mamayev Kurgan, Workshop No. 3 of the 'Red October' plant and part of Mashinnaya Street with in a desperate attack. But the Germans not only managed to repel the attacks inside the city, but even counter-attacked in places. Ambitious goals were also set for the southernmost force – the 28th Army. It was supposed to advance from Astrakhan to Elista and capture it within eight days. But this mission could not be fulfilled either. The Red Army did not have sufficient forces to create a complete encirclement, and many farms and roads between them were not occupied at all. The Russian vanguard units suffered heavy losses and did not represent serious power.

Thus, if the 6th Army had immediately gone for a breakout, it would undoubtedly have been crowned with complete success. It is also likely that rapid and decisive actions could have broken through the fragile ring of the blockade at the end of November. But the German command, which had previously underestimated the strength of the Red Army, now, on the contrary, began to overestimate it. The number of Soviet troops breaking through to Kalacha-on-Don was overestimated several times. German intelligence reported hundreds of tanks driving around the steppe, but mostly this information was obtained from frightened Romanian soldiers. It was not possible to make an accurate assessment of the potential of the Russians due to bad weather. In fact, by 23 November, the Russians had lost half of their available tanks, and there was not enough fuel and shells for the remaining ones. The artillery was far behind the vanguard units, and communication between them had not yet been established. In fact, the blockade ring in the early days was only a chain of weak barriers that could not have repelled German attacks.

But the psychological victory was on the side of the Soviets. Frightened by the imaginary power of the Red Army, the German command fell into a stupor and lost precious time. Instead of quick and decisive action, Paulus began to dig a grave for his army. On the morning of 23 November, he ordered the evacuation of the part of the 'northern barrier' adjacent to the Volga, including the bridgehead on the shore at Akatovka and Vinnovka, which had been a symbol of success exactly three months ago. The 11th Army Corps also retreated from the small bend of the Don to the south-east. This allowed the Germans to quickly reduce the front and free up sufficient forces to form the western and south-western pocket front.

The following fact also shows how much the German generals overestimated the strength of the Red Army. The headquarters of the 6th Army was seriously afraid of Soviet air landings inside the pocket. Moreover, the Germans were afraid of both parachute and aircraft landings. In this regard, all rear units were ordered to double their vigilance and especially pay attention to firing away from the front positions.

Then discussions about 'future prospects' began. In the evening of the same day, Paulus, in his radio message, asked Hitler to give him freedom of action (in fact, to allow a breakout from the pocket), citing the lack of supplies and the unanimous opinion of the majority of his generals. 'Although most of the equipment will be lost in this case, numerous experienced soldiers and some of the reserves will be preserved. I take full responsibility for this difficult decision,' the message said. Paulus' position was supported by the Chief of the General Staff of the Army, General Kurt Zeitzler. He insisted that the current situation would not allow the 6th Army to be relieved by an offensive from the outside. Zeitzler soberly estimated that the Luftwaffe (especially given the simultaneous crisis in Africa) would not be able to supply the pocket by air. And the general's arguments initially impressed the Führer.

Richthofen also openly doubted the possibility of providing supplies to the 6th Army. He immediately said that during the summer offensive, the transport aviation had been severely depleted and at the moment he had only 80 aircraft at his disposal, which would not be able to supply the 'pocket', especially in winter weather conditions. Fibig was also pessimistic and exclaimed: 'A whole army?! This is absolutely impossible!' He was especially confused by the weather. In Southern Russia, according to Fibig, there was an extremely unpredictable climate. The clear weather was very abruptly replaced by clouds, as well as fog and sleet.

As history has shown, the commander of the 51st Army Corps, General Seydlitz, turned out to be the most far-sighted. On 23 November, he drew up his own memorandum on supply needs. According to him, a single division required at least 400 tons of ammunition (at a low level of combat activity) and 800 tons (at high). At the same time, the troops had only meagre fuel reserves, while the minimum required daily was $10m^3$ of gasoline for each division. The food supplies available in the 51st Army Corps numbered only 7 full daily rations of dry rations, 4 full daily rations of bread and 3.5 full daily rations of flour. Summing up these calculations, Seidlitz came to the conclusion that at least 295 Ju 52 aircraft per day (590 tons of cargo) would be needed to supply his corps alone. And during high-intensity battles, at least 1,000 transport planes would have to arrive in the pocket every day.

Seydlitz wrote:

It is not known where to get the number of Ju 52s necessary to supply the army. To do this, you probably need to collect all the available planes from Europe and North Africa. Fuel consumption for the delivery of goods over such a distance will be so high that it can have an impact on strategic plans and the course of the entire war. Even if 500 rather than the planned 130 planes arrive daily, they will still not be able to deliver more than 1,000 tons of cargo. This is not enough to provide an army of 200,000 people conducting active combat. Just as with fuel and ammunition, only a small fraction of the food needs for people will be covered. All the horses will die in the next few days. At the same time, the tactical mobility of the troops will decrease, their independent supply will become more complicated, and the need for fuel grow, on the contrary.

In addition, Seidlitz warned against direct analogies with the successful supply and subsequent breaking of the Demyansk Pocket, which was referred to by many 'optimists' at that time. The terrain on the Valdai hill favoured defence and created problems for the attackers, the distance from the front was small, and the supply needs were significantly lower. But even there, it took several weeks of gruelling battles to break it. Now the Germans were defending themselves in the bare steppe, the nearest positions on the Chir River were 75km away, and the needs of the surrounded group clearly exceeded the capabilities of aviation.

As a result, the chief of the Luftwaffe General Staff, Generaloberst Hans Jeschonnek, turned out to be the main 'optimist'. He assured the Führer that aviation was able to supply the encircled troops in sufficient volume. Reichsmarschall Göring was not aware of the situation at all at that moment, as he was presiding over an oil conference at his

Carinhall estate. Only after the end of the event was Göring informed of the previously-made decision. He did not think deeply and to calculate complex statistical data (later it turned out that Jeschonnek was not good at mathematics and made the grossest mistakes). Instead, the commander-in-chief of the Luftwaffe, like almost all the other people involved in the development of the solution, suggested that the encirclement would be 'temporary' and supported Jeschonnek. Göring assured the Führer that the Luftwaffe would do everything possible to meet the needs of the 6th Army.

Hitler himself was emotionally inclined from the very beginning to declare Stalingrad a 'fortress' ('Festung'). He was sorry to give the Soviets these ruins, for which so much German blood had been shed. And, most importantly, he has already boastfully announced their capture to the whole world.

Thus, when Hitler met with Göring at the Berghof, the figures and calculations previously prepared by Hans Jeschonnek were presented to the Reichsmarschall. As the Reichsmarschall himself later noted, they were presented to him in such a way that he could only agree with them. At the same time, Jeschonnek himself very quickly realized that his initial calculations were incorrect. However, he did not have the courage to directly inform the Führer about this, and the general notified only his immediate superior of his mistake, asking him to inform Hitler about the real situation himself. Göring, who thought first of all about arranging his beautiful life, did not want to spoil the mood for himself and the Führer! Instead, he simply went to Paris to buy at auctions the next works of art for his collections . . .

However, the visionary General Seydlitz was also mistaken in some things. For example, he predicted endless attacks by Russian fighters against transport planes, as well as 'relentless strikes' that would be inflicted against the 6th Army even before the beginning of the relief offensive. In fact, Seydlitz, like other generals, greatly overestimated the power of the Red Army and its successes. In the battles with the Romanian troops, the Russians suffered such heavy losses and used up so many resources that they could not attack for the next three weeks. The battles took on a positional character. This again came as a complete surprise to the German generals, simultaneously creating a 'window of opportunity' for them to save the situation.

On 24 November, Hitler ordered Paulus to hold on, wait for supplies by air and prepare for a breakthrough from the outside. In order to further encourage the drooping spirit of the protege, the Führer awarded him the rank of Generaloberst.

'Will have to perform the task with
all the resourcefulness and skill'

In the resulting pocket there were 12 infantry divisions, three tank divisions, three motorised infantry divisions, one jäger division and one Romanian infantry division (20 divisions in total). As for the total number of the encircled group, it still raises many questions. It is not uncommon to call the numbers 250,000 – 265,000 and even 300,000 surrounded. According to German documents, as of 15 November, the total strength of the 6th Army (those who were on the ration strength) was 149,230. But only 120,000 were Germans, almost 30,000 more (over 10 per cent of those who ended up in the pocket) were 'Hiwis', that is, former soldiers of the Red Army. The actual combat strength of the 6th Army numbered even less – 79,161: the rest were auxiliary personnel (bakers, gunsmiths, handymen, builders, and so on). From the 4th Panzer Army, three German divisions (297th and 371st Infantry Divisions and the 29th Motorised Infantry Division) were trapped in the pocket, which by mid-November numbered about 25,000 (including 3,000 'Hiwis'). It turns out that the German troops in the encircled group should have numbered no more than 150,000 officers and men, including Luftwaffe anti-aircraft gunners and ground crews. Even if we add to this Russian 'assistants' and Romanians, the figure of 265,000 seems difficult to explain . . . Russian intelligence estimated the number of trapped troops at 90,000. According to them, there were 1,400 guns, 10,000 vehicles and 400 tanks in the Stalingrad area.

The size of the huge 'pocket' at the beginning of the blockade was 65km from west to east and 35km from north to south. Initial rough calculations estimated the needs of the encircled group at 750 tons per day. However, this figure was soon reduced to 500 tons. Later, calculations carried out at the headquarters of the 6th Army showed that an absolute minimum of 300 tons per day would be required. Experts proceeded from the fact that the ration for soldiers was almost immediately cut in half, in addition, at that time it was not yet known exactly how many 'eaters' were in the pocket.

As early as 23 November, the air bridge to Stalingrad began to operate. Direct responsibility for the supply of the 6th Army was initially assigned to the headquarters of Fliegerkorps VIII, and officially the Stalingrad air transport operation began only on 30 November. The 9th Anti-Aircraft Division and its commander, Major General Pickert, were responsible for the organisation and management of the reception of aircraft in the pocket, as well as the regulation of the dispatch and delivery of incoming cargo. 'VIII Air Corps is relieved of the tasks of supporting troops and from 30.11 is assigned to the air supply of the 6th Army. An honourable but difficult mission! I am sure that the Russians will counteract with all their might. Will have to perform the task with all the resourcefulness and skill. It will cost a lot of blood, I believe!', wrote Martin Fibig in his diary.

Interestingly, neither before the war, nor during the German offensive on Stalingrad, was there a major air base at Pitomnik. It didn't even appear on the map! The creation of a large airfield in this place began only in October. In preparation for the winter campaign, the headquarters of the 6th Army decided to establish the main Luftwaffe winter airfield east of the Don in the Pitomnik area. Tactical reconnaissance groups, as well as fighter and Ju 87 units were to be relocated there. Construction work was completed in early November. Thanks to this, after the encirclement, the 6th Army had a large well-equipped airfield designed for take-off, landing and parking of hundreds of aircraft.

The Luftwaffe command took desperate measures to increase the number of transport aircraft. In fact, all available Ju 52/3ms were requested for the 6th Army, some of them even being brought back from Africa. First of all, the aviation groups KGr.zbV500 and KGr. zbV700, which were the first to fly into the pocket, were reinforced. By 1 December, 10 more groups had arrived at the Morozovskaya and Tatsinskaya airfields. Most of them received Ju 52s from Luftwaffe flight schools. In addition, as was already the case during the supply of Demyansk, temporary air groups were hastily formed from the instructor pilots of these educational institutions: KGr.zbV20, KGr. zbV21 and KGr.zbV22. They got old He 111Ps and Ju 86s.

In good weather, the transports flew in to the pocket in whole squadrons or groups of five or six aircraft accompanied by fighters. During bad weather, only experienced crews flew in groups, the rest got to their destination one by one. Pilots from the flight schools who were not used to such difficult conditions had the worst of it. The winter cold, the long and dangerous flight to and from the pocket over enemy territory under fire from anti-aircraft guns and facing fighter attacks, frequent icing of aircraft and technical problems, all these presented difficulties even for experienced Ju 52 pilots.

In the first days of the operation of the air bridge in the Stalingrad area, the weather was warm and cloudy, the air temperature was about 0° Celsius. Periodically it snowed, and visibility ranged from 4km to 10km. Sometimes cloud and fog covered the entire sky, reducing visibility to 150–300m. For example, on 29 November, the weather was cloudy in the Stalingrad area and it was snowing. The air temperature was +3 − +5° Celsius.

It quickly became clear that the transport aircraft alone were not enough to supply the 6th Army, so it was decided to additionally use He 111 bombers for this purpose. The first experience of such missions was obtained during the supply of the Demyansk and Holm pockets in February–April 1942. It was considered as a success, and from now on German bombers were regularly involved in transport missions. On 29 November, the 1st Aviation Transport Command (Lufttransportführer 1) was created to coordinate the actions of all air groups based at Morozovskaya (the Germans called it 'Moro' for short), located 150km from the positions of the 6th Army. It was headed by the commander of KG55, 53-year-old Oberst (Colonel) Ernst Kuhl. Operationally, KG27, KG55, part of KG53 and I./KG100 were subordinated to him.

The payload capacity of the He 111 bomber (depending on the type) was 1.5 tons of cargo in the fuselage, 4–8 droppable cargo containers (Abwurfbehälter) Mun C250 or Tank C250 (with fuel), or 1–3 Mun C1000 cargo containers. Bulky loads could not be carried because the entrance hatch of the He 111 was too small. The Mun C250 container contained 50–80kg of food and 100–150kg of ammunition. The Tank C250 container contained 110 litres of fuel. The Mun C1000 container contained 150–250kg of food and 300–400 kg of ammunition.

These containers held not only the essentials for life and war. The German command also took care that the soldiers in Stalingrad were not bored! Pilot H. Nowak from 8./KG27 recalled:

> Out of pure curiosity, I once, before starting a supply mission, carefully examined the contents of one of the supply containers that were stored in the hall. It was filled with completely insignificant things, such as card games, games 'Man-don't annoy-don't annoy' ('Mensch-ögere-Dich-nicht') – stupid marketing products! I do not know how it was possible! Of course, we dropped food, ammunition, and clothing, but the thing just described still shocked me.

In cloudy weather, the He 111s flew in the pocket one by one, each crew choosing their own route, altitude and approach trajectory. The main landmark in the pocket was the characteristic curve of the western part of Stalingrad. In clear weather, in order to protect against Soviet fighters, it was necessary to fly in tight combat formation. But the experienced He 111 crews from KGr.zbV5, who had flown into Demyansk the previous winter, employed the simplest combat formation – the 'chain'. The planes flew in links (triangles and rhombuses) one after the other at a short distance and at the same altitude. Any attacking fighter came under the crossfire of several He 111s at once, regardless of whether he attacked from above, from the side or from below. The 'chain' became a common formation for bombers on such missions.

In cases where landing in the pocket was not possible (due to weather, accidents at the airfield or attacks by Soviet aviation), the aircraft had to drop cargo from the air to a site designated by special signal lights. Sometimes the reset was performed by a radio beacon. In cases where these signals were absent, containers (often the Germans called them 'food bombs' – Verpflegungs-bomben) should be dropped over the eastern half of the blockade ring – closer to Stalingrad. There, the probability that they would be found was higher than in the desert area in the west of pocket. But dumping cargo from the air was considered an extreme measure. There was not enough fuel for transporting containers by vehicle from the drop zones, and in addition, they were hard to spot in the snow because of the white colour of the parachutes.

Meanwhile, the German command was feverishly preparing for an offensive to break the pocket. On 21 November, a new Army Group Don was formed, headed by Generalfeldmarschall Erich von Manstein. The initial plan of Operation Wintergewitter ('Winter Storm') provided for two strikes at once, the first from the Kotelnikovo district to the north-east. The second was from the area of the village of Nizhne-Chirskaya to the east (on Kalach-on-Don). However, due to a shortage of troops, Manstein was soon forced to abandon the double strike. The final Wintergewitter plan, approved in early December, provided for an offensive only from the Kotelnikovo area.

The distance between Nizhne-Chirskaya and the western edge of pocket was only 45km, while the Germans had to cover a distance of 120km from Kotelnikovo. Why did Manstein decide to move such a long way, actually along the positions of the German troops located on the west bank of the Don? Firstly, Hitler demanded not only to rescue the 6th Army, but also to 'restore the situation' in the Stalingrad area. At the same time, he was not going to leave the Caucasus. To achieve this goal, the Germans needed not only to break through to the pocket, but also to push the Russians away from Kotelnikovo, eliminating the threat to the left flank of Army Group A. Secondly, there were purely logistical reasons for this. The railway that led to Stalingrad from the west was blocked by the Russians to the east of Morozovskaya. Therefore, the delivery of troops and tanks to the starting area required a lot of time. But the Tikhoretsk–Stalingrad railway line was free all the way to Kotelnikovo. This made it possible to deliver troops directly to the starting point of the attack.

Soviet front-line intelligence, which, unlike that in the air, worked quite efficiently, carefully monitored what was going on in and around the pocket. They gathered information with the help of agents located in the German rear, actively using the local population. In addition, well-equipped reconnaissance groups were regularly sent into the German rear. The practice of regularly capturing prisoners from forward positions was well established. The scouts even collected gossip that spread in German territory, processed it and compiled fairly accurate reports.

As a result, on 27 November, the Stalingrad Front headquarters received information that 'fresh' German units and tanks were concentrating in the Kotelnikovo area. And it is from there that the unblocking blow would be delivered in the direction of Stalingrad. The Russians were aware of the difficulties in the relationship between the Germans and their Romanian allies. It was the Romanians who were blamed for the crisis and they treated them like cattle. Most of the Romanian soldiers in the pocket had their weapons taken away ('there's no use from you anyway!') and sent to heavy construction work. Soon the Russians also learned that bombers were being used to supply the 6th Army. In early December, intelligence obtained information that the '100th Bombardment Group' (I./KG100) had been transferred from Armavir and Maykop to Morozovskaya.

But Russian intelligence also made serious mistakes. The Soviets were sure that the 6th Army would certainly break out of Stalingrad to the west. Therefore, instead of throwing all its forces into reducing the blockade ring, the Red Army spent a lot of troops and resources on creating defences in the western and south-western sectors of the perimeter of the pocket.

Russian troops also experienced severe difficulties. At the end of November, the Volga began to be covered with ice, and crossing by ships proved impossible. The troops of the 62nd Army stationed in Stalingrad had to be supplied by air every night. At the same time, Soviet aviation did not have proper cargo containers, so supplies were dropped from a low altitude in PD-MM bags. On some nights, transport planes carried out up to 300 sorties to supply the troops. From 20 to 30 November alone, the 8th Air Army dropped 868 bags to its soldiers. In fact, two 'air bridges' worked synchronously in the Stalingrad area at the same time!

Chapter 11

HOT MUD IN A WINTER STORM

'Russians walk in front of positions'

While Manstein was preparing for a relief operation, the Luftwaffe was making desperate efforts to supply the pocket. On 1 December 1942, 42 flights were carried out, of which 17 were by Ju 52s (15 successful) and 25 by He 111s (all completed safely), delivering 85 tons of cargo to the encircled army. A flight was considered 'successful' if the plane was able to land in the pocket and unload the cargo on the ground.

On 2 December, 78 sorties were carried out and 120 tons of cargo were delivered. Gradually, the volume of supplies grew. On 4 December, 88 flights were carried out, of which 64 were Ju 52s (52 successful) and 24 He 111s (22 successful). In total, 143.8 tons of cargo were delivered to pocket, including 55 tons of shells (including 3 tons of shaped-charge rounds for 75mm anti-tank guns), 46 tons of fuel, 12.6 tons of bread, 4 tons of links for tank tracks, 300g of 'Scho-Ka-Kola' (caffeinated chocolate), mail, radio equipment, etc.

On 5 December, only Ju 52s flew to the 6th Army, which completed 37 sorties (29 successfully). At the same time, due to heavy fog, take-off was carried out blind, and over Pitomnik the planes had to make six or seven approaches before the pilots received permission to land and the landing strip itself was accurately detected. On the way back, the crews of the Ju 52s had a new adventure: due to icing, landing in Morozovskaya and Tatsinskaya was prohibited, as a result of which they had to land in Novocherkassk, and in poor visibility and with almost empty fuel tanks! Against the background of these difficulties, the losses of two aircraft that crashed in the Pitomnik area do not seem serious.

On 6 December near Stalingrad, there was continuous low cloud cover with fog at an altitude of 200–300m, with drizzling rain. The Luftwaffe carried out 96 flights to the 'fortress', delivering 72.9 tons of cargo there. On this day, the Luftwaffe suffered heavy losses for the first time. Six planes were shot down and reported missing.

On 7 December, it warmed up to +5° in the Stalingrad area, and it was raining. The snow had melted almost everywhere. Transport aviation carried out 190 flights, most of which fell on He 111 bombers. One hundred and thirty-five aircraft were able to land inside the pocket, delivering a record 362.6 tons of cargo there, including 160 tons of shells, 72 tons of fuel, 2 tons of antifreeze and 50 tons of food (mainly bread), and 704 wounded were taken out by return flights. These figures were encouraging, but the next day the Luftwaffe again suffered heavy losses. Out of 126 planes that took off 13 were lost (about 10 per cent). Most of them suffered accidents due to difficult weather conditions.

On the morning of 11 December, an He 111 landed at Pitomnik with Martin Fibig on board. The commander of Fliegerkorps VIII wanted to find out how things were going in the pocket on the eve of the relief operation. Fibig met with Paulus, who told him that it was necessary to force a corridor through the blockade ring by 18 December at the latest. Otherwise, the 6th Army would have no food reserves left, and have to depend solely on air supplies. 'While there are still 40,000 infantry in combat formations, this number is decreasing accordingly. The volumes delivered by air are not enough. There is not enough fuel, shells for light howitzers and food. The Russians are walking in front of the positions, you can't even shoot at them,' Fibig wrote in his diary. At 13.50, he flew back to Morozovskaya, where the He 111 landed safely at 14.50.

It should be noted that the general took a lot of risks. Taking advantage of the improved weather conditions, on this day the 8th and 16th Air Armies carried out a total of 527 sorties. Russian pilots reported 43 downed planes, including 17 transports. A raid was also carried out on the Bolshaya Rossoshka airfield, where, according to Soviet data, 10 Ju 52s were destroyed. The Luftwaffe actually did suffer heavy losses: 12 aircraft, including 11 Ju 52s and an He 111.

Up until 8 December, Soviet troops tried to squeeze the blockade ring into the circle of the 6th Army with continuous attacks from different directions. But the Germans, despite everything, managed to create a solid defence along the entire stretched perimeter. The headquarters of the Stalingrad Front had to admit that the enemy was able to quickly create reliable lines consisting of strongpoints, barriers and minefields. Due to good interaction with artillery and mortars, the infantry managed to effectively repel all attacks. And to eliminate the wedges, mobile assault detachments with tanks and armoured vehicles were formed, which acted as 'fire brigades'. 'The encircled enemy is fiercely resisting, still shows great perseverance and fights for every metre, for every trench, conducts counter-attacks with tanks,' General Yeremenko and a member of the Khrushchev Military Council said in a report. The brutality of the fighting is evidenced at least by the fact that the 38th Rifle Division alone (mentioned at the beginning of the book) lost 1,700 casualties in three days. The unit practically lost its combat capability and was once again taken to the rear for refitting and reinforcement.

But despite these successes, the 6th Army had already begun to have serious problems. The artillery began to run out of ammunition, and therefore it was necessary to establish limits for their consumption. Howitzers and mortars began to fire much less frequently and less intensively. Soviet pilots noted that starting from 10–20 December, anti-aircraft fire from the pocket became noticeably weaker. A German soldier from the 295th Infantry Division was captured in Stalingrad. He said that in the first days of the month, the food situation deteriorated greatly. Since the beginning of December, soldiers had received an average of 300 grams of bread per day.

On 9 December, Soviet intelligence received numerous reports that strong assault groups were concentrating in the Kotelnikovo and Nizhne-Chirskaya areas, which were about to go on the offensive. Russian reconnaissance planes photographed many tanks, armoured vehicles and trucks in these sectors. Intelligence also reported that the operation to break through to the 6th Army should begin on 14–16 December, and it will be commanded by 'General Monstein [*sic*]'.

Meanwhile, the Germans were finishing the concentration of their assault group. The main striking force was the 6th Panzer Division of General Erhard Raus. It had recently transferred from France and was at full strength. The division consisted of 160 tanks and 30 self-propelled artillery pieces. The morale of Raus's tankmen was very high, they were confident of success. 'The combat capability of the division can be assessed as outstanding. Everyone felt their great superiority over the enemy, believed in the strength of their weapons, in the preparedness of their commanders,' company commander H. Scheibert later recalled. The 23rd Panzer Division, transferred from the Caucasus, was much weaker and exhausted by recent battles. There were only 30 serviceable tanks in it (including several Panzer IIs), and the tankers were largely demoralised. Therefore, this division was assigned an auxiliary role in the offensive. Later, the 17th Panzer

Division was also supposed to arrive, but its combat strength was also very low. All three divisions were combined as part of General Friedrich Kirchner's 57th Panzer Corps.

The weather was a very important factor for the success of the operation. Only with clear weather and good visibility could the Luftwaffe provide effective support to the offensive. Frost was also important for German tankers. Only the frozen soil could ensure rapid progress across the steppe. Therefore, Manstein had to wait a few days before the weather conditions became favourable. However, it was impossible to guarantee clear and frosty weather for the entire period of the offensive!

On the Soviet side, the 51st Army of Major General Nikolai Trufanov stood in the way of the 57th Tank Corps. This unit was severely exhausted and weakened by the fighting and was experiencing serious supply problems. The rifle divisions lacked shells, grenades and ammunition, as well as food.

On 10 December, in the Stalingrad area, the temperature dropped sharply to − 13°, but it was still snowing heavily. The next day, the clouds began to disperse and visibility improved. As a result, the start of the operation was scheduled for the morning of 12 December.

At 05.30, after a heavy artillery bombardment, the 57th Panzer Corps rushed to the attack. As soon as it was light, the Stukas, Zerstörers, Hs 123 biplanes and Romanian IAR-81 fighter-bombers launched the powerful air strikes against the Russian troops. As a result, the 302nd Rifle Division, which was in the path of the main attack, suffered heavy losses, and fled across the steppe in panic. At 13.40, nine Ju 87s from StG2 struck the command post of the 51st Army headquarters. As a result, the shelter was destroyed and eight officers were killed, including the head of the army intelligence department, Colonel Ivan Yurov, communications officer Lieutenant Khramtsov and the chief interpreter (translator) of the army Klimov. The commander of the army, General Trufanov, survived only by a miracle. The Luftwaffe suffered minimal losses in these missions, with only one Ju 87D-3 from 4./StG2 reported missing.

On 13 December, German aviation continued to actively support the offensive. For example, in the morning, the Luftwaffe carried out a very successful air attack against the Abganerovo railway station, which played a key role in supplying the 51st Army. As a result of bomb hits, 22 ammunition wagons exploded there.

Air supremacy allowed the Germans to cross the Aksai River without hindrance and break through to the Verkhne-Kumsky farm, covering about 40km in two days. The successful start of the operation inspired optimism in the German soldiers in the pocket (the news of the breakthrough quickly spread through the trenches and ruins) and the German command. It seemed that the story of the Demyansk pocket was repeating itself.

The only strong Russian unit that was on the way to Stalingrad at that moment was the 4th Mechanised Corps of Major General Vasily Volsky. It had 107 T-34, KV-8 (flamethrower) and T-70 tanks. On 14 December, Volsky threw his tanks at the Germans north of Verkhne-Kumsky. The Russians managed to stop Raus's vanguard, and the next day they attacked the 6th Panzer Division from three directions at once.

On 15 December, a protracted tank battle unfolded on the steppe around the farm. Raus requested air support, but the weather deteriorated sharply that day. At Stalingrad, it warmed up to +2° again, and the sky filled with clouds. Therefore, the Stukas and Zerstörers did not appear, and the German tankers had to fight without the 'Luftwaffe umbrella'. There was also no aerial reconnaissance, as the Fw 189 reconnaissance planes did not fly either. Therefore, Raus did not know where the enemy was and how many tanks he had. The fire of the Russian anti-aircraft artillery was unexpectedly powerful, which was secretly moved to the front line and engaged in direct fire. As a result, by the evening, the Germans, under the threat of encirclement, had to evacuate Verkhne-Kumsky and withdraw to the bank of the Aksai River. This was the first serious setback that affected the course of the operation. The losses of the 6th Panzer Division amounted to 19 tanks (13 Panzer IIIs, five Panzer IVs and a Panzer II).

While the 6th Panzer Division was fighting with the 4th Mechanised Corps, on the right flank the 23rd Panzer Division was fighting with the 13th Tank Corps of Colonel Trofim Tanaschishin. This battle was more successful for the Germans. By 17 December, the 13th Tank Corps had lost 75 per cent of its men and 60 per cent of its equipment. Only 31 tanks (17 T-34s and 14 T-70s) remained in the unit. After that, Tanaschishin's corps lost its combat capability, was withdrawn to the rear, and then disbanded.

On 17 December, weather conditions changed dramatically. A northerly wind blew, dispersed the clouds, the air temperature dropped to – 15°. Taking advantage of this, Stukas from StG2, sirens howling, fell on the positions of the 4th Mechanized Corps. Then they were replaced by Bf 110 Zerstörers from ZG1. The Luftwaffe, taking advantage of the absence of Russian aircraft, attacked targets from a low level, dropped bombs directly on the heads of Russian soldiers and shot them at point-blank range with cannons and machine guns. 'Our aviation was inactive!', reports the war diary of the 4th Mechanised Corps.

The next day, Raus's regrouped 6th Panzer Division went on the offensive again. The Russians fought desperately, but due to constant air attacks they suffered heavy losses and could not move freely. The Luftwaffe also suffered. On 16 December, three aircraft from ZG1 were shot down, and another one was severely damaged. The next day, three Bf 110s were lost, and on 18 December 11 members of their crews were reported killed or missing.

On 19 December, the weather in the Stalingrad area was still good (for aviation and tanks). A north-easterly wind was blowing, and the air temperature was -6°. The Luftwaffe threw in all available forces to support their troops. About 1,000 sorties of bombers and ground-attack planes were carried out. The positions of the Russian troops were subjected to continuous fierce bombardment and shelling. As a result, Volsky's 4th Mechanised Corps was practically destroyed. Having lost 1,300 men and 72 tanks, he abandoned his positions and retreated to the north-east in disarray. 'The enemy managed to break our resistance, mainly due to the massive impact of aviation on the positions of our units. Enemy aircraft carried out 1,500 sorties on December 18 and 19. Our aviation did not protect us,' was how this defeat was explained in the corps' war diary.

German tanks broken through into open country and, in the evening, with a swift rush, reached the Myshkova River near the Nizhne-Kumsky farm. It was a real winter blitzkrieg: in one day the 6th Panzer Division advanced 15km through mud and snow. There were still about 50km to cover to the south-western part of the pocket.

This moment was the culmination of Operation Wintergewitter. Manstein believed that the 6th Army should immediately begin a breakout. At the same time, Hitler, under pressure from his entourage, also agreed with this. However, Paulus showed indecision. He believed that his army was unable to cover 50km due to lack of fuel and ammunition. According to the calculations of the headquarters of the 6th Army, fuel for tanks and trucks could only be enough for 20–25km, the rest of the way the soldiers would have to walk. Paulus insisted that the 57th Panzer Corps should move closer to Stalingrad, creating more favourable conditions for a breakout.

Among other factors, the headquarters of the 6th Army referred to 'frosty weather'. Allegedly, German soldiers would not be able to move across the open steppe in conditions of severe cold. In fact, the weather was rather warm! On 20 December, it was -3° in the Stalingrad area. The Luftwaffe maintained control over the airspace, carrying out about 1,000 sorties.

On 21 December, the 57th Panzer Corps continued its attacks and, with massive support from Stukas and Zerstörers, managed to capture a bridgehead on the northern bank of the Myshkova River. On the following day, the headquarters of the Stalingrad Front expected another full-scale offensive of German tanks in the north-east direction. However, the attack unexpectedly did not follow. On the contrary, the Germans began to strengthen their positions.

Meanwhile, the 2nd Guards Army of General Rodion Malinovsky, consisting of six Guards rifle divisions and three Guards mechanized brigades, hastily concentrated in the area of the breakthrough. Initially, it was intended to strengthen the inner ring of the blockade and eliminate the pocket. But due to the threat of a breakthrough, Malinovsky received an order to deploy his troops along the Myshkova River. As part of this army, the artilleryman Yuri Bondarev fought, who later wrote a book about these events. It was called *Hot Snow*, although it would have been more correct to call it *Hot Mud*!

While the German tanks were racing to the pocket, the air bridge continued to work on the limits of possibility. On 12 December, the Luftwaffe lost 11 aircraft (six He 111s, four Ju 52s and a Ju 86), and two more He 111s were destroyed during an air attack on the Pitomnik air base. The next day, 95 flights to pocket were carried out, during which 133.7 tons of cargo were delivered. This time three transport planes were lost. On 14 December, the Luftwaffe carried out 98 transport flights and delivered 135 tons of cargo. The only loss of the day was a Ju 52 from KGr.zbV700, which made an emergency landing south of Stalingrad on Russian-controlled territory. The Russians found 2,800 litres of petrol in barrels on the plane, and the three crew were taken prisoner.

On 15 December, 57 transport flights were carried out in conditions of continuous cloud, fifty aircraft were able to land at Pitomnik. The 6th Army received 91.5 tons of cargo. One He 111 from KGr.zbV5 was hit by anti-aircraft guns when approaching the pocket and made an emergency landing on Soviet territory (west of the village of Beketovka). The four crew were captured and 800 litres of gasoline and 28 pallets with anti-tank shells were found in the plane. Under interrogation, the German pilots said that 200 Ju 52 aircraft from the 50th, 300th, 500th, 700th and 900th Transport Aviation Groups were based at Tatsinskaya air base.

On 16 December, in heavy cloud, the Luftwaffe carried out 129 transport sorties, and 97 aircraft were able to land at Pitomnik. At the same time, most of the missions were carried out by He 111 bombers. On this day, losses on the air bridge amounted to 11 aircraft (eight

Ju 86s, two Ju 52s and an He 111). On 17 December, 71 flights to the pocket were carried out and 129.9 tons of cargo were delivered. Despite the clear weather and numerous attacks by Russian fighters, the losses amounted to only two aircraft. The statistics of the next day were as follows: 46 missions, 85 tons of cargo delivered, one aircraft lost.

On 19 December, a record was set: 179 transport flights were carried out, most of which were by He 111s: 273.3 tons of cargo were delivered to the pocket (16.4 tons of kerosene, 85.4 tons of bread, 10 tons of butter, 14 tons of sausage, 6.8 tons of ammunition), and 632 wounded soldiers and 32 bags of mail were taken out on return flights. According to Soviet data, the route of the transport aircraft followed the Morozovskaya–Stalingrad railway, over the Logovsky–Marinovka section. The approach to the pocket was carried out from the south-west. The transports followed the same course on return flights. Landings were carried out not only at Pitomnik and Gumrak, but also directly at the front line. The Russian Air Force carried out almost 700 sorties, pilots reporting 23 downed transport planes. In fact, the Russians again failed to interfere with the operation of the air bridge. The losses of the Luftwaffe amounted to only five aircraft. The Soviet aviation's own losses on this day amounted to 19 aircraft.

On 20 December, German aviation carried out 128 transport flights and delivered 215 tons of cargo. Many crews were working at the limit of their capabilities. For example, the commander of 1./KG100, Hauptman Hans Batcher, made three flights to Pitomnik in one day. The first time his plane took off at 05.20, and landed in the pocket at 06.10. Such speed was possible due to the proximity of the Morozovskaya airfield and the precise organisation of unloading and loading of aircraft in Pitomnik. After resting for one hour, Batcher took to the sky again at 07.05 and returned to Morozovskaya at 08.00. The next sorties took place at 10.15 and 13.25. Each time eight wounded soldiers were loaded on board the He 111 bomber. Thus, during the day, one bomber saved the lives of 24 men. Russian pilots and anti-aircraft gunners overestimated their successes as usual. They reported 27 downed transports, although in fact the Luftwaffe lost only one He 111.

December 21st was one of the most successful days in the operation of the air bridge. Luftflotte 4 carried out 180 transport flights to the pocket, of which half were carried out by bombers, and 362.3 tons of cargo were delivered, including 128 tons of food. At the same time, losses were minimal: only two Ju 52s were disabled at the Pitomnik and Tatsinskaya air bases as a result of Soviet air attacks.

The figures of cargo deliveries seemed to inspire optimism. But for modest successes in supplying the 6th Army, they had to pay the price of reduced air support. Cargo turnover was increased due to He 111 bombers being used. It was customary for experienced crews to fly even in zero visibility, in conditions of strong air defence. The He 111s had powerful defensive weapons, and the pilots were able to navigate in difficult situations and fend off fighters. Therefore, the losses of the bombers were several times lower than those of the transports. But at the same time, they could not support their troops on the battlefield and strike at Russian logistics chains. Thanks to the absence of He 111s in the sky, the Soviets were now able to transport their troops and cargo to the front line without hindrance. This played an important role in the deterioration of the situation.

Meanwhile, the changeable weather created an unsolvable problem for the Luftwaffe. Heavy clouds and snow were better suited for supply flights, but interfered with the actions of Stukas and Zerstörers. And clear weather, on the contrary, was good for attacking ground targets, but created great danger for the flights of transport planes (especially Ju 52s and Ju 86s).

In addition, the food situation in the pocket continued to deteriorate anyway. For example, German soldiers from the 297th Infantry Division in mid-December received only 125 grams of breadcrumbs and horsemeat soup per day. By 20 December, this very modest ration was reduced to 100 grams of biscuit.

Escape from Tatsinskaya and the Beginning of the End

After 21 December, Manstein still had chances to break through to the 6th Army. However, further efforts were prevented by another crisis. On 16 December, the troops of the South-western Front launched an offensive on the Middle Don from the bridgeheads in the Boguchar and Vishenskaya areas. The purpose of the new operation code-named Saturn was Rostov-on-Don, in order to cut off all German troops in the Caucasus and the Southern Don. But at the last moment, Stalin changed the plan, directing the axis of the offensive to the south-east – to the rear of Manstein's troops. With greatly superior forces, the Red Army attacked the positions of the Italian 8th Army. Two days later, the defence in this sector began to collapse rapidly, and hundreds of T-34 tanks raced to the south and south-east. Soon, the German air bases, from which the supply of the 6th Army was carried out, were under threat.

On the morning of 20 December, the crew of a Ju 88D-1 reconnaissance aircraft of 2.(F)/Ob.d.L. received the task: to locate the enemy. The scout took to the sky at 10.55. Due to dense clouds, the flight took place at low level – 300m from the ground. Just 40–50km north of the Tatsinskaya airfield (near the Berezovaya River), the crew noticed some vehicles moving in a southerly direction. After making a circle over the column, the pilots realized that these 'machines' were T-34 tanks! Painted in white camouflage, they rolled across the steppe. At the same time, the second Ju 88D from 2.(F)/Ob.d.L. found another unit of Soviet tanks north of the Tatsinskaya–Morozovskaya railway line.

The next day, Fibig, who was at Tatsinskaya at that time, received another alarming message that Russian tanks had reached the Bystraya River and were on the approaches to the village of Skosyrskaya (25km north of Tatsinskaya). At the same time, the only German unit that covered the road from this village to the air base was a small combat group led by the Chief of Staff of Fliegerkorps VIII, Oberstleutnant von Heinemann. It consisted of only 120 men with one 88mm and six 20mm anti-aircraft guns. A little later, a small army detachment joined the Luftwaffe unit, although it did not have heavy weapons.

On 22 December, the first Soviet reconnaissance group consisting of three tanks appeared at Skosyrskaya. Throughout the day, the Germans managed to hold off the attacks. And from Tatsinskaya, despite the 'suitcase moods' that reigned there (Romanian planes left the base in a hurry, without even consulting with their allies), transports with cargo for the 6th Army continued to take off regularly. At night von Heinemann reported that his group was short of ammunition and reinforcements were not coming, while there were more and more Russians, and the noise of tank engines was growing around them.

The morning of 23 December in Tatsinskaya began in a state of general anxiety. Due to the high humidity, aircraft were already icing at an altitude of 80m, which made Stuka flights impossible, and also made aerial reconnaissance difficult. Immediately after dawn, the headquarters Storch of Fliegerkorps VIII flew to Skosyrskaya. The pilot saw that there was still a battle going on in the village, while there were at least 60 Russian tanks around it. At 10.00 Fibig called Richthofen and reported the situation, but he gave a categorical order – 'premature evacuation is prohibited'. Apparently, someone was still hoping that the situation would somehow miraculously stabilise. However, at noon it became known that Skosyrskaya had been captured by the Red Army, and German units were hurriedly fleeing south across the open steppe. By order of Fibig, the Ju 87s that took off from Morozovskaya attacked Soviet tanks twice, which made it possible to hold them once again.

In the evening, the third – highest – level of combat alert was announced in Tatsinskaya. And at 21.00 it became known that at least three tanks had reached the Tatsinskaya–Morozovskaya railway line, after which telephone communication with the Morozovskaya air base was cut off. It seemed to the Germans that the enemy was about to appear from behind the nearest hill, but instead of the Russians, at 23.00 a German reconnaissance group on armoured personnel carriers appeared out of the ominous-looking northern darkness. They reported that the nearest Russian tanks were still 20km away. This news allowed the exhausted Fibig and members of his staff to go to bed.

But the 'sleep of the dead' of the Luftwaffe commanders in Tatsinskaya was short. Already at 02.00 on 24 December, Fibig spoke on the phone with Richthofen, who congratulated him on being awarded the Knight's Cross. And an hour and a half later, the first shells exploded on the outskirts of Tatsinskaya, one of which destroyed the radio mast. Now 'premature withdrawal' was out of the question! At 04.15, Fibig, who had not had enough sleep, left his dugout and went to the aerodrome to lead the evacuation. The village itself looked completely deserted, and visibility was only 100–200m. All this looked threatening, and the Germans feared that at any moment a tank would appear out of the mist.

At 05.00, the risky task of conducting reconnaissance and establishing the exact location of the Russians was entrusted to Unteroffizier Rudolf Kiesch from 2.(F)/Ob.d.L. His Ju 88D-1 with preheated engines climbed to a low altitude, after which he flew around the northern environs of Tatsinskaya. Despite the darkness and light snow, Kiesch was horrified to see the silhouettes of T-34 tanks standing out well against the background of the steppe. They were already only 5–6km away from his base! When the reconnaissance plane returned there at 05.20, shells were already exploding on the outskirts of the airfield. Only after that – at 05.30 – Fibig gave the order for all planes to take off all and evacuate immediately. Ten minutes later, the first Ju 52 rolled over the snow-covered runway to the start. 'It is impossible even to describe the chaos that was going on there. Snow, minus 35° frost and rings of burnt-out planes around the airfield,' recalled navigator Max Lagoda from 2.(F)/Ob.d.L. However, one cannot believe the emotional memories of soldiers written decades after those events. In fact, the weather was warm that day: the air temperature was about 0°!

At 06.00 the artillery shelling of the airfield intensified, and seven minutes later Major von Burgsdorf from the 16th Panzer Division, who had just arrived, reported to Fibig that there was a wild commotion in the village, Soviet tanks and infantry appeared on the streets, and there was no defence anymore. Meanwhile, despite periodic explosions and the whistling of shells, the planes continued to take off and quickly disappeared into the darkness. Soon it was the turn of the staff Ju 52.

Martin Fibig wrote in his diary: '06.15. Takeoff, Visibility of about 500m, the cloud boundary at 30m. "Junkers" takes off very hard, the right motor is running intermittently . . . Almost the entire flight is blind, it is impossible to climb above the clouds – even at 2400 m there is no upper limit yet. No icing – great luck!' At 07.25, Fibig's plane landed safely at the Rostov-West air base.

After the war, German pilots often described this evacuation from Tatsinskaya as 'indescribable confusion and chaos', accompanied by numerous accidents, as if the Ju 52s rushed to the runways from all corners of the huge airfield at the same time, overtaking and cutting off each other's trajectories, while ground personnel in the same hurry loaded onto vehicles and fled to the south-west. In fact, all 108 aircraft left the base safely, no losses of Ju 52s being recorded that morning!

The KGr.zbV22 aviation group based in Tatsinskaya had a worse time, however. As a result of the late evacuation and the subsequent attack of Soviet tanks, it lost 15 of its Ju 86s at the airfield. KGr.zbV21 was luckier. The bulk of its old aircraft managed to escape, and the Red Army soldiers got only three Ju 86s as trophies.

This moment was the culmination of a Russian tank raid into the German rear. Soon, troops at Tormosin, previously intended for a second attempt to relieve the 6th Army, were transferred to this area. With the powerful support of aviation, including He 111 bombers, the Germans managed to recapture Tatsinskaya, throwing the Red Army back to Skosyrskaya. Morozovskaya also managed to be held, thereby delaying the collapse in this sector of the front. Soon Fibig visited Tatsinskaya again, and for some time German aircraft returned there, primarily ground-attack planes.

On 25 December, it became sharply colder near Stalingrad, the air temperature dropping to -15°. Meanwhile, the 57th Panzer Corps, under the onslaught of the Russian 2nd Guards Army, evacuated the bridgehead on the northern bank of the Myshkova River, retreating to the southern bank. And on 26 December, the assault group began to retreat back to Kotelnikovo. From now on, the fate of the 6th Army was sealed. At the same time, there were the first serious interruptions in the operation of the air bridge. Due to the chaos with the urgent relocation on 24 December, only nine He 111s flew to pocket, delivering only a small amount of cargo. The next day, 49 transport flights were carried out and 78 tons of cargo were delivered.

Due to the changed situation, Yeremenko and Khrushchev issued an order to the troops to immediately proceed with the destruction of the 6th Army. In addition, they demanded that the supply of the pocket by air be interrupted. The commander of the Stalingrad Corps Air Defence Area was instructed to create two lines of anti-aircraft guns on the approaches to the inner ring of the blockade, and the 8th and 16th Air Armies were to strengthen the air blockade, using 50 per cent of their fighters to intercept transport aircraft. By 20 December, there were 235 anti-aircraft guns, as well as 241 anti-aircraft machine guns in the western part of the blockade ring. For the Russians, accustomed to firing only barrage fire, it was not too much.

Until Christmas, when the officers and soldiers of the 6th Army believed in imminent rescue from the outside, relative order and discipline reigned in the pocket. The situation was somewhat reminiscent of what happened on the famous liner *Titanic*. After the huge and 'unsinkable' ship collided with an iceberg, most of the crew and passengers did not show much concern. In the first minutes, everyone was sure that everything would be fine with the ship, it would definitely not sink, and help would surely arrive. However, when the trim on the bow began to increase, the boats began to descend, and obvious anxiety appeared on the faces of the sailors, then a slight panic, which intensified every minute. When the bow of the ship began to sink into the water, and there were no signs of outside help, the liner was seized with chaos and confusion . . . So, the Christmas days in Stalingrad roughly corresponded to the situation of the *Titanic*, when people realized that they could drown! The anxiety on the faces of Paulus and his staff was transmitted to the commanders of corps and divisions, from them to the commanders of regiments and battalions. The soldiers, seeing the deteriorating mood of the officers, gradually realized that the Führer might not help them.

The change of mood was felt especially clearly in the places where planes were boarding. The report of the pilot Weltner from KG27 (*Versorgungseinsätze nach Stalingrad*) stated:

> The number of wounded taken with them was determined depending on the condition of walking or only lying down. On average, we invited 12–18 wounded people to our plane, depending on their condition. During the return flight, they were in a euphoric mood. They believed that nothing else could happen, and they were saved. The soldiers seemed surprisingly calm in this situation. Severe weather conditions, insufficient nutrition and constant fighting caused indifference mixed with physical infirmity. Therefore, most of the soldiers were unable to think clearly. It was different with the wounded, with whom we personally contacted during loading and who had a 'return ticket'. They clearly had a strong will to live thanks to the possession of 'tickets' for the

return flight. Despite their more or less serious injury, and despite their fatigue, in many cases they were cheerful and used every opportunity to take a seat on the plane. If, due to the overload of the aircraft, this hope was not justified, their mood became aggressive. They strove with force and recklessness to make their way to the plane. To prevent such events, we supplied bread and part of our onboard food to the troops, who had to organise the loading of the wounded, as well as monitor the wounded. It happened that some of the wounded clung to the entrance hatch (under the fuselage of the aircraft) and curled up, so that take-off was impossible.

The situation of the 6th Army was getting worse. Not only food, but also firewood became scarce in the huge pocket. A third of the soldiers lived in bunkers and basements, while many slept in dugouts among the bare steppe. In December, countless cases of frostbite began and thousands of soldiers froze to death. Of particular concern was the situation of the huge number of wounded. Hundreds of them were taken to the Pitomnik airfield, where they waited for evacuation right in the snow, often dying of cold. Even experienced bomber crews returning to the pocket were really shocked by what they saw there. Nothing like this had been seen in Demyansk.

Before the New Year, the work of the air bridge began to improve again. On 27 December, the Luftwaffe performed 95 flights to Stalingrad, and from the 29th, for the first time, the pocket was supplied at night. On that day, 106 transport flights were carried out and 124.2 tons of cargo were delivered, including 10 tons of sweets for Christmas. The Russian pilots were still powerless to prevent this. On 29 December, they reported 20 downed transport planes. In fact, five Ju 52s were lost, but only one of them fell victim to a Russian fighter.

On 30 December, 91 flights to the pocket were carried out. At the same time, some of the transports landed not on airfields, but directly at infantry positions. For example, at 10.00 in the area of a subsidiary farm (in the northern sector of the pocket), 10 Ju 52s landed. Between 13.40 and 15.40, 13 transport planes landed near the Drevny Val railway station (in the north-eastern part of the pocket). 224.9 tons of cargo were delivered, including 62 tons of food.

By the end of the year, the condition of the bomber squadrons that provided the air bridge had deteriorated significantly. Due to constant breakdowns and heavy wear, fewer and fewer planes remained in combat-ready condition. For example, in KG27, as of 30 November there were 64 He 111s, including 27 serviceable ones. A month later,

KG27 had 56 aircraft, of which only 15 were operational. But the lack of aircraft was compensated for by the dedication of the German pilots. On 31 December, the Luftwaffe carried out 177 flights. At the same time, the commander of 1./KG100, Hauptman Hans Batcher, flew to Pitomnik three times alone. The bomber delivered almost 4 tons of petrol to the encircled troops and took out 24 wounded soldiers.

Chapter 12

THE BRIDGE TO
THE 'AFTERLIFE'

The Führer prayed to God

On 1 January 1943, the soldiers of the 6th Army received a 'New Year's greeting' from Hitler from the Wolfsschanze. It spoke of the 'enormous military successes of Germany', the current situation and the need to hold the defence on all fronts until complete victory. Then the atheist Führer suddenly remembered God . . . 'God spare Europe, if the conspiracy of the Jews succeeds, then Europe will definitely perish. 1943 will be a difficult year, but certainly not harder than the previous one. If the Lord gave us the strength to overcome the winter of 1941 – 1942, then we will hold out this winter and the coming year,' the Führer urged his soldiers. It is characteristic that Hitler did not mention National Socialism in his New Year's proclamation. And in conclusion, he urged everyone to pray for victory: 'We hope, praying to the Lord God, that he will bless us this year, as in the past.'

Richthofen was having tea with Fibig that day. Both were also seized with 'lyrical' thoughts. 'Everything is not so bad if it were not for the ghost of how the fate of the 6th Army will affect all other cases of encirclement,' the commander of Fliegerkorps VIII wrote in his diary. Fibig was surprised why the Soviets had not yet crushed the pocket and stopped the air bridge. The German commanders again overestimated the power of the Red Army! From 19 November 1942 to 4 January 1943, the Russian 8th Air Army lost 309 aircraft, including 145 ground-attack planes, 140 fighters and 24 bombers. Of these, 131 were shot down by German fighters, 60 by anti-aircraft artillery and 66 were missing. Russian aviation was once again defeated.

Meanwhile, the situation was getting worse for the Germans. By 1 January, the nearest units of Army Group Don were still 115km from the inner ring of the blockade. At the same time, the Red Army continued to throw new divisions into battle and pushed the Germans everywhere. On 2 January, the Germans had to evacuate the Morozovskaya air base. At the same time, trains (several hundred wagons) with cargo prepared for the 6th Army were destroyed at the railway station: 3,000 tons of ammunition, 1,500 tons of grain, 540 tons of flour, 200 tons of canned meat and 12 tons of marmalade were lost.

From that moment on, Salsk became the nearest airfield to Stalingrad, and the He 111 bombers relocated to Novocherkassk. The distance to the Nursery from there was 300–330km, almost at the limit of the range of the Ju 52/3m. Naturally, this led to a reduction in the amount of payload in each aircraft. Fuel overspending and excessive engine wear led to the fact that more and more aircraft were under repair and could not participate in the operation. The old He 111Es, He 111Fs and He 111Ps had to be withdrawn from the air bridge altogether, since their range did not allow them to fly to the pocket and back. If the plane was unable to land at Pitomnik and refuel, it might not have enough fuel for the return flight, although some pilots still took this risk.

In the first days of January, the weather was warm and cloudy in the Stalingrad area. On average, 123 tons of cargo were delivered to the 'fortress' per day. However, the needs of the encircled group had also changed in comparison with the end of November. The 6th Army needed less food due to losses and evacuation of some people by air. But at the same time, the need for ammunition and fuel had increased, the stocks of which having greatly decreased due to the fighting.

On 8 January, the Soviet command presented Paulus with an ultimatum, in which it offered the 6th Army the chance to capitulate. The text also mentioned the work of the air bridge.

The German transport aviation, which carries you starvation rations of food, ammunition and fuel, due to the rapid advance of the Red Army, is often forced to change their bases and fly into the pocket from afar. In addition, the German transport aviation suffers huge losses in aircraft from the attacks of Soviet aviation. Her help to the encircled troops becomes unreal. The situation of your surrounded troops is difficult. They experience hunger, sickness and cold. The harsh Russian winter is just beginning. Severe snowstorms, frosts and cold winds are still coming . . .

If they surrendered, the soldiers and officers of the 6th Army were promised comfortable conditions, food and medical care. For Paulus, this was the last chance to save the lives of many men. But Hitler's devoted and at the same time indecisive general, of course, did not take it.

Until 10 January, despite the difficulties, the overall situation in the pocket remained relatively stable. The 6th Army firmly held a huge defensive perimeter, and there was quite heavy vehicle traffic within it. The air bridge also functioned relatively stably. In addition, the weather was comfortable, without severe frosts. Hitler was sure that the 6th Army would hold out for another couple of months, and maybe longer. And he promised to rescue it . . . next spring.

German combat losses were surprisingly small. According to the chief quartermaster of the 6th Army, Oberstleutnant Werner von Kunowski, for the period from 23 November 1942 to 10 January 1943, losses amounted to only 5,000 killed and missing. During the same time, about 20,000 wounded were evacuated by air. As a result, by 10 January, there were approximately 195,000 people in the pocket.

Meanwhile, the air bridge was significantly strengthened. The four-engined planes promised by Hitler arrived, as well as new bomber units. On 10 January, in order to improve the supply of 'Festung Stalingrad', the 2nd Air Transport Command (Lufttransportführer II – LTF II) was formed in Voroshilovgrad (now Lugansk). It was led by the commander of KG27 Oberst Henning von Beust, with Stab./KG27, III./KG4, II./KG53, 15./KG6, KGr.zbV20 and KGr.zbV23 under him. LTF I (Oberst Kuhl) consisted of Stab./KG55, I./KG55, III./KG55, I./KG27, II./KG27, III./KG27 and I./KG100.

But these measures were too late. On 10 January, the situation in the Stalingrad area changed dramatically. In the morning, the Red Army launched an offensive simultaneously on the north-western and southern sectors of the perimeter. The plan of Operation Koltso ('Ring') was to capture the Pitomnik air base with converging strikes and divide the 6th Army into two isolated units. Despite hunger and lack of ammunition, the Germans again put up desperate resistance around the perimeter, and in some places even launched fierce counter-attacks. As a result, in the first two days of the offensive alone, the Don Front lost 8,000 killed and wounded!

On 12 January, the period of relatively warm weather finally ended, and frosts struck. On this day, the Red Army finally managed to break through the front in the western part of the pocket and capture Karpovka. There, surprised Russian soldiers (who were also permanently starving due to lack of supplies) discovered that the 6th Army had a lot more supplies! In Karpovka, they seized two warehouses full of ammunition. There were 3,000 shells, 53,000 rounds of ammunition, 3,700 mortar shells and a large number of weapons. In the south-western sector, the 57th Army captured Rokotino. The Germans unsuccessfully tried to hold a new line of defence along the banks of the Rossoshka and Chervlennaya rivers, but it was no longer possible to hold back the hordes of Red Army soldiers advancing with shouts of 'hurrah'. Returning to the comparison with the sinking *Titanic*, this moment roughly corresponded to the beginning of the final phase of the drama, when the bows of the ship were under water, and the stern, on the contrary, began to rise out of the water. It became finally clear to Paulus' staff and all the commanders that the days of the 6th Army were numbered, and the collapse was only a matter of time (and a short time).

On 15 January, it got colder, dropping to -28° in the Stalingrad area. The 'real Russian frosts' had come, which the recent ultimatum had mentioned. For the Germans, it was worse than the attacking soldiers of the Red Army. On this day, the advanced units of the Soviet 21st Army broke through to the Dubinin farm and Dairy Farm, after which only 4km remained to the Pitomnik air base. To the south, the 57th Army captured Basargino and also advanced to the east.

'A Ring of Dead Metal'

Trying to improve the situation, Hitler took new administrative measures. He ordered Field Marshal Erhard Milch to fly urgently to Taganrog and personally head the command of the air bridge to Stalingrad. The Führer gave this not particularly intelligent, but very active and restless, officer extraordinary powers. Arriving at Luftflotte 4 headquarters on 16 January, Milch hastily formed a special staff there named after himself (Sonderstab Gen.Feldm. Milch). He immediately tried to increase the number of departures in the pocket by various 'administrative' methods. In particular, Milch threatened to personally shoot the officers who allegedly 'disrupted' the supply of the 6th Army. The Field Court of the VIII Air Corps (Das Feldgericht des VIII. Fliegerkorps) was ordered to interrogate 'in court' all the crews who, instead of landing in the pocket, dropped their cargo by parachute. The court had to find out whether a landing was possible or whether there was 'cowardice in the face of the enemy'? In addition, it was necessary to interrogate the pilots who landed in order to obtain reliable information about the state of the airfields in the pocket.

However, these 'harsh measures' were also too late. On 16 January, it got colder, dropping to -32° in the Stalingrad area. On this terrible morning for the 6th Army, an event occurred that finally doomed it. Shortly after dawn, the soldiers of the Russian 298th Rifle Division launched another attack. This time they met no resistance. In the foggy morning haze, the soldiers found only trucks, guns and tanks frozen into the ground. Moving quickly forward, at 09.00 the Red Army soldiers saw a truly apocalyptic spectacle. Dozens of wrecked and damaged planes of various types were standing in a huge space. Many of them were already covered with snow and resembled frozen prehistoric monsters. This unprecedented cemetery of aviation technology stretched for several kilometres into the distance. Anti-aircraft guns stuck out just as motionless; their barrels covered with frost were pointed at the frosty sky. Even more, the soldiers were struck by a giant cluster of 'dead' trucks – there were thousands of them! This was Pitomnik air base, which the German pilots called 'A ring of dead metal'.

In total, the Red Army, according to Russian reports, seized 13,000 vehicles, 1,632 motorcycles, 270 tanks and self-propelled guns, 70 anti-aircraft guns, 350 bicycles and about 300 aircraft in the area of the airfield (almost all of them were faulty). The retreating troops abandoned several ammunition and food depots, as well as two hospitals full of wounded. These poor devils were definitely not destined to return to Germany . . .

On the external front, the situation was also catastrophic for the Germans. On 14 January, the Red Army launched an offensive against the Hungarian 2nd Army south of Voronezh and immediately broke through the defence. The German 2nd Army was already under the threat of complete encirclement. At first, Hitler planned to ban withdrawal in this sector as well and declare Voronezh another 'fortress'! But he no longer had any aircraft at his disposal that could be used for another air bridge. This fact made the Führer more compliant, and soon (albeit belatedly) he gave permission to retreat from Voronezh. In the sector of Army Group Don, the Red Army also continued to advance. On 16 January, the Germans had to evacuate the Salsk air base. The Ju 52 transport groups were once again forced to change their location. They flew to Zverevo airfield (north of the city of Shakhty). Now the 6th Army was separated from the nearest Wehrmacht positions by 275km.

Meanwhile, there were only two airfields left in the pocket that were suitable for landing transport aircraft. These were 'Stalingradsky', which was a small site in the west of Stalingrad, and Gumrak, located

12km north-west of the city centre. Stalingradsky was a civilian airfield where passenger planes landed before the war, while Gumrak was a military airfield where Russian fighters were based until August 1942.

But the problem was that both airfields were in a neglected state. The headquarters of the 6th Army had not expected the sudden loss of Pitomnik, and had not bothered to prepare a reserve air base. This is how feldwebel Ospel from II./KG27 described the condition of Gumrak, who landed there at 11.45 on 16 January:

> The runway in Gumrak consisted of rolled tracks about 400m long, 5–10m wide. The tractor with the roller was still working in the snow. Outside of the rolled track, the snow lay about knee-deep. To the south of the runway lay the wreckage of Bf 109s and Ju 87s. There were craters in the vast expanses around and some planes were parked. The bomb craters at the airfield were filled in. There was no landing cross. A cross made of canvas signs lay outside the runway in the northern part of the airfield. The starting post and the turn signal to the unloading point were missing. Landing was difficult due to the short length of the runway, not very firm snow and surrounding pits. The place is unsuitable for night landings. Unloading teams were not in place. The crew unloaded the plane on their own. There was a fuel tanker for refuelling. The organisation of unloading, the allocation of the wounded for the return flight could not be found.

However, for the Luftwaffe, all this was not an insurmountable problem. German pilots were used to improvising and working even in the most difficult conditions. Therefore, the very next day – 17 January – the work of the air bridge was resumed. For example, Hauptmann Karl Mayer's He 111 bomber from III./KG27 took off from Novocherkassk at 12.30, and landed in Gumrak at 14.05. The plane came in from the south over the village of Beketovka. The crew unloaded the plane on their own, took 10 wounded soldiers on board and at 14.55 set off on the return flight. At 16.10 – already in the dark – the bomber returned to Novocherkassk. The He 111 of the Oberleutnant Thofehern from III./KG27 took off from Novocherkassk at 12.30 and landed in Gumrak at 14.00. The plane passed over Beketovka at an altitude of 4,500m, after which it began to spiral down to the airfield. Fifteen minutes after landing, the officers who organised the unloading arrived. Then the Luftwaffe staff doctor came up, who regulated the boarding of the wounded on the plane. At 15.00, the bomber took off and landed safely in Novocherkassk at 16.20.

Starting the engines and taxiing to the start was complicated by completely desperate wounded who did not get seats in the planes.

Some of them lay down in front of the undercarriage, blocking traffic. Mayer recalled:

> It was established that the garrison of the 'fortress', including the officers, thought that the German relief troops were in front of Kalach-on-Don. The crews of the aircraft did not give any information to questions about where the front line was located. It should be feared that when the real state of affairs becomes known, the onslaught on landing planes will have to be repelled by force of arms.

Despite the catastrophic situation, many officers and men of the 6th Army at that moment still believed in the 'Führer's genius' and possible salvation. They thought that the Wehrmacht was doing everything possible for this. In fact, in mid-January, the German command had already finally put an end to the 6th Army. It was concerned only with a more important task – how to stabilise the collapsing front, plug huge gaps and save other armies from captivity, including those withdrawing from the Caucasus. Manstein and Hitler cynically called on the 6th Army to fight so that it would tie down as many Russian troops as possible and prevent them from being prematurely transferred to other sectors. Freezing and starving soldiers had to make a sacrifice to save the Eastern Front from collapse. And they carried out this mission! As of 10 January the troops of the Don Front operating against the 6th Army numbered 280,000 men (210,000 soldiers), 23,600 guns and mortars, 9,300 vehicles, 41,000 horses, 254 tanks and 222 anti-aircraft guns. At the same time, the Soviet troops suffered quite heavy losses. In the period from 10 to 15 January alone, the armies of the Don Front lost 5,500 soldiers killed and 16,000 wounded.

On 17 January, the 6th Army, gradually retreating to the east, occupied the former inner boundary of the Stalingrad fortified area. This defence perimeter had been hastily built last summer 15–20km west of Stalingrad to deter the advancing German troops. Now it was the other way around: the Red Army was advancing from the west, and the Germans were defending in the east!

'The worst betrayal in German history'

Despite the fact that the German pilots made every possible effort to supply the dying 6th Army and made great sacrifices, its headquarters, headed by Paulus, was extremely dissatisfied with their actions. He considered the traffic insufficient and was outraged that many planes dropped cargo from the air instead of unloading on the ground. Forbidding himself to seriously think about who was truly responsible for the disaster, Paulus and his entourage were looking for culprits, who, in their opinion, were not in the top leadership at all! The commander of the 6th Army once again contacted Manstein and categorically demanded that a Luftwaffe officer 'with the rank of no lower than general' be sent to him for talks. Manstein called Richthofen, who turned to Milch with this question. They decided not to put generals at risk, and the commander of III./KG27, Major Erich Thiel, was sent to the headquarters of the 6th Army. This officer was well acquainted with the situation; he had been to pocket more than once.

On the morning of 19 January, Thiel flew to Stalingrad at the head of the He 111 group. The flight took place in heavy cloud at an altitude of 1,500–2,000m. Guided by the beacon, the bombers reached their destination. From a height of 1,500m, Gumrak was clearly visible from the accumulation of crashed planes and a lot of craters around the runway. Shortly after the planes landed (at 11.00), 10 Russian planes appeared overhead. But anti-aircraft artillery was still operating in Gumrak, and they did not dare to attack lower than from a height of 800–1,000m.

To his surprise, Thiel saw complete desolation at the air base. Neither unloading teams nor soldiers were visible, and numerous 'food bombs', which were delivered here by German pilots at the risk of their lives, were lying everywhere, half covered with snow. Soon the major found himself in Paulus' headquarters dugout, which was still in the Gumrak area. In addition to the commander, the meeting was attended by the Chief of Staff of the 6th Army, Generalleutnant Schmidt, Commander of the 51st Army Corps General von Seydlitz, Oberst Elhlepp, Oberst Rosenfeld and Oberleutnant Kolbenschlag. In response to the claims about the poor operation of the airfield, Paulus burst out with angry curses. He said that every plane that landed save the lives of 1,000 people, while dumping cargo containers did not bring any benefit. Many of them were simply not found, and the army no longer had fuel for vehicles to collect them. The commander of the 6th Army stated:

> The last horses have been eaten. Can you imagine soldiers pouncing on an old horse carcass, opening its head and eating its brains raw? What will I, as the commander-in-chief of the army, say when a person comes to me and asks, Mr. General-Oberst, for a piece of bread? – Why did the Luftwaffe promise that the supply would be carried out? Who is the responsible person who chose this opportunity? If I had been told that it was impossible, I would not have blamed the Luftwaffe, because then

I could have broken through, then when the Russians broke through, I was strong enough to break out of the pocket and today it's too late.

Generalleutnant Schmidt was even more categorical, actually blaming the air force for the impending death of the army: 'And so you come here and want to justify the Luftwaffe, who committed the worst betrayal ever committed in German history? It must have been suggested to the Führer by someone? The Luftwaffe betrayed us, and this is a crime against the 6th Army!'

'The landing in the pocket must be carried out, even if the plane crashes at the same time,' Paulus continued his accusatory speech.

> So the Luftwaffe did not fulfil their duty. It cannot be left to the discretion of the crews whether they can land or not, but they must be ordered that if someone does not comply with this order, he will be court-martialled! The Führer promised me that he and the entire German people feel responsible for the army, and now this is the most terrible tragedy in German military history, because the Luftwaffe failed . . . Look at the people, how they certainly do their duty, because they don't even know the truth.

At the end of the conversation, he told the pilot that he was talking to him from the afterlife, because he was practically dead already . .

Thiel, dejected by what he heard, returned to his plane. It was still not unloaded, but it was already badly damaged by artillery fire, and the flight mechanic had been killed! From 15.00 groups of three to four Polikarpov U-2 light bombers began to circle over the airfield. This continued until night. The weather was cloudless, and the bright moonlight illuminated the 'afterlife' landscape of Gumrak well. Thiel saw how the plane taxied to the start was immediately covered with bombs. U-2s continued to circle over the airfield until 22.00, replacing each other. Only when the snow started falling, the Russians flew away. After that, the familiar hum of engines was heard from the darkness and a single Ju 52 landed. After unloading, 20 wounded were taken on board, Major Thiel going with them. The Ju 52 took off safely and delivered them to Zverevo airfield.

Thiel's conversation with Paulus, the report of which is stored in the archive of Kamfgeschwader 27, actually became a kind of last 'interview' of the commander of the 6th Army before his captivity. The next officially documented conversation with his participation will take place under completely different circumstances!

On the night of 19/20 January, a large number of aircraft landed in the pocket (KG27 alone completed 28 sorties). The last day when many planes landed in the pocket was 21 January. KG27 alone carried out 33 transport flights at that time. Hauptmann Meyer wrote in his report: 'The location of Gumrak could only be found by secondary landmarks. The direction finder itself was overloaded, but it worked satisfactorily. A beacon beeped at the airfield. The airfield area was clearly visible on a moonlit night. The runway was marked with green and white lights. The landing was extremely difficult and feasible only for good crews.'

The commander of the 4th Army Corps, General Erwin Jaenecke, was among the lucky ones taken out on return flights to the 'mainland'. The day before, he was very fortunately wounded by shrapnel, without receiving serious injuries, but received a legitimate reason to leave the 'fortress'. In this regard, many officers who knew Jaenecke told the story that he somehow feigned injury in order to escape from the already imminent Soviet captivity. Subsequently, the general played an important role in the defence of the Kuban bridgehead and the Crimea, but he still could not escape his 'military fate'. After the end of the war, Jaenecke was taken to the USSR, convicted and sent to hard labour. There he experienced even greater hardships than his colleagues from the pocket, who were kept in relatively comfortable conditions, and returned home later than many of them – in 1955.

Earlier, the completely healthy commander of the 14th Panzer Corps, General Hans Hube, was also taken out. But he left Stalingrad on the direct orders of Hitler. When the Führer's favourite refused to evacuate voluntarily ('I can't leave my soldiers'), a detachment of the dictator's personal guard flew after him on a specially allocated Ju 52, who Hitler directly admonished: 'Do not return without Hube'! As a result, the men literally pushed the one-armed general into the plane and delivered him safely directly to Hitler's headquarters.

The third German general who managed to escape capture was Wolfgang Pickert. On 13 January, he flew out of the pocket in his personal plane to meet with Richthofen. And then, after several attempts, he 'could not return', stating that 'it was not possible to land'. Then Milch appeared, with whom Pickert had been well acquainted since the early 1930s. The Field Marshal openly took advantage of his official position to save his friend from predictable 'troubles' and appointed him another officer 'responsible for the supply of the fortress'. However, not from the inside, but from the outside! Oberstleutnant Richard Heitzman was appointed commander of the 9th Anti-Aircraft Division (see below).

Despite all the difficulties and hardships, the 6th Army continued to fight and fulfil its sacrificial mission. From 15 to 20 January, the Don Front lost 6,000 soldiers killed and missing, and another 16,000 were wounded. Thus, in 10 days of fighting, the Red Army lost 32,000 men in the Stalingrad area (15 per cent of its soldiers). But the situation for the Germans continued to deteriorate rapidly. On 22 January, the front was breached in the north-western part of the narrowed pocket. At 15.00, the 51st and 52nd Guards Rifle Divisions of the 21st Army reached the vicinity of the village of Gumrak. In the south, the Russians captured Voroponovo. Now the length of pocket from west to east had been reduced to 20km.

On 23 January, there was frosty and cloudy weather in the Stalingrad area. Soviet soldiers were already 700m from the village of Gumrak. In this regard, German planes trying to land had to choose other sites. One of the crews of KG27 reported:

> After the Gumrak airfield was in the hands of the Russians, we landed in a nearby village on a deeply snow-covered field, along the edge of which the remnants of the troops were moving. The site was marked only with a red landing cross. Shortly after landing, the wheels sank into the snow almost to the axles, so that the plane almost overturned. How would we get out of here?! Several other planes were already in place with broken landing gear after they drove into the craters from the explosions. Our plane was quickly unloaded, I got a fuel tanker and drained so much fuel that it was enough just for the return flight. Suddenly, a crowd of fleeing soldiers in a panic tried to storm our plane to get out of pocket. With pistols, we could still restrain them. Then we invited several seriously injured people and the crew of the damaged plane. Then we rolled to the start. Suddenly, we were attacked by Russian fighters! One burst of shells passed 50 meters in front of us, Ivan did not calculate. It was our salvation! I was rolling slowly over a slightly uneven surface. I tried to lift the plane, but it barely broke away from the snow.

The bomber narrowly avoided disaster, and then by a miracle did not touch the high-voltage line. But the pilot still managed to take off, and then immediately disappeared into the low-hanging clouds that protected him from the Soviet fighters who were waiting around. This He 111 safely reached its air base.

At night, the headquarters of Fliegerkorps VIII received a shocking, albeit expected, message from the pocket: 'There are no more landing opportunities.' On 24 January, the Russians broke into Gumrak, where they seized another 'cemetery' of 120 aircraft of various types, 3,200 vehicles, several ammunition depots and two hospitals crammed with wounded 6th Army soldiers. On this day, Russian airspace observers recorded only 40 transport planes dropping cargo by parachute. Among them were again bombers from KG27. In the Stalingrad area, they came under heavy anti-aircraft fire. As a result, an He 111 from the 9th Staffel was damaged. The pilot, Oberleutnant Gunther Schuldt, had his elbow pierced by a shell. The navigator and the radio operator managed to take control of the plane, blindly bring it to German territory and make a night emergency landing! The 22-year-old Schuldt was sent to a hospital in Taganrog (Lazarett Lw 7/IV). However, the young man was disappointed with his 'military fate'. He did not want to return home a cripple (instead of a hero with an Iron Cross) and appear in such a 'shameful form' in front of his beloved and his family. Therefore, on the evening of 28 January, he shot himself . . .. although the soldiers of the 6th Army could only envy Gunther. Many of them were ready to give an arm and even both legs, just to get a chance to escape from Hell!

Returning again to the comparison with the sinking *Titanic*, by this time a phase had begun in the drama of the 6th Army corresponding to the splitting of the liner's hull into two parts. While the front part was rapidly plunged into the cold abyss, the passengers who had accumulated on the stern were still waiting for their fate. So, the 'passengers' of Stalingrad now clearly understood that the denouement was very close. Some resigned themselves to their fate, others continued to fight to delay the inevitable finale, others came up with various, including the most fantastic escape plans.

On 25 January, a group of three German soldiers, escorted by a Red Army soldier, appeared at the NKVD post near the Karpovskaya railway station. They was travelling in a westerly direction towards Kalach. One of the Russians asked the soldier: 'Where are you taking these prisoners?' In response, there was only a strange mumbling . . On inspection, it turned out that the 'convoy' was a German disguised in Red Army equipment, and the 'prisoners' were officers of the staff of the 9th Anti-Aircraft Division and its commander Oberstleutnant Richard Heitzman! After he formally assumed command of a division that no longer actually existed, he developed a thorough escape plan from pocket. Under the guise of 'prisoners', his group managed to walk 35km in the direction of Kalach, from where they were going to go further in the direction of Rostov-on-Don. According to some reports, it was an unteroffizier from the 9th Anti-Aircraft Division who became the only German soldier who managed to walk through the blockade ring and reach the positions of German troops. However, it has not yet been possible to establish the authenticity of this and the name of the lucky one.

In the following days, individual German soldiers continued to try to break out of the pocket. For example, a Soviet truck with a closed body drove through the positions of the 57th Army from the central part of the city. Its cabin was covered with suspended metal sheets. The soldiers did not shoot at it, thinking that it was the Russians who were 'having fun'. Half an hour later, in the area of the Sklyarov farm, this truck was detained by patrols. There were 12 German officers in it, trying to head west.

Meanwhile, on 25 January, the Soviets finally pushed the remnants of the 6th Army to the western outskirts of Stalingrad. At the same time, the first German units began to surrender. In the evening, the remnants of the 297th Infantry Division and the 20th Romanian Infantry Division led by Generals Drebber and Dimitriou, as well as the 6th Liaison Regiment, surrendered. In total, by this time the Red Army had already captured 17,500 prisoners, and along the way released 2,500 Red Army soldiers from German captivity. But the attackers still suffered heavy losses from the fought 6th Army. From 20 to 25 January, the Don Front lost 16,000 soldiers killed and wounded: another 519 died from frostbite.

After the loss of Gumrak, the last runway for transport aircraft became the Central Airfield (the Germans called it 'Stalingradsky'). Survivors of the battle often referred to it as a 'small ground' on the western outskirts of the city. In fact, it was a normal city airfield, it was just that during the previous battles it suffered a lot of damage. On the surviving part, they only managed to somehow clear the snow. The landing lights there consisted of several dim lamps, and only the bravest and most experienced crews could land. Nevertheless, at least 12 bombers from KG27 managed to land at Stalingradsky before it was lost. Exact information about when and which of the German planes was the last to take off from the pocket has not been preserved.

Mission impossible: Save Paulus?

On 26 January, the last phase of the protracted battle began. In the morning, the 51st Guards Rifle Division 'Voroshilov', which had previously captured Gumrak, broke into Stalingrad from the west and joined units of the 62nd Army in the 'Red October' residential district. The pocket was split into two isolated parts. German soldiers spontaneously surrendered in droves, but many fanatics continued to put up fierce resistance.

German planes continued to drop cargo containers at night. On the night of 26/27 January, 142 aircraft flew to Stalingrad, of which 120 reached the objective and dropped cargo. The crews reported that the cargo drop points were marked and clearly visible, and radio beacons also work periodically. The next day, during a regular meeting, Milch demanded, no matter what, that the 'Fortress' continue to be supplied. On the night of 27/28 January, 80 aircraft dropped cargo containers, and the next night 110. On 26 January only nine bombers from KG27 flew to the pocket, 21 on the next day, 18 on the 28th and 19 on the 29th.

On the night of 29/30 January, 150 planes flew to the city, of which 124 managed to detect signals from the ground and drop containers. One of the crews from 2./KG27 reported:

> In the city, cargo drop points were marked with bonfires. Not far from the target, we dropped the gas and began to descend in a gliding flight. Acoustically controlled Russian anti-aircraft searchlights wildly rotated back and forth, not taking their eyes off us. At the destination, containers with food, as well as boxes with ammunition from the entrance hatch were dropped from about 50 meters high. Something may have fallen into the hands of Ivan, it is unknown. In 'gratitude' he rewarded us with a hell of a fireworks for this. However, we kept coming back safe and sound. In the last actions, we no longer saw military sense, but, at most, a friendly service for valiant fighters in a cruel city.

On this day, Paulus sent a congratulatory telegram to the Führer on the anniversary of the day the Nazis came to power, in which he loyally reported that 'the swastika flag is still flying over Stalingrad.' In response, the grateful Hitler sent a radio message about the assignment of the rank of Generalfeldmarschall to Paulus. At the same time, with the Führer's sanction, he actually handed over command of the 6th Army to the commander of the 71st Infantry Division, Friedrich Roske, who was urgently promoted to Generalmajor. Thus, Hitler legally relieved Paulus of responsibility for the fate of the remaining troops and the likely surrender.

According to the popular version, the assignment of field marshal's rank was a direct hint to commit suicide. But there is reason to believe that Hitler did not want Paulus to commit suicide at all, but wanted to evacuate him from the pocket at the last moment! The fact is that according to the status and German military traditions, a field marshal could no longer command a single army. Consequently, he could leave Stalingrad with a clear conscience to be appointed to a new post. A curious fact found by the author indicates the preparation for this mission.

On 28 January, Russian reconnaissance planes flew around the city at low level. At the same time, the pilots noticed that in the Dynamo stadium, located next to the railway station, the ground was being hurriedly cleared. The next day, a Yak-1 troika from the 629th IAP specially flew to this place to check the information. The pilots again made sure that the clearing of the landing site at the stadium was almost finished and it is ready to receive aircraft. At the same time, one of the reconnaissance planes was hit by fire from the ground.

Dynamo Stadium was located 300m from the building where the last headquarters of the 6th Army was located. Probably, it was there that the Germans planned to fit out the last landing strip for aircraft. The stadium was not suitable for landing He 111 bombers and Ju 52s transports, but a small Fi 156 Storch could have landed there! According to Martin Fibig's diary, on 25 January, the possibility of a Fi 156 landing in Stalingrad 'for the removal of important persons' was discussed at a meeting with Milch. Not only the Dynamo Stadium could be suitable for landing and take-off, but also a wide area near the department store. To do this, it had to be cleared of debris, bomb craters filled in and landing lights prepared. Perhaps Hitler intended to take out of the city not only Paulus, but also some other figures.

In addition to the Fi 156, only one German aircraft, the Ar 232, could perform such a mission. It had a special multi-wheeled chassis that allowed it to land on any flat ground, and Luftflotte 4 had such planes at its disposal! A pair of Ar 232s together with a pair of six-engined Me 323Ds passed combat tests on the Eastern Front. There is no information that these planes flew in to pocket, but they definitely delivered cargo to the front airfields of the Luftwaffe.

Almost all books about Stalingrad claim that Paulus' last refuge was the basement of the Central Department Store. This information is given in the memoirs of his adjutant Wilhelm Adam, as well as in many Soviet books. There is even a corresponding memorial plaque on the preserved building of the department store. However, in the official report of the Don Front on the capture of Paulus, it is reported that this happened in the building of the Executive Committee of the Stalingrad Regional Council! Outwardly, it was very similar to a department store and was located in the next block (it has not been preserved to the present day). Most likely, the evacuation of Paulus really was planned. But in all likelihood there was simply not enough time to prepare for this extremely risky mission. Already in the evening of 30 January, Russian assault groups reached the vicinity of the Executive Committee building, completely surrounding the headquarters of the 6th Army.

Meanwhile, the flights of transport planes continued despite everything. On the night of 30/31 January, Russian air surveillance posts observed at least 15 aircraft dropping cargo containers in the vicinity of the Stalingrad Tractor Plant. In fact, KG27 alone carried out 13 flights to pocket that night, and 110 planes flew to the city in total, 85 of them dropping containers on designated cargo drop points. 'There is wild disorder in the southern cauldron, chaotic firing of flares,' Fibig wrote in his diary. The effectiveness of this mission was hardly high, for which the Luftwaffe made another sacrifice. The four-engined FW-200C-3 'F8+GW', which descended to a low altitude to dump containers, was shot down by ground fire. The burning Condor crashed in the vicinity of Stalingrad. The crew of the four-engined Ju 290V2 was much luckier, which was also damaged by ground fire while flying at low altitude over Stalingrad, but was able to reach friendly territory (and it was already quite far away!). The huge plane was badly damaged during an emergency landing in Kharkiv, but the pilots were unhurt.

In the morning, the Executive Committee building was surrounded by units of the 38th Motorised Rifle Brigade of Colonel Burmakov. After a short negotiation at 10.00 (Moscow time), a group of Soviet officers led by the Chief of Staff of the 64th Army, Major General I.A. Laskin, entered the basement where Paulus was and arrested him.

But the 6th Army continued to fight by inertia. The air bridge also continued to work. On the night of 1 February, 110 planes flew to pocket, most of them dropped cargo on points marked with triangles and swastikas of red lights. The crews of the He 111 bombers from KG55 noted that the entire southern part of Stalingrad was plunged into darkness, while conditional signals were still being sent from the north and even a radio beacon was working. Most of the containers were dumped on the southern outskirts of the Tractor Plant.

On this day, the northern group of the 6th Army was still resisting fiercely. The Red Army managed to capture only a few ruins, while the 62nd and 65th Armies lost about 800 killed and wounded. The defence in the area of the Tractor Plant was very powerful, with a network of well-established strongpoints adapted to long-term circular defence. And theoretically, the Germans could hold out there for another couple of weeks (subject to air supply continuing).

On the night of 1/2 February, 108 planes flew to Stalingrad, of which 85 completed the task. The pilots noted that the pocket was still clearly visible, and until midnight cargo drop points were indicated by appropriate signals. However, towards morning, all the lights disappeared for some reason.

At 08.00 a radiogram came from Stalingrad: 'According to the Führer's order, we defend to the last. Long live Germany, long live the Führer!' Then the radio communication was interrupted . . . Nevertheless, on the evening of 2 February, 12 He 111 bombers flew to Stalingrad again. When the planes reached the characteristic bend of the Volga, along which the dark ruins of the completely destroyed city stretched, the pilots could not see any signs of fighting below. A fire was burning in the north-western part of the Tractor Plant, there was a uniform light of searchlights and launches of signal rockets and flares of different colours everywhere. At the same time, there was no shooting or explosions. At 21.30, Milch ordered to stop the supply operation of the 6th Army and cancel the planned departures of four-engined Condors on the night of 2/3 February. In fact, on the afternoon of 2 February, the remaining German units surrendered. 'One of the selected and equipped with advanced technology armies of invaders and enslavers has ended its historical path with an inglorious defeat,' the war diary of the Don Front reported pathetically. During 1 and 2 February, 45,000 German soldiers (including 24 generals) surrendered. Most of them died in a typhus epidemic and did not return to their homeland. From a purely formal point of view, this sacrifice did not seem useless to some. From 10 to 30 January alone, the casualties of the Don Front amounted to 57,000. The 21st Army alone suffered 20,000 casualties in January, including 4,000 killed and missing. This made up a third of its total number!

The pocket really did tie down large Red Army forces. Due to snow and disruption of railway transport, the released troops arrived at other sections of the front only by the end of February. But by that time the Wehrmacht had already overcome the crisis, and Army Group South launched a counteroffensive. But in strategic terms, it was still a complete collapse.

From 30 November 1942 to 2 February 1943, the Luftwaffe carried out 5,996 sorties to supply 'Festung Stalingrad'. But only in 4,691 cases was the mission completed (the cargo was delivered). At the same time, 3,520 aircraft landed in the pocket, and another 1,171 dropped cargo from the air, delivering 8,250 tons of cargo, including 4,000 tons of food, 1,562 tons of ammunition and 1,736m^3 of fuel. The average figure, therefore, was 138 tons per day. Also, 24,994 wounded, 1,088 ordinary officers and men and 5,150 people who held various posts and technical specialists were evacuated by air, in total over 31,000 people (about 15 per cent of the number of people who were originally encircled).

Against the background of these achievements, the sacrifices made by the Luftwaffe were not so great. Total losses amounted to

409 aircraft. Of these, 234 were total losses and 175 suffered over 25 per cent damage by German standards. The losses of the bomber squadrons were lower than those of the transport units. For example, I./KG100 lost eight aircraft and four crews during the supply operation of the 6th Army.

CONCLUSION

The second summer campaign of the Wehrmacht on the Eastern Front was primarily distinguished by the complete absence of any strategy and common sense. The plan of Operation Blau, which was actually an effort to 'finish what was started' in 1941, designated the capture of oil fields as the main goal. The German generals planned an offensive to a depth of 1,500km (approximately equal to the distance between Berlin and Moscow!), assigning routes for panzer and under-strength infantry divisions through desert areas with almost complete absence of railways and highways, without any calculations of the needs of troops for fuel, ammunition, food and even water.

But they still 'thought' about covering the gradually lengthening flanks, deciding to entrust this responsible and risky mission to poorly armed and poorly trained allied troops led by incompetent and stupid generals. At the same time, the frankly delusional plan to capture the Caucasus did not provide for any alternative options in case 'something goes wrong'. Except maybe 'dig in and stand to the death' . . .

When the offensive began and led to some impressive successes, the already adventurous Operation Blau began to transform rapidly, taking more and more strange forms. At the same time, all operational decisions were made by the German command on the move, depending on the situation, as unpredictable difficulties arose, and the priorities and goals of the military campaign changed in a strange and unexpected way. So, it turned out that Stalingrad, which did not figure at all in the Blau plan, eventually became the site of the decisive battle of 1942 on the Eastern Front.

However, the same can be said about the Soviet command. Frightened and broken by the military disasters near Kerch and Kharkov, when entire armies were captured, Joseph Stalin faltered and in early July authorised the retreat of the Red Army to the Volga, which turned into a stampede. But then the red dictator suddenly changed his mind and issued the famous order 'Not a step back!' Russian historians are still sure that this document 'inspired soldiers to great feats' and 'strengthened discipline'. In fact, its consequences were a sharp increase in the number of deserters and collaborators. The fact that the Soviets 'stood up to death' in Stalingrad, the Germans perceived as proof that this city had some huge strategic importance (although not fully understood) and even a mystical and sacred meaning for the Stalinist regime.

Otherwise, how to explain the complete confidence of the Nazi military leaders that after the capture of Stalingrad, victory in the war was bound to come? The Russian military leaders, who considered the Germans very smart, were sure that since the enemy was so stubbornly climbing into these ruins, regardless of time and losses, it means that they knew more about this city than they did. Well, and so on in a circle . . . At the same time, the disastrous practice for the Wehrmacht, due to the lack of reserves and lack of forces, simply to 'waste' its elite divisions as a whole, was compensated by even more wasteful spending of troops in the Red Army.

In fact, the attack on Stalingrad, the subsequent endless assault on the city and the natural collapse showed the true level of the Führer's 'generalship genius', his intellectual abilities and unconscious motives. Which for some reason, to this day, some do not cease to admire, trying to write off the collapse of the Third Reich solely on the numerical superiority of opponents and individual 'fatal decisions' (at this point they turned the wrong way, at that point they stopped at the wrong time).

After the collapse of Operation Barbarossa and the winter crisis of 1941/42, the power of the Wehrmacht was seriously undermined. The German army could still successfully defend and advance, but it could no longer win a decisive victory over the growing Red Army. However, Hitler never admitted his mistakes and decided to take a chance. He drove his troops into the barren desert on the border of Asia, eventually giving the Soviets the perfect chance for revenge. Thanks to the powerful support of the Luftwaffe, the Wehrmacht managed to capture most of Stalingrad with weakened and 'depleted' divisions and hold the stretched flanks of the 6th Army for a long time. At the tactical and technical level, German aviation was several times superior to Soviet aviation and was capable of carrying out any mission. But in view of the complete absence of a coherent strategy from the Wehrmacht command, all these successes ultimately came to naught, and the endless stretching of the front over huge distances led to a predictable dispersion of forces.

For the Germans themselves, the impressive achievements of the Luftwaffe eventually played a dramatic role. Believing in the 'omnipotence' of his aviation, which, as it seemed, could fend off any threat and plug any gap in the collapsing front, Hitler and his entourage blithely decided that any problem could be solved with its help. The consequence of this was the creation of an air bridge to Stalingrad, which had no analogues in the history of warfare. However, stupidity, unsupported illusions and a persistent desire for collapse, of course, led to the predictable result.

For the Germans, the word 'Stalingrad' has become a symbol of disaster and shame for many years. For Russians, it has become a source of pride, a symbol of the invincibility of their army and a model for the education of their people. Unfortunately, 80 years later, the fate of Stalingrad was repeated . . .

REFERENCES AND SOURCES

Archives

Central Archive of the Ministry of Defence of the Russian Federation (TSAMO RF):

Foundation 500. Shap. Inventory 12642. Case 676.
Foundation 202. Shap. Inventory 5. Case 557.
Foundation 203. Shap. Inventory 2843. Case 116.
Foundation 22360. Shap. Inventory 0143466cc. Case 0010.
Foundation 22344. Shap. Inventory 0222520c. Case 0004.
Foundation 27687. Shap. Inventory 0926920. Case 0001.
Foundation 33468. Shap. Inventory 0015395c. Case 0008.
Foundation 27588. Shap. Inventory 0405812c. Case 0015.
Foundation 16533. Shap. Inventory 0100055c. Case 0001.
Foundation 341. Shap. Inventory 5329. Case 1.
Foundation 20257. Shap. Inventory 1. Case 6.
Foundation 1212. Shap. Inventory 1. Case 7.
Foundation 220. Shap. Inventory 220. Case 92.
Foundation 220. Shap. Inventory 220. Case 93.
Foundation 206. Shap. Inventory 262. Case 79.
Foundation 206. Shap. Inventory 262. Case 66.
Foundation 206. Shap. Inventory 262. Case 78.
Foundation 229. Shap. Inventory 161. Case 938.
Foundation 48. Shap. Inventory 451. Case 98.
Foundation 220. Shap. Inventory 220. Case 86.
Foundation 220. Shap. Inventory 220. Case 87.
Foundation 320. Shap. Inventory 4522. Case 10.
Foundation 3368. Shap. Inventory 1. Case 2.
Foundation 230. Shap. Inventory 568. Case 34.
Foundation 48. Shap. Inventory 451. Case 141.
Foundation 48. Shap. Inventory 451. Case 125.
Foundation 20247. Shap. Inventory 1. Case 5.
Foundation 20014. Shap. Inventory 1. Case 17.

Foundation 22088. Shap. Inventory 0575799. Case 0001.
Foundation 3167. Shap. Inventory 1. Case 4.
Foundation 341. Shap. Inventory 5328. Case 58.
Foundation 206. Shap. Inventory 262. Case 99.
Foundation 1131. Shap. Inventory 1. Case 13.
Foundation 469. Shap. Inventory 6046. Case 39.
Foundation 1319. Shap. Inventory 1. Case 4.
Foundation 331. Shap. Inventory 5041. Case 33.
Foundation 469. Shap. Inventory 6046. Case 39.
Foundation 3428. Shap. Inventory 1. Case 10.
Foundation 226. Shap. Inventory 648. Case 23.
Foundation 335. Shap. Inventory 5113. Case 120.
Foundation 243. Shap. Inventory 0002928. Case 00011.
Foundation 1212. Shap. Inventory 1. Case 7.

National Archives and Records Administration (NARA):
NARA T-312 R-1458.
NARA T-312 R-1684.
NARA T-312 R-1683.
NARA T-312 R-1682.
NARA T-312 R-1681.
NARA T-312 R-1683.
NARA T-314 R-1159.
NARA T-315 R-2188.

Archive of Kampfgeschwader 27 (Boelcke Archive).

Published Sources

Astrakhan Party organisation during the Great Patriotic War. Collection of documents and materials. Astrakhan, 1962.

Dierich, W., *Kampfgeschwader 55 'Greif'*, Stuttgart: Motorbuch Verlag, 1994.

Hayward, Joel S.A., *Stopped at Stalingrad: the Luftwaffe and Hitler's Defeat in the East, 1942–1943*, University Press of Kansas, 1998.

Hazard, M., *La Stukageschwader 2 'Immelmann'. Tome 01. Collection Histoire des Unités n°10*, Lela Presse, 2018.

Horn, J., Über allen Fronten. Chronik des Kampfgeschwaders 6 1941 bis 1945, Dresden: Eigenverlag, 2018.

In the days of severe trials. Stalingrad Party organisation during the Great Patriotic War. 1941–1945. Collection of documents and materials. Volgograd, 1966.

Kovalev, I.V., *Transport in the Great Patriotic War (1941-1945)*, Moscow: Nauka, 1981.

Loktionov, I.I., *The Volga Military Flotilla during the Great Patriotic War*, Moscow: Voenizdat, 1977.

Stalingrad: The Price of Victory, Moscow: ACT, 2005.

Soviet River Transport in the Great Patriotic War, Moscow: Voenizdat, 1981.

Vanchinov, D.P., *The War Years of the Volga region*, Saratov: 1980.

Weiss, W., *Chronic Kampfgeschwader Nr. 27 Boelcke. Teil 3. 01.01.1942 – 31.12.1942*, Aachen: Helios Verlag, 2005.

Weiss, W., *Chronic Kampfgeschwader Nr. 27 Boelcke. Teil IV. 01.01.1943-31.12.1943*, Aachen: Helios Verlag, 2007.

INDEX

175